MODERN SPORTS OFFICIATING
A PRACTICAL GUIDE

MODERN SPORTS OFFICIATING
A PRACTICAL GUIDE

RICHARD CLEGG/
WILLIAM A. THOMPSON
Long Beach City College

Fifth Edition

WCB Brown & Benchmark

RAP 3044502 ✓

Book Team

Editor *Chris Rogers*
Developmental Editor *Scott Spoolman*
Production Coordinator *Karen L. Nickolas*

WCB Brown & Benchmark
A Division of Wm. C. Brown Communications, Inc.

Vice President and General Manager *Thomas E. Doran*
Executive Managing Editor *Ed Bartell*
Executive Editor *Edgar J. Laube*
Director of Marketing *Kathy Law Laube*
National Sales Manager *Eric Ziegler*
Marketing Manager *Pamela Cooper*
Advertising Manager *Jodi Rymer*
Managing Editor, Production *Colleen A. Yonda*
Manager of Visuals and Design *Faye M. Schilling*
Production Editorial Manager *Vickie Putman Caughron*
Publishing Services Manager *Karen J. Slaght*
Permissions / Records Manager *Connie Allendorf*

Wm. C. Brown Communications, Inc.

Chairman Emeritus *Wm. C. Brown*
Chairman and Chief Executive Officer *Mark C. Falb*
President and Chief Operating Officer *G. Franklin Lewis*
Corporate Vice President, Operations *Beverly Kolz*
Corporate Vice President, President of WCB Manufacturing *Roger Meyer*

Cover design by Dale Rosenbach

Cover photos, left to right: Photo by David Klutho / Focus West; Photo by Rick Stewart / Focus West; Photo by C. Bernhardt / Focus West; Photo by Mike Powell / All Sport.

Copy Editor *Karen Dorman*

Consulting Editor *Aileene Lockhart*

Library of Congress Catalog Card Number: 91-76154

ISBN 0-697-12610-2

Printed in the United States of America by Wm. C. Brown Communications, Inc., 2460 Kerper Boulevard, Dubuque, IA 52001

10 9 8 7 6 5 4 3 2 1

This book is lovingly dedicated to the "subtle influence" of our family members—without whose qualities of "judgment," "hustle," "poise," "consistency" and "rapport" this book would not have been written.

Contents

Preface

Organized sports have enjoyed another decade of growth and progress. Has, however, the art of sports officiating kept pace? An obvious weakness in the preparation of sports officials is the lack of contemporary textbooks on the subject. *Modern Sports Officiating* represents an attempt to bridge this gap.

This guide is designed for college courses in sports officiating, for supervisors of school sports, community recreation programs, and individuals preparing to enter the sports officiating field. In addition, the book is intended to provide special direction for physical education and recreation major students and prospective coaches.

The approach presents a current, understandable, and practical framework beneficial to both prospective and experienced sports officials. The emphasis is on *what to do* and how and *why to do it*. It was not possible nor was it the desire of the authors to cover all the playing rules and officiating mechanics of each sport. The reader is referred to instructional literature from the National Federation of State High School Associations, the National Collegiate Athletic Association, the National Intramural-Recreational Sports Association, *Referee* magazine, and other sports organizations.

Chapter One serves as an introduction to sports officiating. Special emphasis is given to the development of a sound philosophy of officiating, to clarification of the personal requirements of an official, and to the roles played by a sports official. Chapter Two presents practical advice for the beginning official. Chapters Three through Ten deal specifically with selected sports—baseball and softball, basketball, football, soccer, swimming and diving, track and field, volleyball, and wrestling. The format for the sports chapters includes sections on *the game, officials and their responsibilities, basic penalties and rulings, mechanics, problem calls,* and *miscellaneous considerations.* Chapters One, Two, Three, Four, Five, and Nine, and final editing were the responsibilities of Richard Clegg. Chapters Six, Seven, Eight, and Ten were the responsibilities of William A. Thompson.

This edition reflects important additions and revisions. All chapters have been updated regarding recent changes in rules and mechanics.

The production of the first five editions of *Modern Sports Officiating* has been greatly enhanced by the assistance of many people who have offered general and specific suggestions, critiqued manuscript drafts, and done the typing. The authors wish to acknowledge their indebtedness to all those who assisted in the preparation of this book.

A special note of appreciation is extended to sports officials/ administrators Len Friedlund, Bob Gildersleeve, Fritz Gorham, and Diana Stevens for their exceptional expertise and consideration over two or more editions with specific chapters of, respectively, softball, flag/touch football, basketball, and volleyball.

Richard Clegg
William A. Thompson

MODERN SPORTS OFFICIATING
A PRACTICAL GUIDE

Officiating Requirements

Welcome to the challenging but rewarding job of sports officiating. If you love sports and are willing to work, you can develop a skill which is personally satisfying and beneficial to the American sports scene. There are no shortcuts to true officiating success any more than there are to true athletic success, but enthusiastic effort on your part can lead to a stimulating addition to your life.

The Officiating Scene Today

The continuous and phenomenal growth of sports programs in this country has produced a great need for qualified sports officials. There is virtually no ceiling to the prospects for advancement of officials who are gifted and eager to learn. Athletic coaches, administrators, and recreation personnel at all levels of competition are constantly seeking competent officials. They know that good officiating helps to produce a healthy, educational, and sportsmanlike environment associated with a fair determination of the winner. They wish to hire officials who will be effective in reaching these goals. The same leaders know, on the other hand, that poorly trained, incompetent sports officials create tensions and generate frustration among players, coaches and spectators— sometimes with serious consequences. They prefer not to hire such officials.

Photo by Robert Beck/Focus West

To put it simply, the official is the essential *third dimension* of an athletic contest. The player, the coach and the official interact. Depending upon their abilities and attitudes, they produce a variety of possible results—not merely a winner and a loser, but also satisfaction or disappointment, thrills or mediocrity, cooperative teamwork or antagonism, mutual respect or distrust. Any sports expert will acknowledge the contribution of this *third dimension* to the quality of athletic competition.

The challenge for the prospective official is to develop his or her capabilities to the point where that which is expected of a sports official can in fact be produced, regardless of the difficulties presented. Achieving a high degree of competence is chiefly the result of concentrated study and game experience, supplemented by continuous evaluation and efforts to improve.

Officiating is not a simple or easy avocation. It is a challenging task. New officials should prepare themselves thoroughly if they contemplate a continuing career in officiating. By the same token, a new official would be mistaken if he or she were to enter into officiating casually or for the sole purpose of financial gain. Officials should direct themselves toward meaningful developmental goals if they expect to be successful.

Our purpose in this chapter is to establish a clear and comprehensive concept of sports officiating. The goal of the reader might be to develop an intelligent, realistic understanding of what competent sports officiating is and what it demands. Consider the following questions:

1. What is the fundamental aim of sports officiating?
2. What are the essential ingredients for effective sports officiating?
3. What qualities should a competent sports official possess?
4. What are the financial aspects of sports officiating?
5. What are the legal aspects of sports officiating?
6. What are the various roles to be played while officiating?

The Fundamental Aim: To Cause the Game to Progress Smoothly within the Rules

The official's overriding goal is to promote the normal progress of a contest, as it was meant to proceed, with as little interference as possible. This is *not* to say that rule enforcement should be neglected to the slightest degree, but rather that the competent official should not merely be concerned about penalizing rule infractions. *Preventing rule infractions before they occur* is also an important concern.

A contest which is frequently and unnecessarily interrupted by the official's whistle leaves no one satisfied. Under such circumstances, the official rather than the players becomes the dominant factor. Players and coaches alike respect the official who, within the playing rules, provides for continuous and uninterrupted action.

Rule violations can be prevented in two general ways: (1) by establishing a subtle but unquestioned influence over the game; and (2) by actively preventing specific infractions.

Establishing a Subtle Influence

In almost all cases, players wish to avoid rule infractions because penalties hurt. Players—especially well-trained players—will avoid many rule violations when they have cause to avoid them. The competent official capitalizes on the desires and abilities of the players by establishing a controlling influence over the contest *early in the contest*—for example, in the first two to four minutes of a basketball game.

In order to accomplish this, the sports official must be completely "warmed up," both mentally and physically, on the first play of the game in order to make *any* necessary ruling without hesitation. The quality of "early control" established, or not established, can influence the entire game. When the official's influence is felt from the start, the game progresses as it was meant to progress. Two important ways in which you as an official can establish this influence are:

1. *By being in a position* to call the play at all times, so that the players are constantly aware of your presence.
2. *By reacting immediately* to rule infractions, especially early in the contest.

When opponents, *on their own,* try to compete in accordance with the spirit and letter of the rules, the result is satisfying and rewarding to all concerned. Such a situation is not always found in athletic competition, but the dedicated official constantly seeks it. Athletics benefits from officials' efforts to produce this type of competitive environment.

Active Prevention

Obviously, more than just a subtle officiating influence is sometimes needed in athletic competition. A decision by the official and the enforcement of the prescribed penalty are needed. At other times, however, it is appropriate and advisable for the official to anticipate the impending infraction and to "talk the athletes out of" committing it. Direct action can and should be preventive as well as punitive.

Considerable experience and background in the particular sport are necessary in order to know when and when not to issue warnings. Generally, in the higher levels of competition fewer warnings and less preventive officiating are appropriate. Nevertheless, there are moments in all sports and at all levels of play when this type of preventive officiating can be accomplished appropriately and unobtrusively. Here are a few examples:

1. In football the head linesman cautions a lineman who has been lining up in a position very close to "offsides." Before a kick-off the umpire reminds members of the receiving team, "no blocking below the belt."
2. In basketball post play, the "lead" official warns opposing centers to "watch your hands" in order to prevent pushing for position. Before free throws the trailing official issues explicit warnings to "watch the lines."
3. In baseball, the plate umpire warns the batter about stepping out of the batter's box when swinging the bat. While dusting off the pitcher's plate, the base umpire informs the pitcher with a "near-balk move" just what balk might be committed.
4. In track, the starter forewarns the sprinters to avoid "rolling starts." The relay lane judges show the athletes the exact areas within which the baton must be passed.

Such warnings not only help to eliminate needless and unwanted infractions but they also can establish a positive player-official relationship.

To summarize, the primary aim of the competent official is to cause the game to progress smoothly and with as little interference as possible. Preventive officiating is superior to "whistle-happy" officiating, but *does not* eliminate the responsibility for unhesitatingly enforcing the rules.

The Essential Ingredients

Regardless of the sport in which you are involved, you must meet four fundamental requirements if you wish to be considered a successful official:

1. You must enforce the rules intelligently.
2. You must show integrity.
3. You must build sound human relations.
4. You must show primary concern for the individual athlete.

Intelligent Rule Enforcement

The rules of sports have evolved through the concentrated attention of many experts over a period of many years. As such, the rules *command respect and demand enforcement.* The athletes are not adequate or appropriate rule enforcers. The official is there to enforce the rules—to show respect for the sport and for the players by *knowing* the rules and *enforcing* them. To do otherwise usually brings the unwanted consequences of disorganized games, unsportsmanlike acts, and even the danger of injury.

Applying the rules requires the use of *judgment* on the part of the master official. In certain instances apparent rule violations will be ignored, while in other instances virtually invisible acts will be ruled upon immediately. Preserving the ideal of the sport through rule enforcement is the chief concern.

Judgment by the official in applying the rules is largely based upon the wisdom of Oswald Tower, former member of the basketball National Rules Committee. Tower said, in effect, that *the purpose of the playing rules is to penalize a player who, by reason of an illegal act, places an opponent at a disadvantage.* Thus, in rulings where judgment is permissible, the competent official is more concerned about the *effect* of an illegal act than about the act itself. For example, the slightest push of a shooter in basketball can affect his shot; if it does, an infraction has occurred and should be ruled. There are many other examples, some of which are specified in subsequent chapters.

Authorities agree that the Tower philosophy is essentially correct, because when properly employed, it assures that the spirit of the game prevails rather than exact or petty enforcement. Two cautions should be noted:

1. The philosophy does not apply to all rules or even to most rules. A player is in bounds or out of bounds, a swimmer did touch or did not touch, the throw did or did not beat the base runner on a force play at second base, and so forth. In most cases, the official is asked, not to exercise judgment, but *to call immediately* what has been seen.

2. When the philosophy *does* apply, the official must know and understand the correct rule interpretation so that the decisions rendered are as consistent as possible. The philosophy permits flexibility, but inconsistency *and* flexibility would soon bring trouble.

The concept of consistency leads us to the second essential ingredient of effective sports officiating.

Absolute Integrity

The official wants to see the game progress correctly, without bias or inconsistency. In spite of pressures, the official should not be unduly influenced by the score, the time remaining, or the reactions of players, coaches or spectators, nor be influenced by the direction of previous decisions. To a considerable degree, the capable official sees each movement of the competition as a moment in itself, unconnected with what had happened previously.

In certain instances, great courage and personal confidence are required in order for an official to rule with absolute integrity. No one, not even the home coach, admires a "homer" official. Regardless of the circumstances, the sports official must be completely honest in all phases of the job, especially in applying the rules, but also in relationships with fellow officials, players, and coaches.

Personal integrity can also be shown by what officiating assignments you *do not accept.* An official should never accept an assignment which creates a compromising situation. Contests should not be worked in which an official has a close relationship with the involved schools, players or coaches. Those who hire officials actively avoid making such assignments, but in many instances only the official is able to sense a potentially compromising assignment.

Personal integrity can be shown by your relationship with officiating associations, coaches, and players. Generally, these relationships should be businesslike—not political. So-called "preferred assignments" will eventually come to the qualified official, regardless of political maneuverings. The official who is not gifted is merely baiting his or her own trap when assignments are attained for which he or she is not qualified. Unfortunately, large officiating associations, because of the official's anonymity, frequently create the impression that influence is more important than ability. Ultimately, such an impression is false.

Finally, personal integrity can be shown through reliability in meeting all accepted assignments and meeting them on time. The only officiating "sin" more serious than arriving late is not arriving at all. It is evident that officiating integrity is a product of personal honesty and reliability. A potentially outstanding official can rise or fall according to the integrity demonstrated.

Sound Human Relations

It has been said with considerable truth that officiating is more like an art than a science. Building sound relationships with fellow officials, players, coaches, and spectators while under the fire of intense athletic rivalry calls for "an artist's touch."

Relationship with fellow officials. For the most part, officials are on their own at the contest. If their mutual support and teamwork break down, problems in other relationships will certainly increase. Here are a few specific suggestions for producing effective teamwork among officials:

1. *Always* arrive early enough to consult with your fellow officials before the game so that you can agree on mechanics and rule interpretations and begin to become acquainted with one another.
2. *Never* argue with a fellow official.
3. Agree in advance about who will call what and who will not call what. Remove all doubt about this potentially sensitive issue. Stick with the advice of association directives whenever possible.
4. Agree in advance about how you may assist one another in making decisions which require assistance.
5. Decide in advance the circumstances, if any exist, in which one official may overrule or cancel the decision of another. This practice is permissible in a few sports—although it is to be avoided. Nonetheless, such a potentially sensitive issue should be discussed in advance.
6. Avoid the temptation to "explain" your fellow official's decision. Assuming such a responsibility has the potential for damaging relationships at several levels, including those within the officiating team.
7. More experienced officials should take the initiative to advise inexperienced officials. Suggestions may be given *before* and *after,* but seldom during, the contest.

Relationships with players. Good relationships between players and officials are of fundamental importance to effective officiating. Coaches and spectators can sense the quality of player-official relationships, and this influences their evaluation of the official. Officials should be neither overly friendly nor aloof in their dealings with players. Players tend to distrust an official who seems to be trying to win a popularity contest with both teams. They prefer an official to act like an official who has an important job to do.

The degree to which an official should try to be helpful varies considerably according to the sport and the level of play. In professional sports a particularly helpful official would be treated with amazement, amusement, or scorn. In youth contests, on the other hand, a competent official will not hesitate to actually teach the rules at appropriate moments.

A domineering or dictatorial official upsets the players. Officials must be, or at least act, humane and approachable. An official must show respect for the players in order to gain respect. Hustle and enthusiasm greatly increase player respect.

When unsportsmanlike acts occur, whether directly involving the official or not, these acts should be penalized immediately, but in as calm a manner as possible. Unsportsmanlike acts usually create excitement and emotional reactions in players, coaches, and spectators (and often officials) alike. What is especially needed under such circumstances is not anger or revenge but an accurate and efficient penalty enforced as confidently and calmly as possible.

Relationships with coaches. As implied by the rules of most sports, contact between the coaches and official should be businesslike, friendly, respectful, and *limited*. The coach is concerned about an official's mechanics and judgment and is not likely to be concerned about whether or not an official wishes to be a friend. Occasionally, coaches become extremely upset with officials. Under such circumstances, considerable tact is needed. Often the upset coach is the type who can be calmed down almost as easily as he or she became excited. A brief, calm, businesslike, but not unfriendly explanation of the decision may prevent serious consequences.

The sports official must always remember the importance of a game to the coach—the time and dedication that has been applied towards a successful effort. Most coaches sacrifice financial return for the sake of athletes. Emotional reactions to an official's decisions often exemplify loyalty to their athletes and their "cause" rather than a personal vendetta against the official. The official should not overreact to the excited coach, but neither should he or she neglect obvious infractions by the coach. If there is a choice between protecting the coach or the game, the game comes first.

Relationships with spectators. "Crowd control" is the chief responsibility of the host school or organization, but the official also bears an indirect responsibility and exerts considerable influence. While the official's attention is directed principally to the game and the players and partially to the coaches, he or she cannot ignore the presence of spectators, in all reality the *fourth* dimension of sports (players first, coaches second, officials third, spectators fourth).

The trend of an athletic event can be harmed by intense spectator reactions. An obviously upset official unintentionally adds fuel to the fire. A hustling, efficient, and calm official can do much to neutralize potentially explosive circumstances.

In summary, sound human relations must be a part of competent officiating because sports involve human beings with opposing goals and loyalties. These human beings possess different backgrounds, abilities and emotional responses. In fact, some of them simply do not like officials. The sports official can seldom satisfy everyone, nor should this be the aim. He or she should show respect for others, avoid antagonizing anyone, and be approachable and businesslike. Primary attention should be directed toward the best officiating job that can be produced. When, in part because of high-quality officiating, the contest is played skillfully and fairly, the basis for common good will has been established.

Your Foremost Concern: The Individual Athlete
The capable official has a primary concern for the protection of the players. In many instances his or her actions are based on this concern. The master official:

1. Wants to prevent injuries and knows that in many sports good officiating can prevent damaging and unnecessary accidents.
2. Understands the importance of, and encourages sportsmanlike behavior.
3. Knows that correct rulings can motivate player improvement through the trial-and-error learning process.
4. Does not discourage questions on the rules, because he or she knows that players don't know all the rules.
5. Wants to keep all the players in the game and knows that in many cases the disqualification or ejection of a player can be prevented.
6. Is willing to eject or disqualify a player when the rules and spirit of the game demand such action, because the appropriate development of the given player, the protection of other players, and the quality of the game itself are involved.

The official who is able and willing to use "protection of the players" as a guide will be amazed at its effectiveness, especially in making difficult decisions. To test this theory, try it against any seemingly hopeless officiating situation that you can imagine. Ask yourself in this imaginary situation, what should be done for the players' protection? Perhaps the indicated decision will not be completely popular with all people, but it will be the *best decision available* if it is based upon concern for the individual athlete. The beginning official should be constantly reminded of this responsibility to the players.

Qualities of a Competent Official

If one hundred different sports officiating experts submitted their own lists of the essential qualifications of a master official, one might expect one hundred different listings. If asked to place a given set of qualifications in order of their importance, the same experts might again be expected to differ in their opinions. Thus, the qualities selected by the authors and the following list bear no claim of infallibility or even comprehensiveness. The selected qualities are meant to clarify the game-by-game requirements of successful sports officiating.

The qualities were derived from survey and interview responses from scores of recognized officials and coaches, as well as the personal experiences of the authors. The purposes of the list are (1) to specify the requirements of effective officiating; (2) to guide and motivate improvement; and (3) to suggest guidelines for the evaluation of officials (either self-evaluation or evaluation by those who hire officials). *Good eyesight* was not included, although its importance cannot be questioned.

I. Precise Knowledge of Playing Rules
The rules of any game provide the direction for play. Officials are expected to see that the game is played according to those rules. Mastery of game rules is a continuing effort. Early in their training prospective officials study rule and case books, discuss rules in detail in the officiating association class meetings, and are tested on their knowledge of the rules. The most effective means of resolving confusion and promoting understanding of complex sections of the rules is to participate in smaller study groups. Some competent officials make it a practice to review briefly the total rulebook the night before an assignment and find it helpful to analyze difficult sections of the rules on the day of the game. Following the game, officials independently should critique their individual effort and the performance of the officiating unit. This will allow for immediate attention to deficiencies in the understanding of the rules while situations are still fresh in the mind. Officiating associations in some areas of the country meet socially during the off-season in an effort to keep their officials posted on rule changes for the coming season. *Referee* magazine provides regular and reliable updates of the playing rules.

II. Judgment
Judgment in an individual contest should be based primarily upon a thorough knowledge and understanding of the playing rules. No official ever has said or probably ever will be able to say, "My judgment is complete and perfect." Development of good judgment is a never-ending process. The official who *continues* to study the rules and to apply officiating experiences to personal improvement is the official who will succeed. Good judgment is a foremost qualification of the top-notch

official, because it permits correct, unhesitating decision making under any game circumstances. It also develops the respect and approval of players and coaches alike.

When an official is able to make one sound decision after another, control of the game becomes evident. The game progresses as it was meant to progress, with the players and the action rather than the official in the spotlight. Competitive playing or coaching experience in a given sport greatly helps the judgment of a new official, but such experience is certainly not enough in itself.

III. Good Mechanics

Officiating mechanics refer to the routine procedures surrounding what the official does. The two primary areas of mechanics are "signaling" and "positioning." When more than one official is involved, "teamwork" becomes a third category, and additional signaling and positioning responsibilities are then necessary. The mechanics of signaling, positioning, and teamwork are each of essential importance to assure a professional performance.

Signals may be executed by mechanical device, voice, or gesture, depending upon the sport and the circumstance. Sharp, unhesitating, and unhurried signals are necessary both to communicate decisions and to build the confidence of participants and observers in your abilities. Correct positioning is necessary to permit you to see (rather than guess) what you are hired to see. Teamwork procedures are necessary (1) to provide balanced coverage of all conceivable actions and (2) to minimize or eliminate disagreement among the officials.

When proper mechanics are observed precisely, the game progresses without confusion or unnecessary delay. There is nothing complicated or magical about the officiating mechanics of any sport. Good mechanics are not difficult to develop *if correct habits are established early in the official's career.* Difficulty does occur when the new official unsuspectingly forms incorrect positioning, signals, or teamwork habits. Mechanics, good or bad, are habitual actions. It is much easier to learn the correct habit than to unlearn an incorrect habit later.

Like playing rules, officiating mechanics are clearly specified and have evolved from the efforts of many people for many years and, therefore, should command the respect and acceptance of new officials. The first two obligations of a new official are to begin (1) to learn and understand the playing rules and (2) to develop the correct habits involved in officiating mechanics.

IV. Hustle

By the colloquial definition, "hustle" means to move or act with resolute energy. With the possible exception of good judgment, no quality commands more respect and approval than hustle. Hustle is highly valued on the athletic scene by all concerned, including fellow officials. It is the quality which improves athletes most, which coaches wish most to teach, and which is greatly admired and respected by spectators, coaches, and athletes alike.

Depending on the particular sport, hustle can be demonstrated in several different ways. It is broadly defined here to include such related attributes as alertness, physical effort, dedication, and enthusiasm. Hustle—or the lack of it—*is apparent,* regardless of the sport you happen to be officiating. A hustling official will see more, display better mechanics, and enjoy the work more. The opposites are true of the official who is somewhat lazy or disinterested. As one dimension of the sports scene, the official is expected to demonstrate this valued attribute. But whether hustle is expected or not, the hustling official will certainly do a better job. Coaches continually rank hustle high on their list of positive officiating qualities.

V. Decisiveness

The effective official converts a controversial or judgmental decision into an accepted decision through decisiveness. The usual result is a continuous contest apparently decided by the skills of the players, not an interrupted game "unfairly" affected by the "questionable" decisions of an official. The experienced, competent official realizes that judgment is not subject to formal protest in any case—that unnecessary and hopeless controversy can be avoided by ruling decisively on close decisions. *The closer the decision, the greater the decisiveness needed.* Compare these examples with your personal experience.

1. In football, when the ball carrier is struggling close to the goal line, the sideline official (head linesman or field judge) should (a) signal immediately whether or not a touchdown has been scored or (b) aggressively close in on the action if not yet certain. Either action conveys the impression of expert coverage decisively executed.
2. In basketball, when the period ends just before a "try" is in flight, the trailing official immediately and decisively should cancel the potential basket before the try reaches the basket.
3. In wrestling, a fall which is very close to being merely a near-fall should be accompanied by a much more decisive signal than the obvious fall.

When there is a hesitant, indecisive, delayed decision, one opponent or the other is sure to believe that the decision was incorrect. Since a decision must be made in any event, the competent official makes his or her decisions decisively.

VI. Poise
Athletic contests are exciting and, therefore, frequently arouse the emotions of the participants and spectators. Contests can get out of hand when emotions run high. Officials cannot control the emotions of others, but they are expected to control their own and to show poise, regardless of the circumstances.

Confidence and calmness are the basic components needed. Persons who lack personal confidence or who cannot control their emotions and excitement do not usually make good officials. Such persons add to existing tensions when they overreact in pressurized moments. On the other hand, the poised official contributes to a controlled atmosphere. During tense moments, gestures and movements become deliberate, almost slow, whenever possible. The greater the momentary tension, the greater the need for calmness (e.g., removing a player from the contest for unsportsmanlike conduct). Obviously, to maintain poise under extreme tension is not easy. To do so under certain circumstances requires nearly superhuman personal control. Most outstanding officials have developed the habit, consciously or unconsciously, of *acting* calmly at a time when, in fact, they are very excited.

Athletic contests should be governed by the abilities of the players and the playing regulations, not by uncontrolled emotions. The sports official sometimes is the only person in the position and with the authority to return the game to the "healthy excitement" of properly supervised athletic competition.

VII. Consistency
If a count were taken of the officiating qualities most frequently criticized by and most upsetting to coaches and players, inconsistency would undoubtedly lead the list. Coaches and players expect the rules to apply equally to both teams. True consistency is open to misinterpretation by players, coaches, and spectators, and even by officials. True consistency results, not from attempting to even up both sides but, from applying the *correct rule interpretation* to each separate competitive act. The underlying truth is that *no two competitive situations are exactly alike.* If an official applies accurate judgment according to the letter and meaning of the rules to each separate decision, the decision will be consistent—because the *correct rule interpretation is unchanging.* Proper judgment and interpretation are the sources of consistency.

VIII. Courage

This quality is related to integrity and objectivity. Nevertheless, no list of necessary officiating qualities could be complete without emphasizing that personal courage is necessary for effective sports officiating.

It takes a degree of courage merely to don the black and white striped shirt and report to the contest. Unfortunately, sports officials in the United States traditionally do not arouse immediate feelings of congeniality and comradeship from players, coaches, spectators, and other officials. Unknown officials have to prove themselves, and everyone is aware of this.

Crucial and difficult rulings may be needed at any moment, and these are made by courageous officials just as accurately and unhesitatingly as routine decisions. Courage is a personal quality, but it also is largely based on the official's ability and willingness to understand and accept officiating responsibilities. Competitive rules empower and obligate the official *in behalf of athletes and coaches* to make the indicated rulings, including the tougher decisions, to the best of his or her ability. Two of the *most unfavorable* things that can be done are to (1) avoid a decision where a decision is required, or (2) make a decision merely because the players, coaches, and/or spectators demand it.

IX. Rapport

References regarding rapport have already been made in the section dealing with sound relationships. Rapport refers to the quality of relating effectively to others. Good rapport with others is a desirable quality in any line of human endeavor; its importance in sports officiating is crucial.

While conscientiously meeting the many requirements of the job, the official must not neglect human relationships. The experienced official can show a humane and friendly nature without compromising performance; he or she knows that there are enough problems without creating additional difficulties in human relationships. Each official will discover individual methods of establishing rapport with fellow officials, players, coaches, and spectators. Your individual methods should reflect your individual personality.

Regardless of the individual personality, rapport will usually become evident if you:

1. Demonstrate courtesy and respect for coaches and players.
2. Show a sense of humor at appropriate moments.
3. Are approachable and receptive to questions.

X. Objectivity

As human beings, officials, like others, *can* be influenced by various pressures. But unlike many others, the official is *not supposed to be* influenced by external pressures. Perhaps an official's pre-game preparation should include mentally pledging: "I solemnly swear to call what I see and only what I see and *not* to be swayed by how people react, by my previous calls, or by self-seeking motives (including my own motives)."

Most officials benefit from, first, consciously recognizing their own susceptibility to being influenced and, second, seriously attempting to improve their complete objectivity in each game. Otherwise, the temptations of a given moment in the competition can lead the normally well-meaning individual to make a *popular* decision rather than a *correct* decision.

Perhaps the plate umpire in baseball best personifies the need for objectivity. The effective plate umpire does not try to "even them up" when making close ball and strike decisions, even though he or she is in a perfect position to do so. Each pitch is a different pitch. Each pitch is a ball or a strike, regardless of which player or team is at bat, what the score or the count is, or what was called previously. The less-than-great umpire, without realizing it, is tempted to "help" a team or a player (or oneself), and the result is an inconsistency which seriously harms the game. Soon no one knows what to expect. The suggestion most commonly associated with sports officiating in the United States is, "Call them as you see them." The fact that this phrase is not yet trite, in spite of its continuous usage, demonstrates the importance of objectivity to sports officiating.

XI. Reaction Time

Assuming that judgment is correct, decisions which are made quickly have a greater chance of being accepted without question. An official with a slow reaction time is open to question. An official with fast reactions frequently can make the decision almost simultaneously with the moment of the action. Thus, a "subtle influence" on the game is quickly and firmly established. The slow-reacting official sometimes compensates by developing the poor habit of "anticipating" impending infractions and, consequently, calling infractions that did not occur.

The extent to which reaction time can be "improved" is open to question. Experimental evidence appears to indicate (1) that different individuals have different but definite physiological limits in the speed of their reactions or reflexes, and (2) that the speed of executing any given act can, within the individual's limits, be quickened by practice. A beginning official can expect some early quickening and improved control of whistle and signals *while learning the particular reaction.* Following this initial learning period, the speed of reactions to various situations will become stabilized within individual limits. It is clear, in any case, that a person with severe limits upon basic reaction time ought not to become a sports official.

XII. Conditioning and Appearance

These two qualifications are related since both can be improved up to minimum levels. Also, they both are associated with the pride and dedication of the official.

Conditioning. In several sports the quality of officiating performance can be limited by the physical condition of the official. Such is certainly the case in basketball, football, baseball, and wrestling. To put it simply, in most sports good conditioning is necessary *throughout the contest* to enable you to: (1) be where you should be; (2) maintain your alertness and good judgment; and (3) hold up your end of the teamwork with your fellow official. A tired official cannot meet all the requirements of good officiating. The primary components of good officiating condition appear to be good cardio-respiratory endurance and strong legs. Most outstanding officials, especially those holding sedentary full-time jobs, put themselves through a graduated conditioning program prior to the start of each season. By doing so they avoid early season injuries, especially torn muscles, and measure up to expectations at their first assignment of the year. A jogging/running program is strongly recommended.

Appearance. A certain razor company once increased its sales through the slogan: "Look sharp! Feel sharp! Be sharp!" This slogan presents excellent advice to sports officials. "Feel sharp" has implications for physical and mental preparation, especially for conditioning. "Be sharp" suggests that an official react quickly, hustle, and display good judgment and mechanics. We are concerned here with "looking sharp."

Most officials' associations have minimum dress regulations which should be observed. An official who reports for duty in an unkempt, dirty uniform does not inspire the confidence of players and coaches. Such officials start the game at a disadvantage.

Adequate conditioning and appearance *can* be attained. It makes no sense, nor is it justifiable, for an official to report for a game in an unfit or sloppy condition.

A review of the qualities advocated indicates the impossibility of your becoming a *perfect* official. How many officials have you observed who consistently demonstrate all of these qualities to the maximum degree? The point to be made here, however, is that you or any other prospective official can improve each of the qualities. Both your performance and your enjoyment of officiating will depend greatly upon your efforts to improve continually.

Financial Aspects

The potential for both personal and financial gain makes sports officiating for hundreds of thousands of people throughout the world a very special and important pastime. For hundreds of others—for the relative few who have become "big league" sports officials in college and professional athletics—sports officiating has developed into a major source of income.

The range of compensation for officiating is great. Many sports officials volunteer. The Super Bowl pays $5,000, plus expenses. In high school sports, football pays the most, followed in descending order by basketball, baseball, wrestling, soccer, softball, and volleyball. The fees that officials earn for high school varsity games generally run in the $30 to $45 * range, plus mileage expenses for distant contests.

College football and basketball officials make as much as $400 to $450 per game, plus expenses, down to $50 per game for junior colleges. Four year college baseball umpires can expect to make from $60 to $175 per game.

At the professional level, NBA and major league baseball officials / umpires make from $37,500 to $115,000 plus possible post-season opportunities. Minor league officials make much less. NFL officials start at around $600 per game to a high of about $2,000 per game for some officials.

On the expenses side of the ledger, there are costs for uniforms, equipment, membership, travel, and meals. Start-up expenses for uniforms, equipment, rule books, officiating organization fees, etc., will run from $100 or less for most sports to as much as $350 to fully prepare a baseball umpire. Also, officials who join officials' organizations must plan to take the time to attend several meetings and pass written and sometimes practical examinations. Mileage and / or meal expenses are not normally provided for local high school officiating assignments.

*The April 1989 issue of *Referee* magazine shows an actual range of $12 to $53.

Legal Aspects

Legal activity has greatly increased in all phases of American life today, and sports officiating is no exception. In recognition of this trend, *Referee** magazine includes a section in several issues each year, "Law" which deals with the legal aspects of sports officiating. Among the *legal issues* referred to in this excellent periodical have been assault and battery, liability for player injuries, defamation of character, discrimination in hiring, and others.

Among sports officials' activities which may subsequently lead to legal action are the pre-game check of facilities and equipment, assistance provided to physically injured participants, enforcement of playing rules, game control, suspending play due to weather, and others. Fulfilling virtually any officiating responsibility conceivably might lead to legal actions.

It is beyond the scope of this book to present comprehensive coverage of the many and varied legal ramifications of sports officiating. Here are some common sense suggestions to help protect the sports official from adverse legal consequences.

1. Become a student of the legal aspects of sports officiating.
2. Carry out meticulously and thoughtfully all officiating responsibilities which relate particularly to injury prevention, game control, and proper relationships with players, coaches, and others, including the media.
3. Avoid first-aid treatment other than protecting the victim from further injury.
4. If in doubt whether to suspend competition because of weather/facility/equipment conditions, suspend it.
5. Control your temper or stop officiating.
6. Take notes on important game circumstances and keep them for a period of time when the circumstances could possibly involve legal aspects.
7. Don't disregard *your own* legal rights.
8. Have access to a lawyer, preferably one who knows something about athletics.

Referee is published monthly, $47.40 per year in U.S., $59.50 in Canada and Mexico. Direct subscription inquiries and all other mail to Referee, P.O. Box 161, Franksville, WI 53126. Phone 414/632–8855.

Officiating Roles

As the action and tempo of a contest progress and change, the official must frequently assume several different roles, depending upon the particular circumstances. It may be necessary for the sports official to assume partially the role of educator, salesman, psychologist, "in-house" attorney, and/or statesman. The competent official recognizes the particular need under the given circumstance and assumes the indicated role.

As an Educator
The rich developmental and learning potentials of competitive sports can be understood and fostered. During competition an athlete is constantly responding, achieving, or falling short, all of which result in behavior changes. The chief behavioral changes created through athletics are skill- and knowledge-related. They are also attitudinal, social, and personal in nature, because athletes are usually strongly motivated and emotionally involved. The official inevitably serves as an integral part of these significant learning processes. A good example of courtesy, respect, and emotional stability and effort can be demonstrated. When needed, the rule and its proper interpretation can be briefly explained.

As a Salesman
The official can influence athletes and coaches toward fair, clean, and sportsmanlike conduct by exemplifying in his/her own behavior a combination of respect, empathy, firmness, subtle suggestion, and encouragement.

As a Psychologist
The often strong and emotional feelings of players, coaches, and spectators can be understood and, to a point, accepted. Through demonstrated understanding, respect is shown and respect gained. The "psychologist official" understands that excessive "all-win" approaches, although not purely justified, have become habitual in many people, and that habits and attitudes resist change. Such an official is ready to penalize unabusively those excesses contrary to the rules, but realizes that he or she may be able to influence but *cannot change* habitual approaches. Such an official recognizes that, like any human beings, players, coaches, or spectators become excited, elated, frustrated, embarrassed, infuriated, etc. Such an official is prepared to accept and deal with his or her own emotions in a mature fashion so as not to "add fuel to the fire."

As an "In-House" Attorney

It *is possible* for others to damage you or for you to damage others as a part of your officiating activity. Devote a corner of your mind to legal considerations. Become a student of the legal aspects of sports officiating.

As a Statesman

Beyond knowing the rules, ruling accurately, and executing the mechanics—the official can and should maintain a grasp of overall responsibilities, capabilities, and motivations related to a specific contest. Such a grasp will enable the official to respond and communicate clearly, logically, and wisely, and to deal with emergencies appropriately. All truly outstanding sports officials exemplify this role.

Summary

There is an urgent need for qualified sports officials, both men and women, to meet the demands of an expanding sports scene. Regardless of the level of competition, the benefits of athletic competition are greater when the contest is guided by capable sports officials. The results of competition should depend entirely on the preparation, ability, sportsmanship, and effort of players and coaches, on game strategy, and on luck. By applying the rules consistently and with good judgment, by setting an example of and encouraging good sportsmanship, by dealing with emergencies objectively and humanely—the official can exert a tremendous positive influence on the game.

Sports officials should be guided by an overall purpose of enabling the contest to progress smoothly, with as little interference as possible. The essential ingredients of effective sports officiating are (1) intelligent rule enforcement, (2) absolute integrity, (3) sound human relationships, and (4) a focus upon the protection of the individual athlete.

Competent sports officials continuously strive to improve themselves, and they measure their performance against standards such as the "qualities of a competent official" described in this book. They also are prepared to assume several different roles, according to the demands of the particular situation.

Sports officiating is a difficult but rewarding avocation. The primary rewards will relate more to personal development and satisfaction than to financial gain. When sports officials are well trained, highly dedicated, and fully aware of the total requirements of their responsibilities, athletic competition will benefit.

2

Getting Off to a Good Start

The first few games you work can be of particular importance to your future as an official. A general pattern of relative success, adequacy, or failure becomes evident to you—and to the players and coaches for whom you work. (Obviously, the quality and direction of your work can change in either direction after these initial assignments.) Early success will encourage and motivate you to further improve your knowledge, judgment, mechanics, and mannerisms. Early failure or mediocrity can hamper your development as a sports official. Premature discouragement undoubtedly is the greatest cause of a high "drop-out" rate during the first year of officiating. Much of this discouragement can be *avoided* through intelligent preparation and a more complete understanding of certain pitfalls which threaten the potentially successful career of the inexperienced official.

Our purpose is to provide you with practical suggestions which will help you to achieve success during your early officiating assignments. *Anyone* can follow these suggestions. The only requirements are time and effort.

Preliminary Preparation

If you follow the suggestions of this section, you will be prepared in a general sense for the mental, physical, and emotional realities of your first assignment.

Photo by Brian Drake/Focus West

1. **Watch as many games as you can, not as a spectator but as an official.** Whether you are watching the game in person or on television, * imagine yourself as being one of that game's officials. Live the game with them. Make decisions with them or criticize their decisions. Imagine yourself blowing the whistle, signaling, talking with the team captains, dealing with the emergencies that are a part of that game, and so forth.

   It is beneficial to watch any game at any level—professional, college, high school, or recreational—but the benefits are greater if you can arrange to see contests at the same level as that of your first expected assignments. The requirements at each level are somewhat different.

   Try to arrive at the game in time to observe the officials during the pre-game activity. Bring a notebook and plan your analysis of the officials in an organized fashion. Know in advance what you are looking for. You might organize your notes under some of the following categories:

   a. What were the strengths and weaknesses of each official?
   b. What happened in the game that (1) created problems or (2) caused the game to progress well from the officials' points of view?
   c. Were there any particularly good or particularly poor decisions or mechanics? What were they and how much did they affect the game?
   d. Specifically, how well did the officials communicate, maintain good position, react decisively, know their rules and mechanics, and show good judgment?
   e. If you had the opportunity, how would you advise each official regarding individual improvement? (Refer to the twelve qualities discussed in Chapter 1.)

   In officiating basketball and football, perhaps the most common and the most difficult fault for the inexperienced official to correct is that of habitually focusing complete attention on the ball, to the exclusion of action away from the ball. This habit can and must be broken. It can be corrected to a considerable degree before your first assignment if you actively avoid overattention on the ball while watching other officials work. When you watch any game, *watch it as an official.*

2. **Participate actively in officials' meetings.** Unfortunately, many sports officials, especially the experienced officials, approach training meetings of the local officials' association with a degree of apathy.

---

*The advent of instant replays and reversals of officials' rulings based on review of TV tapes, while controversial in some quarters, has enhanced significantly the development of prospective sports officials.

Such an approach can "rub off" onto the young, prospective official and will hamper development. Regardless of the attitudes of other officials, these meetings *can be* great learning experiences if they are approached in a positive and active manner. There is a wealth of knowledge and experience available to you at these meetings. You can find the answer to almost any officiating question that you have. You can gain the acquaintanceship of locally outstanding officials. Strong sports officials take pride in their work and are pleased to assist the less experienced official.

3. **Secure adequate officiating equipment.**   Until you earn a reputation as a qualified sports official, you must at least *look* the part. Avoid the undesirable shortcuts of wrong colored shoes, socks, belts and jackets. Don't use a cheap whistle. Such compromises almost certainly will return to plague you. Until you demonstrate your skill, you are only an image, an impression. You might as well present a favorable professional image. Your first few assignments will be challenging enough in themselves without adding to the burden by *appearing to be unprepared.*

4. **Be sure that you are in good physical condition.**   You will be surprised at how physically tiring your first games will be. The inexperienced official is tense and feels a need to overhustle. An inexperienced official runs farther than is necessary and does not know how or when to conserve energy.

5. **Volunteer your services at preseason scrimmages.**   There is no substitute for direct experience. All coaches who plan preseason competitive experiences for their teams would like some of these to be officiated. The preseason scrimmage presents an opportunity for the official, as well as for players and coaches, to tune up, to identify and correct weaknesses in advance. An added benefit is the appreciation and good will of coaches which you gain by volunteering to help. Many new officials have found that their willingness to donate services before the season has resulted in more assignments later.

6. **Concentrate on the basics first.**   You cannot "learn it all" before the first assignment. In fact, you will *never* learn it all. Too much concern over minor details early in your career bogs you down and is confusing to the learning process. For example, a new basketball official should not expect to know and demonstrate every hand signal at his or her first game, such as for an intentional foul, lack of action, and three-, five-, or ten-second violations. On the other hand he/she must know and use correctly the correct signals for beckoning a substitute, personal foul, score or no score, and pointing the direction following a violation.

The "basics" for your early attention are:

a. A knowledge of the common rules and penalties.
b. An understanding of the fundamentals of positioning mechanics.
c. The ability to use routine signals properly.
d. A determination to employ the fundamental aspects of teamwork with fellow officials.

Pregame Preparation

This section is meant to help you feel prepared in a specific sense for each of your first officiating assignments.

1. **If possible, know the teams and the playing areas.** The veteran official sometimes has an added advantage over the neophyte because of advance knowledge about the opposing teams, their coaches, and the playing site. Such an official is better prepared mentally for the job because without prejudging the game to be worked, he or she knows the playing styles, the coaches' mannerisms, the number and emotional involvement of spectators, and characteristics of the playing area, such as space, obstacles, surface, timing device, and special ground rules.

   The new official cannot possibly gather and digest all this information before his or her assignment, but by means of advance preparation can learn some of it. Local newspapers can be checked, other officials can be asked, even games or practice sessions may be observed.

2. **If possible, plan to travel to the game with a fellow official.** A phone call or two a few days in advance of the contest can help to produce a better officiated game. There is no end to the number of points that can be discussed by officials working together in any sport. In all sports there are difficult rules interpretations and difficult circumstances with mechanics that can be identified, clarified, and agreed upon. Mutual respect and confidence can grow during the trip. A good relationship with a fellow official is especially rewarding for the inexperienced official.

3. **Plan to be at the game early.** Do not accept an assignment if you cannot be there, dressed and ready, approximately one-half hour before the game's scheduled time. Estimate your travel time conservatively to avoid being late. The hurried official who runs onto the court two minutes before the center jump is asking for trouble and is creating a very bad initial impression.

4. **Be well rested and sharp.** Occasionally the official will experience a game in which one near-impossible situation after another will occur.

If tired and dull-witted, these "near-impossible" situations *become impossible.* Be sure that you get a good night's sleep before each assignment. Avoid large meals immediately before the game.

5. **Never anticipate an easy game.** Fortunately, you will have easy games from time to time, but you will enjoy these more and *get more of them* if they come as pleasant surprises. It is not suggested that you should be worried or fearful, or that you prejudge an assignment, but that you approach each assignment with the same kind of respect and seriousness as that of a former nonswimmer approaching deep water. Your chances of meeting the challenge of a really tough game will be better.

At the Game

Each individual official soon develops an individual officiating personality and habit pattern. Until these become apparent and are further implemented and improved, the inexperienced official needs guidelines which will help to avoid trouble. Here are some suggestions.

1. **Don't try to oversell yourself.** Many new officials understandably want to prove immediately to players, coaches, and spectators alike that they are not only capable but friendly and personable; such an overall impression, however, will develop only as a result of the job done. You want such an impression to prevail after the game more than before the game. A coach who does not know an official may distrust one whose approach is overly cordial or personal. You must be approachable, but as an "official" in every sense of the word, you are expected to maintain *distance* from players, coaches, and spectators.

    To summarize this important but rather subtle point it is suggested that you let good, positive relationships grow naturally and without force, based mostly on the skill and hustle that you demonstrate and partly on your willingness to cooperate and be approachable.

2. **Actively try to avoid the common mistakes frequently made by inexperienced officials.** Awareness of these common mistakes can help you to avoid them and will also reassure you that most inexperienced officials do make them. Following are some of the mistakes most commonly made, with suggestions on how to avoid them:

    a. *Over-anticipating.* Nothing can be called until it *happens.* It is better to be a split-second late in your decision than to rule incorrectly, or to rule on something that simply did not happen or that had no effect on the competition.

b. *Rushing your signals.* The cause of this is the same as for over-anticipation, that is, over-anxiousness. Tell yourself: "Don't rush, let it happen"; be deliberate, then signal in a decisive manner when you know it happened. Many rushed signals are not even seen; thus the effect of a given decision is diminished or lost. See the section on "Poise" in Chapter 1.

c. *Not enforcing the rules.* As an inexperienced official, you will probably approach your early assignments cautiously. Occasionally, this caution can result in overlooking rule infractions which, you might rationalize "really didn't affect the game that much," or which "the other official was in a better position to call." If you experience this type of difficulty, it is sometimes helpful to remind yourself that both teams and both coaches depend on you for a fair outcome of the game. You must try to enforce the rules.

d. *Being out of position.* The veteran official maintains good position habitually; the new official must compensate for lack of habits by mentally anticipating the flow of action. It is helpful to remind yourself constantly, during "dead spots" of the game, about the basic positioning mechanics found in any sport. Just before the jump ball in basketball, for example, the outside official can anticipate two or three possible movements depending upon the outcome of the jump.

e. *Overreacting to complaints.* Remind yourself that no matter how hard you work, or even how competently you perform, complaints will come to all officials in all sports. Your reaction to "beefs" early in your career will be of great importance to your development. Even when you *know* your decision was correct, react to the complaints with calmness and firmness. If the complaint concerns your judgment, nothing can be done about it. If, on the other hand, a rule interpretation is involved and you are not certain about the rule, you might wish to confer quickly with a fellow official. Incorrect rule interpretations can and should be reversed immediately.

Perhaps the most difficult circumstance for a new official is a confrontation with a coach who habitually baits officials. If such a coach decides that you have "rabbit ears," you will soon be in serious trouble. Under such circumstances, try to think of the game and the players—not of the coach or of yourself. Disregard the first taunts. If they continue, approach the coach in a no-nonsense manner—*inconspicuously and positively, but not in anger.* You will be helping the game, the players, and yourself (not to mention the coach) if you can regain control and settle the coach.

f. *Showing your nervousness.* Experience is the best cure for nervousness, but even the totally inexperienced official can use human traits to combat undesirable nervousness. Constantly talk yourself into being *deliberate,* not rushing. Be an actor. Even though you may be quite unsure of yourself, you don't have to *show* your lack of confidence. Actively *simulate* a confident manner. Play the role of the most poised official that you have ever seen. If you really throw yourself into this type of role-playing you will be amazed at the results.

After the Game

Certain procedures following each early assignment can guarantee improvement. These procedures are commonly overlooked by new officials. The idea is simple: be sure that you complete the learning process of each early assignment.

1. **After the game discuss it with fellow officials.** The other officials have seen you in action, they know what kind of a game it was, and they know something about officiating. Ask them for suggestions. Preferably, take notes on what they tell you.
2. **Keep your own "book" on your personal improvement.** As soon as possible after each early assignment, write down every significant fact that you can remember. Evaluate not only your own performance but that of the other officials. You can learn from their strengths and weaknesses as well as from your own. Your notebook might include some of the following sections:

   a. New rule interpretations that you learned.
   b. New mechanics or techniques that you observed in the other officials.
   c. Your identifiable weaknesses in terms of rules, mechanics, judgment, and relationships in this particular game.
   d. Questions to ask at the next officials' meeting.
   e. Specific goals for improving at the next assigned game.

Many of the best and most experienced professional and college sports officials keep such a notebook because they know that there is always room for improvement. Certainly the values accruing to an inexperienced official are greater.

Hard work and intelligent preparation guarantee relative success for every athlete. The same is true for sports officials. Just as a college freshman basketball player would, you also should set high standards regarding preparation for your first sports officiating season.

Good Luck!

3

Baseball and Softball

The Game

Baseball, "The Great American Pastime," remains today a significant part of this country's sport scene, having become the nation's first great spectator sport during the nineteenth century. More and more players have joined and strengthened this tradition as softball and Little League Baseball were created and flourished. Today, more than forty years after his death, Babe Ruth may still be the most familiar name in American sports. The umpire, although sometimes maligned, has always been an integral part of this heritage.

In baseball and softball, umpires as well as players face stern individual tests within a team setting. The major challenges for the umpire involve (1) gaining the near-perfect position necessary to rule on close calls in a "game of inches," (2) matching split-second action with split-second decisions; and (3) teaming with fellow umpires to cover the "anything can happen" situations that arise.

In the first few games, the beginning baseball or softball official will learn that this is a unique game which imposes unique demands on its officials. First, the umpire, especially the plate umpire, is more completely alone than officials in most other sports. This means that an umpire must possess a high level of personal confidence in his or her ability as an umpire. The umpire makes the decision, an isolated decision, and must live with it and make it stand, with little or no backing from anyone else, including his/her fellow umpires.

Second, the beginning umpire will learn that to argue with a baseball or softball official is commonplace and traditional—more so than in other sports. Despite efforts to restrict complaints and histrionics, they remain a "part of the game," a reality that each official must learn to tolerate to a degree, *yet permit only so far and no farther.* This means that the umpire must show patience and must understand the game, its players, and coaches. Under no circumstances, however, should the umpire tolerate ridicule, continuous badgering, profanity, or other gross demonstrations of disrespect.

The third challenge involves the extensive and precise rules of baseball and softball and the need for continuous study. To an amazing degree, almost every freak play that ever has happened or could happen is covered in the rules. (See Play Rulings, page 57.) There is no substitute for knowing the rules.

Fourth, almost every game produces several very close ball-or-strike and safe-or-out decisions. The umpire must possess *finely tuned eyesight* and *fast reactions* in order to rule correctly, immediately, and decisively.

Fifth, the umpire, as well as the spectator, will often find the pace of a baseball game to be hypnotically repetitive. The effect of such a pace, especially on the field or base umpire, can lull one to sleep. *Steady concentration* is a must. The better umpires—both base and plate umpires—frequently ask themselves during a game, "What could happen next?"—in order to maintain their alertness. Also, due to the pace of the game, both *physical* and *mental endurance* is required. The umpire is expected to rule just as effectively in the seventh or twelfth inning as in the first inning.

Finally, baseball and softball are games that do not progress according to a time schedule (unless there is a predetermined time limit). It is a seven, nine, or extra inning game which could last an hour and a half or *four* hours and a half.

Consider the aforementioned challenges and demands. It has been said that umpires are the only professionals who are expected to be perfect and then get better through experience. Many umpires work both baseball and softball games, since the requirements, basic skills, and equipment are very similar for each sport. * Since softball field distances are shorter than baseball, the game seems faster. The emphasis in umpiring as well as in playing softball is on *quickness* and *anticipation.* The differences in umpiring baseball and softball will be emphasized in

---

*One important caution should be observed: the "look" of a fast pitch softball pitch to the respective plate umpire is diametrically different from a baseball pitch. Plate umpires seeking to switch from one of these great sports to the other can expect difficulties at first. Significantly different are the angles of delivery, the "breaks" of various pitches, and even the elapsed time.

each applicable section of this chapter. A special section on slow pitch softball appears in the "miscellaneous considerations" section.

Officials and Their Responsibilities

The officials include the umpires and the scorer. From one to six umpires may officiate in baseball, and from one to four umpire softball games, depending on the level of play. The vast majority of games, however, are officiated by just two umpires: the *plate umpire* (or the umpire-in-chief) and the *base umpire* (or field umpire). The major emphasis in this chapter is on the two umpire system.

Officials' Uniforms and Equipment

Baseball umpires now wear gray pants and softball umpires wear dark blue pants. All umpires wear a light blue shirt, an umpire's cap, black polished shoes, black socks, and a trouser belt of black leather. Umpires working a given game should be dressed alike, other than differences specified for the plate umpire. The plate umpire should wear metal-reinforced shoes, shin guards, an inside or outside chest protector, a sturdy mask with a throat protector, and a protective supporter and cup. The plate umpire also needs an accurate watch (not worn), a small whisk broom easily containable in a ball bag, and a navy blue or gray ball bag (matched with the pant color) attached to the belt at the hip. All umpires in a crew, particularly the plate umpire, should have a ball and strike indicator. The umpires should never be without a cap. Three styles of umpire caps are now available: short visored (plate umpire only), long visored (base umpire only), and "combo" visored (either umpire).

Plate Umpire

The umpire-in-chief takes a position behind the catcher. He or she renders decisions on balls and strikes and almost all fair and foul batted balls. The plate umpire has general responsibility for the conduct of the game, establishes, as is necessary, special "ground" rules or other regulations, informs the official scorer of changes in the lineups, and has the sole authority to forfeit the game. The plate umpire is constantly making decisions involving, among others, an approximate 200 pitches per game. The plate umpire runs the game and sets the tempo.

Base Umpire

The base umpire varies field position according to the game situation and makes almost all of the decisions at the three bases. The field umpire has equal responsibility with the plate umpire for all rulings, including discipline and control, with the exception of those specified for the plate umpire. The base umpire covers a large territory, while the decisions rendered are fewer and more irregular. This official tends to be in the background far more than the plate umpire.

Umpires

Each umpire may rule on any matter not specifically covered in the rules. Each may disqualify any coach, player, or substitute, and banish any other person from the playing field. One umpire may seek the assistance of another umpire on any decision, * but *under no circumstances may any umpire seek to reverse the decision of a fellow umpire.* Umpires are encouraged to work both as plate and base umpires to enhance their opportunity for advancement. A degree of personal flexibility is necessary to adapt to either position, since the responsibilities of each are so different.

Official Scorer

Because of the complexities of baseball and softball statistics, the official scorer has a demanding job. One of ten baseball rules (Rule 9) and one of twelve softball rules (Rule 12) deal solely with scoring. The official scorer, therefore, should be a conscientious, meticulous, and dedicated person, preferably one who is avidly interested in baseball or softball.

The official scorer operates semi-independent of the umpires. Normally, the only contact with them occurs when there are lineup changes or questions concerning the scoring of a run or the number of outs. In certain lower levels of baseball, the scorer is required to report immediately to the plate umpire a player batting out of turn in order to alleviate technicality rulings.

Basic Penalties and Rulings

The intent here, as in other chapters, is to emphasize the essentials and to present a logical framework for better understanding of the rulebook itself. There is no substitute for concentrated study of baseball and softball rules.

The Four Cornerstone Rulings of Baseball and Softball

There are four routine decisions in baseball and softball: ruling whether each pitch is a *strike* or *ball;* whether a batted ball is *fair* or *foul;* whether a baserunner is *safe* or *out;* and whether or not a batter is out

---

*See "Teamwork" section, p. 48.

because a fly ball has been caught. At least ninety percent of all umpiring decisions involve these four decisions. The last of the four is usually a clear-cut, uncomplicated ruling: If any batted ball, fair or foul, is caught by a defensive player before the ball touches the ground or other fixed object, the batter is out.

The plate umpire shall call a pitch a "strike" if (1) the batter swings and misses or (2) if the batter does not swing and *any part of the ball passes over any part of home plate between the batter's armpits and top of the knees.* Thus, strikes may be categorized as "swinging" or "called." The softball strike zone is wider than the baseball strike zone because the ball is larger (softball cf.: 12"—baseball cf.: 9"). The difference is even greater in 16-inch slow pitch (see Slow Pitch section at end of chapter). A strike is also ruled when there is (1) a foul ball with less than two strikes on the batter; (2) a "foul tip" (even on the third strike); or (3) a fouled bunt attempt with two strikes on the batter. All other pitches which are not batted are ruled "balls" by the plate umpire. Three strikes constitutes a "strike-out," or four balls results in a "base on balls" being awarded to the batter.

Each batted ball is ruled to be a "fair" or a "foul" ball. A batted ball is foul when it is *first touched, contacts any unnatural object, or leaves the park outside the foul lines,*—that is, to the right of the first base line or to the left of the third base line. All other batted balls are ruled to be fair balls. The baselines and all the bases, including home plate, are in fair territory. A ground ball bouncing directly over first or third base is a fair ball, even if the first bounce beyond the base is outside the baseline. When a batted ball is touched near the first or third base line, the *position of the ball,* not the position of the player, is the deciding factor.

Only when a play is made on the runners is it necessary to signal a decision that the baserunner is "safe" or "out." The common reasons for ruling a baserunner "out" are either when the runner is tagged by a defensive player while the runner is not in contact with a base, or when the runner is "forced" out. In force play situations, it is necessary merely for the defensive player to have the ball and be in contact with the given base. A force out situation is created when the batter batting a ground ball (or a fly ball which is not caught) and becoming a baserunner "forces" runners to advance to the next base. Plays made on the batter-runner attempting to reach first base are always force plays. No baserunner except the batter-runner is forced if first base is not occupied. If all bases are occupied, a ground ball creates a force play at all three bases and home plate. If a *succeeding* runner is forced out, the "force" is removed for the *preceding* runners and preceding runners must be tagged.

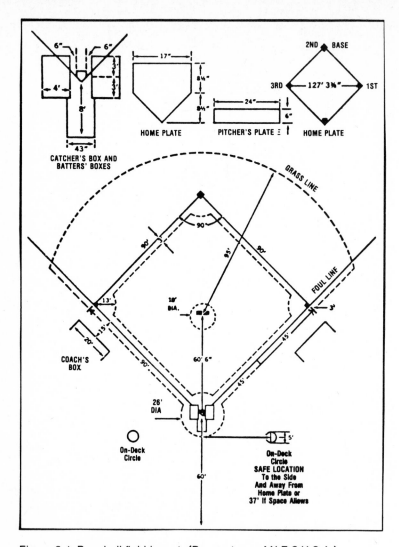

Figure 3.1 Baseball field layout. (By courtesy of N.F.S.H.S.A.)

Rule Differences: Baseball and Fast Pitch Softball
The basic rule differences are:

1. Baserunning. In baseball, baserunners may "lead off" bases before a pitch. In fast pitch softball, baserunners must maintain contact with their bases until the pitch is released. The softball umpire should rule a baserunner(s) out if (1) the runner(s) leaves the base before a pitch is released; or (2) the runner(s), following a pitch or a play, fails to return

OFFICIAL DIMENSIONS
FOR SOFTBALL DIAMONDS

Prepared by The Amateur Softball Association

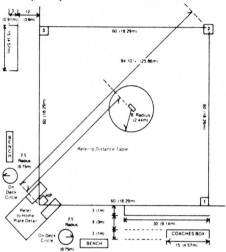

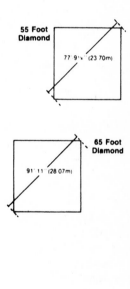

55 Foot
Diamond

77' 9¼' (23.70m)

65 Foot
Diamond

91' 11' (28.07m)

DISTANCE TABLE				
ADULT				
GAME	DIVISION	BASES	PITCHING	FENCES
Fast Pitch	Women	60' (18.29 m)	40' (12.19 m)	200' (60.96 m)
	Men	60' (18.29 m)	46' (14.02 m)	250' (76.20 m)
	Jr. Men	60' (18.29 m)	46' (14.02 m)	250' (76.20 m)
Modified	Women	60' (18.29 m)	40' (12.19 m)	200' (60.96 m)
	Men	60' (18.29 m)	46' (14.02 m)	265' (80.80 m)
Slow Pitch	Women	65' (19.81 m)	50' (15.24 m)	250' (76.20 m)
	Men	65' (19.81 m)	50' (15.24 m)	275' (83.82 m)
	Co-Ed	65' (19.81 m)	50' (15.24 m)	275' (83.82 m)
	Super	65' (19.81 m)	50' (15.24 m)	300' (91.44 m)
16 Inch	Women	55' (16.76 m)	38' (11.58 m)	200' (60.96 m)
Slow Pitch	Women	55' (16.76 m)	38' (11.58 m)	250' (76.20 m)

YOUTH				FENCES	
GAME	DIVISION	BASES	PITCHING	Minimum	Maximum
Slow	Girls 10-under	55' (16.76 m)	35' (10.67 m)	150' (45.72 m)	175' (53.34 m)
Pitch	Boys 10-under	55' (16.76 m)	35' (10.67 m)	150' (45.72 m)	175' (53.34 m)
	Girls 12-under	60' (18.29 m)	40' (12.19 m)	175' (53.34 m)	200' (60.96 m)
	Boys 12-under	60' (18.29 m)	40' (12.19 m)	175' (53.34 m)	200' (60.96 m)
	Girls 14-under	65' (19.81 m)	46' (14.02 m)	225' (68.58 m)	250' (76.20 m)
	Boys 14-under	65' (19.81 m)	46' (14.02 m)	250' (76.20 m)	275' (83.82 m)
	Girls 16-under	65' (19.81 m)	46' (14.02 m)	225' (68.58 m)	250' (76.20 m)
	Boys 16-under	65' (19.81 m)	46' (14.02 m)	275' (83.82 m)	300' (91.44 m)
	Girls 18-under	65' (19.81 m)	46' (14.02 m)	225' (68.58 m)	250' (76.20 m)
	Boys 18-under	65' (19.81 m)	50' (15.24 m)	275' (83.82 m)	300' (91.44 m)
Fast	Girls 10-under	55' (16.76 m)	35' (10.67 m)	150' (45.72 m)	175' (53.34 m)
Pitch	Boys 10-under	55' (16.76 m)	35' (10.67 m)	150' (45.72 m)	175' (53.34 m)
	Girls 12-under	60' (18.29 m)	35' (12.19 m)	175' (53.34 m)	200' (60.96 m)
	Boys 12-under	60' (18.29 m)	40' (12.19 m)	175' (53.34 m)	200' (60.96 m)
	Girls 14-under	60' (18.29 m)	40' (12.19 m)	175' (53.34 m)	200' (60.96 m)
	Boys 14-under	60' (18.29 m)	46' (12.19 m)	175' (53.34 m)	200' (60.96 m)
	Girls 16-under	60' (18.29 m)	40' (12.19 m)	200' (60.96 m)	225' (68.58 m)
	Boys 16-under	60' (18.29 m)	46' (12.19 m)	200' (60.96 m)	225' (68.58 m)
	Girls 18-under	60' (18.29 m)	40' (12.19 m)	200' (60.96 m)	225' (68.58 m)
	Boys 18-under	60' (18.29 m)	46' (12.19 m)	200' (60.96 m)	225' (68.58 m)

Figure 3.2A Softball field layout.
(By courtesy of Amateur Softball
Association of America.)

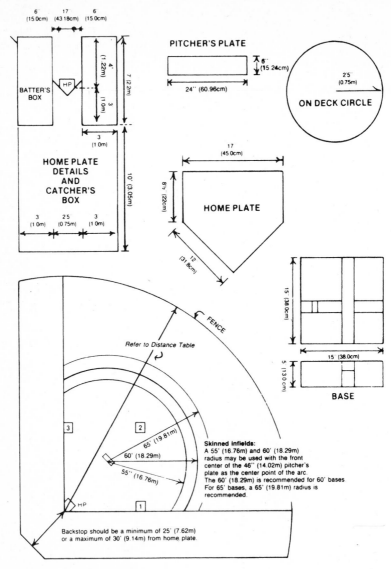

Figure 3.2B Softball field layout. (By courtesy of Amateur Softball Association of America.)

to the base or advance to the next base, once the pitcher has the ball within an eight-foot radius of the pitcher's plate.

The technical nature of the above rules, and the "close calls" they produce, impose added demands on softball officials. Baseball and softball baserunning rules are the same regarding tag-outs, force-outs, interference, obstruction, appeal plays, etc.

2. Pitching. One pitching delivery is implied in softball rules and two, "windup" and "set," are specified in baseball rules. The set position is used for the purpose of holding runners close to their bases before the pitch. A violation of the pitching rules results in an "illegal pitch" in both softball and baseball. In baseball, an illegal pitch with one or more runners on base becomes a "balk." The penalty for an illegal pitch in both baseball and fast pitch is to call a "ball" on the batter and rule the ball dead. When a balk is called in baseball, each baserunner is advanced one base and the ball is ruled dead, but a ball is not called on the batter. In fast pitch, an illegal pitch with runner(s) on base results in the advance of any baserunner(s), the ball becoming dead, *and* a ball called on the batter. These penalties are not enforced and the ball remains alive if action resulting from an illegal pitch causes the batter to advance at least one base and causes all baserunners to advance at least one base. (The intent of the rules is to avoid interruption of game action if the offensive team gains the same or greater advantage without the penalty.) The plate umpire and/or base umpire should immediately and loudly call "ILLEGAL PITCH" or "BALK," but *withhold* any "dead ball" and enforcement rulings until after any extra action following the pitch, such as a batted ball or wild pitch.

Listed below are selected pitching rule interpretations for both baseball and softball. Violations of these should be ruled *illegal pitches* or, when in baseball there are runners on base, *balks.*

From the *baseball windup position,* the pitcher may not:

1. execute more than two pumps;
2. stop or alter his or her windup motion, once started; or
3. lift the pivot foot clearly off the pitcher's plate.

When executing the *baseball* set position, the pitcher must:

1. come to a complete stop before pitching;
2. not separate the hands without immediately delivering a pitch or throwing to an occupied base;

3. step towards home plate on a pitch or towards the particular base when attempting a "pick-off";
4. deliver the ball once committed to home plate or first base by any habitual movement; and
5. not assume a pitching position without the ball, or drop the ball, or feint toward the batter or runner at first base.

The *softball* pitcher must:

1. start the delivery with the pivot foot or both feet in contact with the pitcher's plate;
2. take the signal from the catcher with hands separated, the ball in either hand;
3. bring hands together;
4. step toward the batter;
5. take no more than two revolutions in a "windmill" motion; and
6. pitch underhanded, the wrist being below the hip and the wrist not farther from the body than the elbow.

Obviously, pitching rules are complicated. Considerable observation and experience as well as a thorough knowledge of the rules are required before an umpire can rule accurately and consistently.

Other than the above differences, plus differences in field dimensions and equipment regulations, the rules of baseball and softball are almost identical. Most successful baseball umpires can adjust to softball umpiring, and vice versa.

Mechanics

Mechanics are defined as the standard operating procedures for officials working a game. The focus here is on the two umpire system.

In baseball and softball umpiring mechanics, voice and hand signals make a considerable impression on the spectator but are comparatively uncomplicated and few in number. The major attention must be devoted to *positioning* mechanics, especially by the base umpire, and to *teamwork* mechanics. Positioning and teamwork are of great importance in umpiring because of the problems imposed by the combination of *speed of action* and *distance.* The two umpires are responsible for covering action at all four bases and occasionally in the outfield and foul territory. The normally high velocity of batted or thrown balls creates problems for an umpire who started in or moved towards the wrong position or who was unaware of teamwork coverage guidelines, that specify which umpire is responsible for which decision and for which playing area.

Plate Umpire Positioning

Plate umpire positioning mechanics are the same in baseball and softball. The major differences between the two sports in calling balls and strikes concern the respective ball sizes and the respective time elements and movements of the pitches. These differences do not create major problems for an umpire with good eyesight and quick reactions. Because of the shorter pitching distance, the typical softball fast pitch obviously takes less time to reach home plate. The movement or "break" on a pitch in fast pitch softball or baseball can be remarkable, depending on the pitcher's ability.

The difference between a called ball and a called strike can be as slight as you wish to imagine; an inch, a quarter of an inch, or a sixteenth of an inch. In order to reduce the margin of error, it is necessary for the *plate umpire* to secure and maintain a low position close to the catcher. Most important, the view of the pitch must remain unobstructed by the catcher and the batter. The plate umpire should *stay with* the pitch and avoid the natural tendency to "back off" or to "raise up" as the pitch arrives. A natural tendency to "blink," especially when the batter swings, can be reduced through practice.

Previously, there were two recommended plate umpire positions: the National League (inside corner) position, commonly known as "working the slot," and the over-the-top position. Currently, all umpiring organizations, including both major leagues and the federation softball associations, favor the inside corner position. The beginning umpire will find that it is easier to umpire from the inside corner (that side edge of the plate closest to the hitter) with an inside chest protector rather than with a "balloon" type protector.

Base Umpire Starting Positions

It should be emphasized from the outset that base umpire starting positions can be varied somewhat according to the particular situation and the preferences of individual umpires. Before each pitch the base umpire should find a position which promotes a feeling of readiness and confidence and does not obstruct the vision or movements of any defensive player or baserunner. Many umpires have found that a slight movement towards the batter with each pitch keeps them alert and not flatfooted but ready to "get the jump" on the next play.

With no runners on base, the starting positions are approximately the same in baseball and softball in the two umpire system, although in softball the umpire is closer to first base. With runners on base, the baseball base umpire is positioned inside the baseline, while the softball field umpire stays behind the infielders. The behind-the-infielders position enables the softball field umpire to determine whether baserunners leave too soon and also reduces congestion in the smaller infield area.

Figures 3.3 and 3.4 show the basic starting positions for the two umpire system in baseball and softball.

Base Umpire Positioning on Specific Plays

Base hits to the outfield. On any base hit to the outfield (except when an outfielder might "trap" a fly ball) the field umpire wants to be inside the baselines as quickly as possible. This will shorten considerably the distance to be run and allow a view of both the ball and the runner. The base umpire should attempt to maintain a slight lead on the batter-runner in order to provide sufficient time to get set for a ruling at second or third base without "racing" the batter-runner.

Putouts at first base. The mechanics here are far more complicated than one would think. The principles are (1) to move as far as possible in the direction of the pitcher's mound to a position about fifteen to twenty feet from first base *without obstructing the throw* and (2) to *get set* before making a decision. The base umpire moves farther toward the pitcher's mound when the throw is from the third baseman than would be the case on a throw from the second baseman. * A position closer than fifteen feet restricts the umpire's perspective. The umpire should watch the ball as he or she moves into position, and continue to watch the ball as it is thrown. *Just before the throw arrives* at first base, the umpire should quickly transfer vision to the first baseman's base-tagging foot to be certain that it is in contact with the base. At the precise moment that the ball reaches the mitt, the umpire wants to have achieved a position where peripheral vision permits a simultaneous view of both the mitt and the foot. Also, on very close plays, some experienced umpires will allow the *sounds* of the ball and of the batter/runner's foot to influence the decision made. (Which sound occurred first? The ball or the foot?) In some cases, when the ball is "in the dirt" a slight hesitation is necessary before making the decision.

Force double plays and sacrifice bunts. Considerable experience is required to enable the base umpire always to move in the correct direction on second-to-first double plays and sacrifice bunt plays. The

---

*ASA mechanics call for the base umpire to move no further toward the pitcher's area than a 45° point (that is, a point bisecting the angle between the right field foul line and a line from first to second base). In softball *or* baseball, there is little or no advantage to positioning yourself beyond the 45° point.

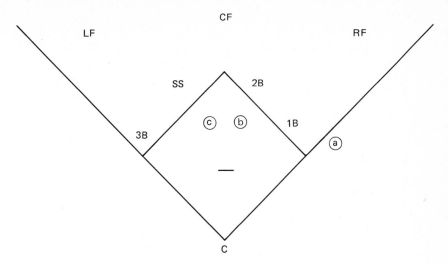

Figure 3.3 Baseball base umpire starting positions in the two-umpire system (before the pitch). a—No baserunners; b—Runner on first; c—Runner on second, third, first and second, first and third, or bases loaded.

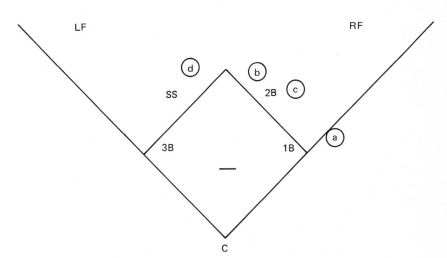

Figure 3.4 Fast pitch base umpire starting positions. a—No baserunners; b—Runner on first; c—(fast pitch only) Optional position, runner on first; d—Runner on second, first and second, or bases loaded. (For slow pitch see page 56.)

underlying principle is to move toward the base where the play will be the closest. On double plays, the base umpire must not overanticipate and turn the head too quickly toward first base after the first play at second base. Look first for a dropped ball by the pivot man or for interference by the baserunner near second base, either of which would cancel the need to look at first base.

Attempts to steal second base. This is a much easier call in softball than in baseball because the entire play is in front of the softball base umpire. In softball, all you need to do is (1) check for the runner leaving too early and (2) adjust your position to a point where the tag can be viewed—about ten feet from second base to the outfield side, but not behind the runner. Since most slides on steal attempts are executed to the outfield side of the base, your angle should favor the outfield side of the base in order to avoid being screened out by the runner's slide.

In baseball, the umpire is positioned inside the baselines. The umpire must first concentrate on the possibility of a balk and then use anticipation and peripheral vision to detect the steal attempt. As the play develops, the umpire moves towards second base parallel to the baseline while watching the catcher's throw. *The first time that the umpire should see the runner is when the ball arrives at second base.* Inexperienced umpires have a tendency to take their eyes off the catcher's throw in order to glance at the runner or even turn toward first base rather than toward second base as the play develops. There is no advantage whatsoever for the umpire to observe the runner. On this play, as in most baseball plays, *nothing can happen without the ball.* As the tag is being attempted, the umpire should get set on both feet and avoid signaling any decision while moving. If there is considerable impact at the moment of the tag and the runner appears to be out, the umpire should delay the signal momentarily in order to be certain that the fielder has held the ball. Ask to see the ball if you are not certain.

Signals

There are no differences between the basic baseball and softball signals, which are shown in Figure 3.5.

Umpires coordinate voice signals with hand signals. The principle is to use greater voice volume and greater hand signal decisiveness for close decisions than for obvious decisions. By saving emphatic voice and gestures for close decisions, the umpire "tunes in" to the pace of the game and reduces the chance of arguments on close decisions. Voice signals should be used only to call foul balls and *never* for fair balls. This practice helps to prevent confusion.

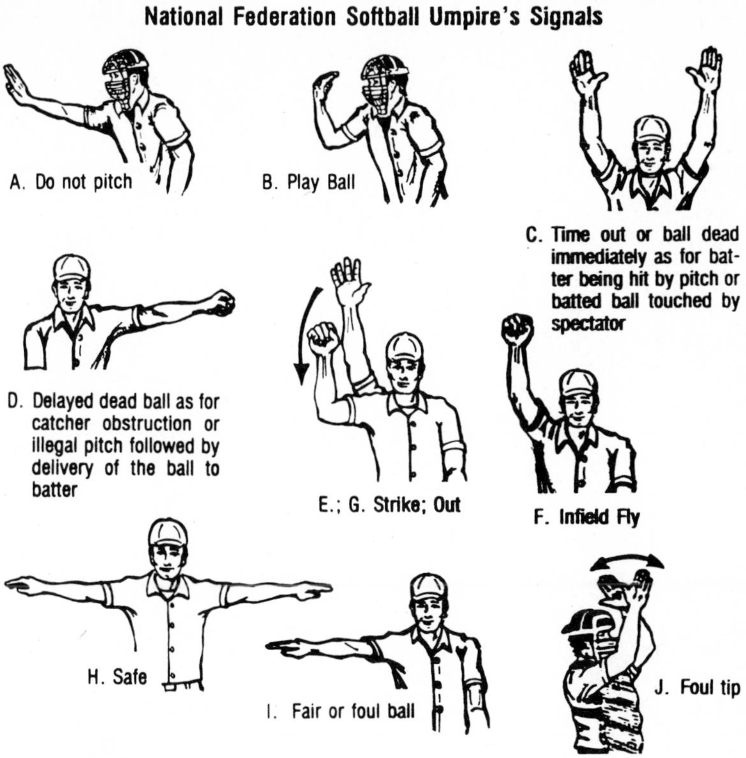

National Federation Softball Umpire's Signals

A. Do not pitch

B. Play Ball

C. Time out or ball dead immediately as for batter being hit by pitch or batted ball touched by spectator

D. Delayed dead ball as for catcher obstruction or illegal pitch followed by delivery of the ball to batter

E.; G. Strike; Out

F. Infield Fly

H. Safe

I. Fair or foul ball

J. Foul tip

Figure 3.5 Umpire's signals (By courtesy of N.F.S.H.S.A.)

Giving the count. The plate umpire should routinely communicate the count on the batter (number of balls and number of strikes) whenever there may be doubt about the count and always when there are either three balls and/or two strikes. The lower the level of play, the more often the count should be given. The count is signaled by steadily holding up both hands, the fingers of the left hand indicating the number of balls and right hand, the strikes. A fist shows either no balls or no strikes. When three fingers are shown, the middle, ring, and little finger should be used. Usually, the count is called as well as shown. The number of balls is called first, followed by the number of strikes. The best moment to give the count is immediately after the catcher has returned the ball to the pitcher; this is a good moment for attention. The voice should be loud enough to be heard and the signal steady and deliberate.

Teamwork

Umpires must constantly be ready to assist each other, in addition to carrying out their individual responsibilities. Following are the primary situations where the base umpire assists the plate umpire or vice versa. These situations apply to baseball and softball alike.

1. *Did the batter swing?* Since the plate umpire must concentrate attention on the pitched ball, there are times when he or she is not able to rule accurately on whether or not the batter completed the swing. The batter must do two things to swing—cause the end of the bat to pass over home plate *and* clearly offer at the pitch. (If the wrists "break" however slightly and the bat passes over home plate, that *is* a swing.) Frequently, the base umpire has a clearer view. The plate umpire should step out in the direction of the base umpire to clearly indicate that assistance is needed on the call. The base umpire should immediately respond by giving the "strike" signal or the "safe" signal to indicate a ball.

2. *Was the force or tag really made?* Either umpire can assist the other at any base on tag or force plays. A common example occurs when, after a ground ball is hit to the infield, the throw pulls the first baseman off the base towards home plate, and the first baseman must go for the tag. The plate umpire usually (not always) has a better angle to see whether or not the tag was actually made. (Signal with a fist for a tag or spread arms for a missed tag attempt.)

3. *Fly ball putouts.* In a two umpire game, one official must watch the catch and the other umpire watches the batter/runner and other runners tag the bases. There must be agreement in advance as to who does what. The advice here is that the plate umpire always watch the catch and the base umpire the tag except when the base umpire must run to the outfield to rule on a near-catch. This will provide a consistent coverage procedure. (Signal with a fist for a catch or spread arms for a muff or trap.)

4. *Plate umpire calls at third base.* Routine mechanics call for the plate umpire to make all decisions at third base when, with first base occupied, there is a base hit to the outfield. This arrangement provides for accurate initial coverage at first and second base (field umpire) and third base and home plate (plate umpire). If there is a decision made at third base by the plate umpire, the *base umpire* must be prepared to rule on any subsequent play at home plate! The plate umpire should move about half way down the third base line as the play develops and prepare to make the initial decision at either third base or home plate. The base umpire is ready to make any decisions at either first or second base, and possibly to assist the plate umpire by making any secondary calls at third base or home plate. If there is a play to call at third base, the plate umpire

must clearly commit to that play in order to establish which umpire is responsible for subsequent action, as well as to provide good coverage at third base. Note that with no runners on base, the base umpire will stay with the batter/runner all the way to and including third base, since there will be no secondary call to be made at second or first base.

There are two other situations when the plate umpire assumes responsibility for rulings at third base.

1. With a runner on second base or runners on first and second, a ground ball is hit to the infield and the first play is to first base. The plate umpire takes a subsequent play at third.
2. With a runner on first base, a bunt is fielded by the third baseman who throws to first. The plate umpire takes subsequent play at third. (The movement of a "heads-up" catcher to cover third can help to remind the plate umpire of this responsibility—but the plate umpire must be "heads up" regardless of the catcher.)

As a general rule, the base umpire will make the first call at any base when there are batted balls to the infield, with or without baserunners.

Problem Calls

Baseball and softball problem calls can be placed in two general categories: (1) calls where the complexity of the rule creates difficulty; and (2) calls where the complexity of mechanics creates difficulty.

Problem Rules

In addition to the four cornerstone rulings discussed previously, five other rule categories frequently create problems for the umpire. Rule book coverage of these rules is difficult for the inexperienced umpire to comprehend, let alone to master to the point where he or she can rule without undue hesitation in a game situation. One of these five categories, *pitching rules,* has been discussed earlier.

The purpose of what follows is to introduce these difficult rulings to the prospective umpire. This must be supplemented by study of the rules, and by observation and discussion. The four additional rule categories are:

1. Interference and obstruction;
2. Appeal plays;
3. "Book rules" for the awarding of bases; and
4. The infield fly rule.

It is interesting to note that, while the four cornerstone rule areas dominate the umpire's attention during a game, very few of the baseball and softball rules refer to them. The bulk of the written rules refer to pitching rules and the four rule categories listed above.

Interference and obstruction. For the most part, baseball and softball are noncontact sports. Inevitably, however, physical contact between opposing players, a player and an umpire, or a player and a spectator will occur. As in basketball, these cases of physical contact, whether intended or unintended, will frequently result in one team gaining an unfair advantage. On such occasions, a ruling is called for by the umpire in order to nullify the unfair advantage. For example:

1. Base umpire contacts a batted ball before an infielder can make a play (ball is dead, batter awarded first base);
2. Baserunner contacts batted ball before an infielder can make a play (ball is dead, base runner out, batter awarded first base); and
3. Catcher contacts batter's swing (ball is temporarily alive, batter awarded first base or accepts the result of batted ball, whichever is of greater benefit).

Such situations can be complicated or simple, obvious or very negligible. While they occur rarely, especially where highly skilled players are involved, they *do occur* from time to time. The suggestions for the umpires are that they:

1. Know what is interference and what is not.
2. Try to anticipate interference situations.
3. Know the rule and the penalty.
4. Rule firmly and without undue hesitation, if possible.

A delayed or weak interference decision almost inevitably will lead to an argument.

For the purpose of definition, *obstruction* refers to when a defensive player *who is not making a play, or is about to receive a thrown ball, hinders a baserunner.* Note that obstruction can occur without actual body contact. "Obstruction" is always by the defense against the offense. For example, a fielder who does not have the ball and is not playing the ball "impedes the progress" of the baserunner. All other examples of illegal contact or hindrance are commonly called *interference* (a violation by the offense). In all interference/obstruction situations, regardless of who is involved, there are four basic questions to be answered by the umpire:

1. Who interfered with whom?
2. What is the penalty?

3. Is the ball immediately dead? *
4. Where are the other runners placed after the interference/
   obstruction is ruled?

The following guidelines should be considered in making the call. The baserunner has a "right of way" on the baseline in all cases *except* when a fielder is making a play on a *batted* ball, in which case the fielder is "boss" and all others must give ground. In most cases, there is some form of *physical contact* before interference or obstruction is ruled; person to person, ball to person, equipment to ball, etc. Any umpire who detects interference or obstruction should call it, regardless of that umpire's position relative to the play.

Appeal plays. In appeal play situations, the umpire is *required not to rule unless the offended team appeals for a ruling.* Among the possible appeal situations are: the batter bats out of order, the baserunner fails to touch a base or home plate, and a baserunner fails to "tag up" on a fly out. (Exception: In high school baseball only batting out of order is an appeal play; when the runner fails to touch a base or tag up properly, the high school umpire makes the call, without appeal, when the ball becomes dead.)

   Appeal plays need not be a cause for particular concern if the umpire will pay heed to two principles which are always in effect during such situations:

1. The umpire must say or do nothing before the appeal to indicate to the offended team or anyone else that a successful appeal might be made.
2. No appeal may be granted *after the next pitch* following the rule violation, or after the defensive team has left the field.

The ball must be in play at the time of the appeal in baseball but not in softball, which now utilizes the "instant dead ball process" in order to simplify appeal plays.

"Book rules." These refer to the number of bases awarded to baserunners when a live ball goes out of play. The most important facet of the "book rule" is the overthrow. The award of bases is always two bases from *where the runners were when the throw was released,* if the overthrow was by an infielder or outfielder, and one base if the overthrow was from the pitcher at the pitcher's plate. For example, if a

---

*The ball is always immediately dead in interference situations and is almost always alive, if temporarily, in obstruction situations.

baserunner was just past second base and the batter-runner was not quite to first base when an overthrow from the outfield was released, a run would score and the batter-runner would be entitled to second base. In order to rule accurately, the umpire should "take a picture" of where the runners were when the throw was released. Whenever a live ball goes out of play, the umpires should immediately call "dead ball" and award the bases as indicated. The "book rules" should not be confused with special ground rules which relate to the peculiarities of a given ball park, which are established before each game by the umpires and coaches.

Infield fly rule. When all the requirements of an infield fly are met (see below), the plate umpire (who has a better perspective) should immediately shout, "INFIELD FLY RULE; IF FAIR, THE BATTER IS OUT" and signal the infield fly rule (see Figure 3.5). If this is called, the batter is irrevocably out, and the runners are not forced to advance, whether the fly ball is caught or not—but may advance at their own risk. All of the following requirements must exist before this rule can be enforced:

1. First and second or first, second, and third must be occupied.
2. There must be less than two outs.
3. A batted fly ball must be high in the air and, in the judgment of the umpire, it must be easily handled by an infielder.
4. It must be a ball that was batted, not bunted.

The only reason for this rule is to prevent the defensive team from converting this given situation into a force double or triple play by intentionally failing to catch an infield fly. Fellow umpires should remind themselves about the rule whenever first and second are occupied or the bases are loaded and there are less than two outs.

In a similar circumstance, a line drive or fly ball that is intentionally dropped is dead immediately; the batter/runner is out and no runners may advance.

Problem Mechanics

Rundown plays. When a baserunner is trapped between two bases by the defensive team, each umpire should take responsibility for one "end" of the play. The danger any time two umpires are involved in the same play is that one will rule "safe" and the other "out." This danger is usually eliminated if the decision is made only by that umpire who is located at the end of the rundown where the tag is made. The other umpire *must not* make the decision unless asked to do so by the umpire responsible for the tag.

Multiple baserunners touching the bases. The golden rule of umpiring is to "watch the ball." Umpires also must strive to see whether or not the baserunners tag each base in the event that there is an appeal. On extra base hits with two or more baserunners, it is difficult to watch both the ball and the baserunners. Generally, the plate umpire observes home and third, the base umpire first and second. Basic vision remains on the ball until a runner nears a base, when the umpire glances quickly to determine whether or not the base was tagged and then once again watches the ball. When a base is missed, the umpire should mentally note which runner was involved, because a possible appeal may not be granted unless the runner, as well as the base, is identified by the appealing team. (See also item 3, page 48.)

Tag plays. The most difficult problem in a tag play is attaining an adequate angle of vision so that neither the baserunner nor the defensive player screens the umpire's vision of the tag. No matter how close the umpire is to the play, he or she cannot see the tag if directly behind either player. The ideal angle would be at about 90 degrees from the runner and the fielder, but somewhat more behind the runner than the fielder. The angle is even better if the umpire is *away* from the direction of the baserunner's slide. Otherwise, the slide can screen the umpire's vision at the last moment. A brief delay on the decision is advised when the runner appears to have been tagged out; then the umpire doesn't have to change a decision if the ball subsequently is found to have been dislodged from the fielder. There is an explosive quality to a tag play, especially when it occurs at home plate. This tends to add to the importance of a correct decision. In softball and high school baseball a runner should be declared out, and possibly disqualified, if he or she deliberately crashes with great force into a defensive player, including the catcher, who is holding the ball and attempting to tag the runner.

Miscellaneous Considerations

One-Umpire Games
One-umpire games are not uncommon in slow pitch. Many lower classified scholastic and community leagues cannot afford more than one umpire. In addition, there are times when one umpire is not able to work an assigned game, leaving the other official to work the game alone. Most experts agree that the best place for one umpire is behind the plate, although some baseball umpires prefer to move behind the pitcher when there is a runner on first. The deciding argument is that the most crucial influences of an umpire are *calling balls and strikes and fair*

and foul balls. Therefore, one umpire should sacrifice accuracy on a few decisions on the bases to maintain consistency and control of the strike zone and fair and foul territory.

Opinions vary regarding the advisability of using a volunteer base umpire. Many umpires and coaches prefer one umpire rather than taking a chance on an untrained person. The suggestion here is to avoid the use of a volunteer unless both coaches want a volunteer. Do not confuse a volunteer umpire with excessive instructions. Try to get the volunteer into the correct starting position before each pitch and provide encouragement and simple suggestions between innings.

A satisfactory job cannot be done by one umpire, even in slow pitch softball. In baseball, imagine yourself, as a plate umpire, when a runner from first base is attempting to steal second, trying to rule on a close tag at second base. Imagine the fast pitch softball plate umpire, with a left-handed batter at the plate, trying to decide *while the pitch is on the way* whether or not the runner on first base left too soon. Fortunately, one-umpire games have been greatly reduced or eliminated in most areas of the country.

The Artistry in Plate Umpiring

There is much that plate umpires can do to promote their own cause and the cause of a smooth running and enjoyable game. Plate umpiring can either be a very lonely and thankless job or a cooperative and rewarding one, depending somewhat on the artfulness employed. Here are some suggestions:

1. Do not assert yourself any more than is necessary to keep the game going and under control.
2. Save your decisiveness in signals and voice for the close and crucial calls.
3. Take advantage of every possibility to promote good will and positive relationships without compromising your authority.

The plate umpire can build sound relationships with key players, the pitcher, and the catcher—especially the catcher. The plate umpire should communicate often with the catcher without being overly friendly and without interfering with the tempo of the game—should encourage the catcher to "stay down" on low pitches. In a friendly but firm manner, the umpire specifies to the catcher such routine matters as the number of warm-up pitches between innings and acceptable methods of getting a new ball into play. The pitcher's good will is almost as important as the catcher's, though more difficult to affect. Nevertheless, a feeling of near-comradeship frequently develops between a good plate umpire and the pitcher. Both are almost entirely on their own, both have difficult jobs, and both know that they depend somewhat on mutual good will.

Slow Pitch Softball Umpiring
Many baseball and softball umpires enjoy the relative informality of
umpiring slow pitch softball. The general differences between umpiring
softball and 12-inch slow pitch are summarized below. (There are slight
differences between 12-inch and 16-inch slow pitch rules.)

The batter. A batter is declared out who bunts or chops (strikes
downward) a pitch. It is possible in slow pitch for the batter to hit a "foul
tip" that does not rise above the batter's head and that can be fielded
by the catcher. This is a *strike;* the batter should not be ruled out unless
there already were two strikes on the batter.

Baserunning. Base-stealing is not permitted (with the pitch or following
the pitch). Baserunners may leave their bases only when a pitch is hit or
the pitch reaches home plate.

Pitching. A pitch is in the strike zone if any part of the ball passes over
any part of home plate between the batter's back shoulder and knees.*
The pitch must have an arc of at least six feet, but not go higher than
twelve feet above the ground. Pitchers are not required to step towards
home plate when delivering a pitch, but must pause for at least one
second before the delivery.

Mechanics. The plate umpire is responsible for decisions at third base
as well as home plate. The only time the base umpire would rule at third
base would be following a play at home plate which involved the plate
umpire. As is shown in Figure 3.6 the base umpire takes only two
different starting positions before a pitch.
    The plate umpire takes a semi-upright stance at a location where
he/she can see the entire strike zone.

Officiating Evaluated by Coaches
What qualities do you appreciate in a baseball official?

1. Clear and confident
2. Firm and friendly
3. Consistent
4. Dependable
5. Hustles
6. Good position

*More and more slow pitch leagues are turning to the "strike zone mat" as a helpful tool
for calling strikes and balls. A pitched ball which lands on home plate or the mat is
automatically called a strike by the plate umpire. The mat is placed behind and adjacent to
home plate.

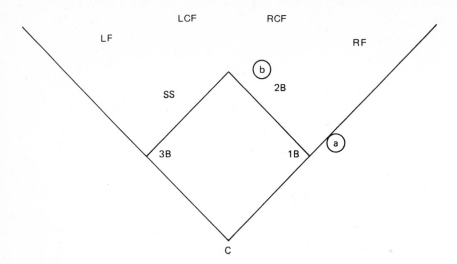

Figure 3.6 Base umpire starting positions for slow pitch. a—No runners or runner on third base only; b—All other combinations of runners.

7. Knowledge of the rules
8. Appearance
9. Dedication to the game

Miscellaneous Comments
1. Quality officials feel each game they work is important.
2. The preferred official has the ability to command respect and get along with people without having to flaunt authority.

Officiating Evaluated by Officials
What is the most difficult play to call in baseball?

1. The steal of home
2. The half swing
3. The pulled foot of the first baseman when the official is on the infield
4. Calling the overhand curve

What is the most difficult phase of mechanics in officiating baseball?

1. General field coverage with only two officials
2. Pick-offs at first and third
3. The plate umpire attempting to cover the tag-up at third base on a sacrifice fly to right field

Miscellaneous Comments

1. It is necessary to "think ahead" to assure the best possible position to cover the play in a two-umpire system.
2. An instinctive approach to the game, acquired through experience, is of utmost importance.

Play Rulings (2)

Situation: B1 hits ground ball which rolls along third base line and touches both outside and inside the line. Ball bounces directly over third or touches third. It alights on foul or fair ground. *Ruling:* Fair ball.

Situation: With R1 on first, B2 hits foul which goes directly to the catcher and: (a) is caught by him or her; or (b) is dropped by him or her. In either case, R1 advances to second. *Ruling:* In (a), it is a foul tip and is treated the same as any other strike, hence R1 has stolen second. In (b) R1 must return to first.

Situation: In a high school game of seven innings, how many innings constitute a regulation game if the game is called? *Ruling:* At least 4½ innings if the home team is ahead.

Situation: With R1 on first, B2 steps out of batter's box and then: (a) strikes at a pitch but misses; or (b) hits a foul or a fair ball. *Ruling:* No infraction in (a), unless B2 interferes with a throw by F2. In (b), B2 is out as in 7-3-1 and R1 returns to first.

Situation: R1, R2, and R3 are on third, second, and first bases, respectively, when B4 hits an infield fly ball which the umpire calls out. R3, thinking the ball will not be caught, advances past R2 just beyond second. The fly ball strikes R2 while he or she is off second base. *Ruling:* Ball became dead when it struck R2. The play results in a triple out play. B4 is out by the infield fly rule. R3 is out for passing a preceding runner, and R2 is out for being hit by a batted fair ball. (2)

BIBLIOGRAPHY

1. Amateur Softball Association of America, *1991 Planning Rules and Umpires Manual,* Oklahoma City, Oklahoma, 1990.
2. National Federation of State High School Associations, *1991 Official High School Baseball Case Book,* Kansas City, Missouri, 1991.
3. National Federation of State High School Associations, *1991 Official High School Baseball Rules,* Kansas City, Missouri, 1991.
4. National Federation of State High School Associations, *1990 and 1991 Official High School Softball Case Book and Umpires Manual,* Kansas City, Missouri, 1990.
5. National Federation of State High School Associations, *1991 Official High School Softball Rules,* Kansas City, Missouri, 1991.

4

Basketball

The Game

For good reason, athletic experts commonly believe basketball to be
the most difficult and demanding sport to officiate. It is also a game in
which opportunities for advancement of well-qualified officials are
virtually unlimited. This great team game, invented and developed in the
United States, combines the elements of fast and abruptly changing
action, excitement and strong emotions, imprecise limits on the physical
contact of players in a limited playing area, frequent penalties for rule
violations, and close proximity of loyal (and biased) coaches, if not
biased, coaches, reserves, and spectators. Each of these elements has
important implications for basketball officials.

Basketball officiating requires a thorough knowledge of intricate
mechanics and complex and changeable rules, sound judgment based
on an understanding of the game, fast reactions and good physical
condition, personal confidence and courage, and a considerate yet firm
court personality. It has been said with considerable truth that
basketball is a great game for players and spectators, and a tough one
for coaches and officials.

There is a continual need for well-qualified basketball officials.
More high school and college basketball games are played each year in
this country than in any other sport. In addition, the demands and
difficulties of basketball officiating cause attrition among officials. The
tremendous growth in girls basketball has created an even greater

Photo by David Klutho/Focus West

shortage of qualified basketball officials. The reasonable practice of a man-and-woman team or a two-woman team working a high school basketball game is with us and can be expected to spread. The presence of the female official has been accepted, and initial success is triggering a greater interest by prospective female officials.

From the official's viewpoint, basketball is a game of judgments— judgments which are constantly scrutinized by players, coaches, and spectators. Physical contact among opponents is inevitable. Much of this contact is incidental to the progress of the game and should not be penalized. The basketball official is constantly analyzing player contact and action preceding the contact, applying the Tower philosophy (see page 7) and judging—(1) Was the contact technically illegal? (2) If illegal, did it place an opponent at a disadvantage? (3) Who was responsible for creating the disadvantage? (4) Should a penalty be applied? and finally, (5) What is the appropriate penalty (to be enforced without undue hesitation)? A given contact situation can be as borderline as imaginable. Fortunately, both high school and college basketball rules include rather extensive "comments on the rules" which deal with judgment of physical contact. The learning official should read and reread these comments until they become a part of oneself, because decisions must be based on the rules and made instantaneously as well as accurately. The ability to consistently apply the "advantage-disadvantage" theory is the mark of a good basketball official.

Because of the exciting and sometimes emotional nature of the game and because of the frequent penalties and closeness to the action of biased viewers, *good mechanics* are of super importance to a well-officiated basketball game. In no other sport are the demands of positioning, signaling, and teamwork more continuous and crucial. Because of the rapid pace of the game, all phases of mechanics must become habitual. Otherwise, the official will "pay the price" for being a step late, out of position, hesitant, and apparently indecisive. The many routine movements and procedures prescribed for basketball officials must be converted into reflex reactions and habits.

A particular mechanics problem constantly challenging any basketball official is that of maintaining a position on the floor where he or she is able to see all relevant action. Good positioning in basketball officiating is made difficult by the rapidity of action and the constant possibility of players obstructing play. The official should attempt to be close to the action, but not too close (almost never closer than five or six feet during live ball action). The basketball official should constantly move, anticipating ball and player movement in order to obtain an angle of vision through the action.

Basketball officiating is hard physical work. It demands *good physical condition,* especially cardio-respiratory fitness. In an average high school game, the official will walk quickly, skip, trot, run, and sprint two to three miles. When both teams fast break and press defensively, this per-game distance may be doubled—at a faster rate of speed. The obvious solution is to *train* prior to and during the season—work out regularly, get adequate rest, and observe a common sense diet, especially immediately before and after games. The official who is physically drained near the end of a game is more likely to lose control and "blow" a crucial, game-deciding decision.

The *psychological demands* of basketball officiating can be and frequently are excessive—especially when a game has drawn a large excited crowd, the stakes are high, the score is close, and/or unsportsmanlike acts occur. The officials have a profound influence on the tempo and outcome of such games. Their decisions, mannerisms, and relationships with others are in the spotlight. Only human beings themselves, the officials must "reach back" to master their own emotions and set examples of poise, courtesy, and courage.

Basketball rule changes during the past two decades have decreased the relative number of free throws attempted and reduced interruptions of game action. Nevertheless, the rules provide more opportunities than in any other sport for unimpeded scoring (free throws) as a means of penalizing rule infractions. This important aspect of the game underscores the extensive (some say "excessive") influence of basketball officials on this great game.

Officials and Their Responsibilities

The two floor officials are the referee and the umpire. They are assisted by one or two scorers and one or two timers seated at one side of the court. An "official scorer" and an "official timer" are designated before the start of the game. Current rules permit three floor officials, a referee and two umpires, when both teams agree. While most college conferences have gone to three officials, the likelihood of three in high school is doubtful because of the cost factor. However, some state associations have authorized the use of three officials. The increased tempo of the game and the adoption of the three-point goal may dictate that high schools go to three officials. The latter has changed many a coaching philosophy in that the perimeter game has taken on greater importance both offensively and defensively.

Officials' Uniforms and Equipment

The floor officials' uniforms are entirely black and white—standard black and white vertically striped, short sleeved knit shirt and *black* pants, belt, socks, shoes, and shoelaces. Each official should have available *two* high quality whistles with cords and rubber caps over the whistle stem. A navy blue jacket is recommended for half-time and before the game. (2:8) Some college conferences have gone to the solid gray shirt.

Referee

The referee is responsible for the following important areas:

1. Prior to the game, designate the official scorer and the official timer.
2. Decide if a goal shall count if there is disagreement.
3. Rule on any matters of disagreement between the scorers and timers.
4. Approve the score at the end of each half. (Approval at the end of the game terminates the jurisdiction of the officials.)
5. Forfeit a game.
6. Make decisions on points not covered in the rules.

   The referee tosses the ball at center to start the game and each overtime. Designated pregame responsibilities of the referee include (1) inspecting and approving all equipment (ball, baskets, backboards, court, timing devices, etc.), and (2) prohibiting dangerous player equipment as described in the rules. The referee is also responsible for having each team captain notified three minutes before each half is to begin.

Floor Officials

No specification of *umpire* responsibilities appear in the rules. Other than the specific responsibilities outlined for the referee, the floor officials work the game as equals. Neither the referee nor the umpire has the authority to set aside or question decisions made by the other official. Their jurisdiction over the game begins at least fifteen minutes before the scheduled starting time and continues until approval of the final score by the referee. Said approval does not require an examination of the scorebook.

Scorers

The scorers record field goals made, free throws made and missed, and a running summary of points scored by each team. They record personal and technical fouls and time-outs, and notify the nearest floor official

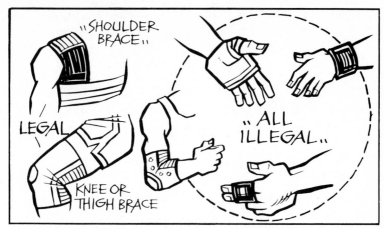

A brace, guard or cast made of leather, plaster, pliable (soft) plastic, metal, or any hard surface—even though covered with cloth or padding—may NOT be worn on the finger, hand, wrist or elbow. If properly padded, hard substances may be worn on the upper arm, shoulder or leg. A head protector or face mask, meeting specific criteria and approved by the referee, may be worn by a player to protect a facial or head injury.

If a player is detected wearing jewelry, that player shall remove the jewelry immediately or be required to leave the game. The head band is also illegal. To be legal, the head band may be no wider than 2 inches and must be made of nonabrasive, unadorned, single-color cloth, fiber, soft leather or rubber. A medic alert bracelet or device is not considered to be jewelry and may be worn if properly secured and covered so it poses no danger to any player.

Figure 4.1 Legal and illegal player equipment. (By courtesy of the N.F.S.H.S.A.)

when the limits of each has been reached. The scorer also records held balls for the alternating possession procedure and is responsible for the possession arrow. The official scorer sounds a horn or buzzer when it is necessary to gain the attention of the floor officials—for such matters as entering substitutes, reaching the limits above, correctable errors, etc. The signaling device may be used immediately if (or as soon as) the ball is dead, and, in the case of a correctable error, the ball is in control of the offending team. It is strongly preferred that the device not be sounded for an entering substitute after a floor official has handed the ball to a player for a throw-in or free throw. In case of a mistaken horn when the ball is alive, the horn should be disregarded. The sound of the official scorer's signaling device should be different from that of the timer.

The running summary of team points scored is particularly important. In case of discrepancies which cannot otherwise be resolved, the referee must accept the team scoring totals recorded in the running summary of the official scorebook. The home team's scorebook is the official scorebook unless previously ruled otherwise by the referee.

Timers

The official timer is responsible for starting and stopping the game clock and for regulating the duration of time-outs and intermissions between periods. The timer should have a stop watch or table clock available as a backup for a faulty scoreboard clock. The operating panel of electric scoreboard clocks normally contains a manual timer suitable for regulating team time-outs and intermissions after the first and third quarters. The duration of half-times is normally shown for all to see on the game clock. The timer sounds his or her horn or buzzer *fifteen seconds* before the termination of a time-out or intermission as a warning to coaches and players that play is about to be resumed. The timer may be called on to help determine whether a try for a field goal was in flight before time expired at the end of a period.

The scoreboard clock should be *started* when (1) on a jump, the ball is legally touched by one of the jumpers; (2) on a throw-in, the ball touches or is touched by a player inbounds; and (3) on a missed free throw attempt, the ball touches or is touched by a player inbounds. The clock should be *stopped* whenever a floor official's whistle sounds (for fouls, violations, held balls, or time-outs) and a floor official signals by vertically extending his or her right arm. (Mechanics call for the whistle and signal to be executed simultaneously.) Usually, the whistle is the best cue, but when the crowd is noisy the timer may need to rely almost entirely on visible signals. The clock is not stopped, nor a floor official's whistle sounded following a field goal. The scorer and timer should recognize that they are important game officials.

A considerable amount of teamwork—between floor officials and timers and scorers, and between the timers and scorers themselves—is needed in order to provide a smoothly administered basketball game. Scorers and timers need to thoroughly read all applicable rules before the season, and briefly review them before each game. Well before the start of a game, the referee should set the stage for good teamwork by discussing proper procedures and responsibilities with the scorer and the timer.

Basic Penalties and Rulings

Floor officials call two broad types of infractions, *fouls* and *violations*. The penalties for fouls are greater than for violations:

1. Free throws may be awarded; and
2. Offenders are disqualified when a foul is "flagrant," or when a fifth personal foul is called on a player, or a third technical foul (second in college) is called on a player, coach, or follower. On a flagrant foul or a third technical foul the player must leave the vicinity of the bench. The disqualified coach or bench personnel must go to the team's locker room or leave the building.

Fouls fall into two categories, personal or technical. Personal fouls can only take place during live ball action. Technical fouls may be called when the ball is alive or dead, but often they are called during a dead ball period. The list below shows all basketball rulings and, where applicable, their penalties.

Personal Fouls
The intent of penalizing personal fouls is to provide greater freedom of player movement by penalizing illegal contact. *Actual physical contact* between opponents must take place for a personal foul to be ruled. The contact must affect play. "Incidental" contact which places neither opponent at a disadvantage should be ignored. Illegal contact includes holding, pushing, charging, tripping, rough tactics, and impeding progress illegally.

Table 4.1   Comprehensive List of Basketball Penalties and Rulings

Rulings	Penalties
Fouls	
Personal Fouls	
Act of shooting	
—if shot is made	One free throw
—if shot is missed	Two free throws
Player control (including airborne shooter)	Possession to offended team
Intentional	Two free throws plus possession to offended team at the spot nearest the foul
Flagrant	Two free throws and offending player disqualified plus possession to offended team at the spot nearest the foul
Double	Ball awarded to team next entitled to possession under alternating possession procedure
False double	Penalize each foul and enforce order of occurrence
Multiple	One free throw for each foul
False multiple	Penalize each foul
All other personal fouls	
(common fouls)	Before bonus-penalty takes effect: possession to offended team at nearest out-of-bounds spot
	After bonus-penalty takes effect: one free throw; bonus free throw if first successful (1 and 1)
Technical Fouls	
Nonflagrant	Two free throws to any offended player (including substitute) plus possession at division line
Flagrant	
Flagrant technical foul for bench conduct	Two free throws to any offended player (including substitute) plus possession at division line. Charge technical to both head coach and offender if the offender is known. If not known, charge coach.

Table 4.1 *continued*

Rulings	Penalties
Violations	
Basket interference or goaltending at opponent's goal	If on free throw, one point * If on field goal, two points
All other violations	Possession to offended team at nearest out-of-bounds point
Other Rulings	
Jump ball	Ball awarded to team next entitled to possession under alternating procedure
Call or grant team's request for time-out	

With the exception of certain personal fouls, discussed later in this section, the penalties for personal fouls are as follows:

Number of Team Fouls Each Half	Penalty
Prior to the *fifth* team foul each half in high school games and the *seventh* in college games	Award possession of the ball to the offended team at the out-of-bounds spot nearest to the point of the foul.
Beginning with the *fifth* team foul each half in high school games and the seventh in college games	Award a free throw to the player fouled; award a *bonus* free throw if the first is successful.
In college beginning with the tenth foul	Two free throws

The "bonus rule" demonstrates the intent to increase penalties against teams which commit more personal fouls. Player control fouls count toward the number of team fouls but free throws are never awarded on a player control foul.

Personal fouls in the act of shooting. The intent of basketball rules is to impose a greater penalty when a personal foul is committed against a shooter. The penalty varies according to whether or not the field goal try is successful. If successful, the goal counts and the offended shooter is awarded one free throw. If unsuccessful, two free throws are awarded. * The official's major problem regarding act-of-shooting fouls, as

*Goaltending a free throw is also a technical foul.

*In college a shooter fouled during an unsuccessful three-point try is awarded three free throws.

BASKETBALL COURT DIAGRAM

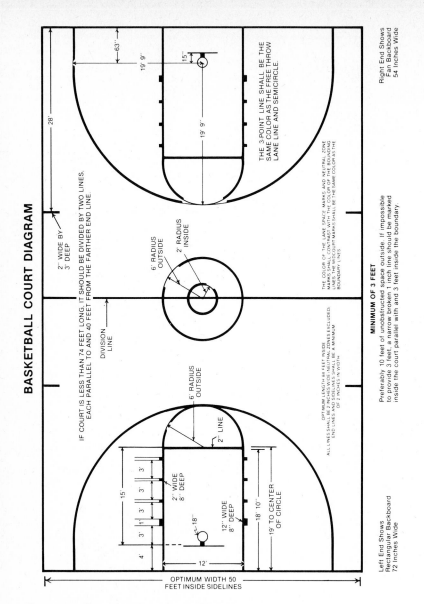

THE 3-POINT LINE SHALL BE THE SAME COLOR AS THE FREE THROW LANE LINE AND SEMICIRCLE.

IF COURT IS LESS THAN 74 FEET LONG, IT SHOULD BE DIVIDED BY TWO LINES, EACH PARALLEL TO AND 40 FEET FROM THE FARTHER END LINE.

DIVISION LINE

6' RADIUS OUTSIDE

2' RADIUS INSIDE

2'' WIDE BY 3' DEEP

28'

63''

19' 9''

19' 9''

15''

6' RADIUS OUTSIDE

2'' LINE

15'

3'

3'

3'

3'

3'

1'

3'

4'

2'' WIDE 8'' DEEP

12'' WIDE 8'' DEEP

18''

18' 10''

19' TO CENTER OF CIRCLE

12'

OPTIMUM WIDTH 50 FEET INSIDE SIDELINES

OPTIMUM LENGTH 84 FEET INSIDE END LINES (2 INCHES WIDE, NEUTRAL ZONES EXCLUDED) END LINES AND SIDELINES SHALL BE A MINIMUM OF 2 INCHES IN WIDTH

ALL LINES SHALL BE 2 INCHES WIDE.

THE COLOR OF THE LANE SPACE MARKS AND NEUTRAL ZONE MARKS SHALL CONTRAST WITH THE COLOR OF THE BOUNDING LINES. THE MIDCOURT MARKS SHALL BE THE SAME COLOR AS THE BOUNDARY LINES.

MINIMUM OF 3 FEET

Preferably 10 feet of unobstructed space outside. If impossible to provide 3 feet, a narrow broken 1 inch line should be marked inside the court parallel with and 3 feet inside the boundary.

Left End Shows Rectangular Backboard 72 Inches Wide

Right End Shows Fan Backboard 54 Inches Wide

Figure 4.2 (By courtesy of the N.F.S.H.S.A.)

distinguished from "common fouls," lies in deciding whether the illegal contact occurred before, during, or after the shot. If clearly before or after the shot, the penalty is the same as if no shot had been attempted. The penalty for an act-of-shooting foul should be invoked when illegal contact occurs after a player "begins the motion which habitually precedes the release of the ball" and until "the ball is clearly in flight." When an offensive player is driving to the basket for a shot, the official should penalize for an act-of-shooting foul if the illegal contact clearly took place after the offensive player picks up his or her dribble in preparation for the shot. Illegal contact against a player attempting to tip-in is not an act-of-shooting foul because the player is not in control of the ball, which makes such illegal contact a common foul. However, if the tapped ball has left the tapper's hand prior to the foul it is considered to be a try and will count if it goes in.

Player control personal fouls. When illegal contact occurs while the offending player is holding or dribbling the ball, a player control foul is called. The offended team is awarded possession of the ball at the out-of-bounds spot closest to the infraction, regardless of the number of personal fouls previously charged to the offending team. The intent of this penalty is to impose an equitable penalty and to avoid an unnecessary delay in game action. The most common example of a player control foul is when a player with the ball charges into a defensive player. When a player control foul is called on a player who was in the act of shooting, an apparent *field goal cannot count.* (The ball became "dead" when the illegal contact occurred.)

A significant expansion of the high school player-control foul rules was made effective in the 1983–84 season. The definition of "player control" now includes the "airborne shooter." Thus player control continues, in the case of an offensive player attempting a shot while driving to or jumping towards the basket, until the airborne shooter returns to the floor. This change makes it impossible for a basket to count if the responsibility for contact is the shooter's. Furthermore, if the *defensive player* is responsible for the contact on such a play, two free throws are awarded. This rule change should prove to be successful in reducing dangerous body contact situations and in simplifying the judgments of floor officials.

Intentional personal fouls. A floor official should call an intentional foul whenever an illegal contact was deliberate, designed, or premeditated. The degree of roughness is irrelevant to calling an intentional foul. Two free throws are awarded to the offended player and his or her team is awarded possession out of bounds nearest the spot of the foul. Since judging a person's intentions can be risky, officials should call intentional fouls with discretion. Most, but not all, intentional fouls are committed by trailing teams on defense near the end of the game. The intent of this rule is to discourage the gaining of an unfair advantage and to maintain the integrity of the game. A specific signal has been developed that the calling official should execute immediately when calling an intentional foul. (See Figure 4.8, page 84.)

Flagrant personal fouls. Physical contact which is unsportsmanlike and violent or savage results in a severe penalty—the offender is disqualified, two free throws are awarded to the offended player, and the ball is awarded to the offended team out-of-bounds nearest the spot of the foul. Examples of flagrant fouls are viciously kicking, kneeing, or striking an opponent with the fist or elbow, and running under an opponent who is in the air.

Judgment and courage are needed to make this call. When ruling a flagrant foul, the official should strive to regain a controlled emotional atmosphere by demonstrating poise and courtesy. Showing anger or disgust will not help. The intent of this penalty is to prevent injuries and to maintain control and enforce sportsmanship in physical contact situations.

Other types of personal fouls are *double, multiple, false double,* and *false multiple fouls.* A double foul occurs when two opponents commit *personal fouls* against *each other* at approximately the same time. A personal foul is charged to each player, and the ball is put in play by the team next entitled to possession under the alternating procedure. There can also be a double technical foul which results in two free throws for each team and utilization of the alternating possession to resume play.

A multiple foul should be called when two or more *teammates* commit personal fouls against a *single opponent* at approximately the same time. Both teammates are charged with a personal foul, and *one free throw for each foul* is awarded to the offended player, with no bonus free throws. Double and multiple fouls are rarely called, but should not be overlooked. The first illegal contact taking place causes the ball to be dead. Subsequent contact is considered incidental unless flagrant.

False double and false multiple fouls should be ruled when an additional foul occurs *while the clock is stopped* after a previously ruled foul. The second foul would be by the *same team* that committed the previous foul in a *false multiple* foul situation—and by the *other* team in order to create a *false double* foul situation. In the false double foul situation the penalty for each foul is enforced in the order of occurrence.

Technical Fouls

Unlike personal fouls, technical fouls may be charged against coaches and team followers as well as players. In addition, technical fouls may be charged against a team or against individuals, while personal fouls may be charged only to individual players.

Eight team technical foul infractions and twenty-two individual technical foul infractions are specified in high school basketball rules. Examples of team fouls are stalling tactics, exceeding the allotted number of time-outs, and having more than five players on the court. Unsportsmanlike conduct is the most common cause of individual technical fouls—conduct by players, coaches, or followers, such as baiting an opponent, speaking or gesturing disrespectfully to an official, and inciting undesirable crowd reactions. Grasping the ring, interfering with the ball after a goal, and failing immediately to pass the ball to the nearer floor official are also specified as causes for technical fouls.

Penalties for technical fouls are more severe than for personal fouls. When a nonflagrant and nonintentional technical foul is called on a player, the foul is charged to the offender; *any* player on the offended team is awarded two free throws, and the offended team gets ball possession for a throw-in at midcourt. The penalty against a player for a flagrant technical foul or intentional technical foul is the same, except that the offender is disqualified and the offended team is awarded two free throws. Good judgment is needed in calling flagrant technical fouls. The official must attempt to show poise and a degree of courtesy, especially when a coach is involved. Any technical foul called on a coach, team attendant, or follower results in two free throws and possession of the ball for a throw-in. The purposes of technical fouls are—from the pregame warmup period until the final score is approved by the referee—(1) to enforce technical requirements specified in the rules, such as team rosters, substitution procedures, number of players on the court, proper uniforms, (2) to enforce minimal respect, courtesy, and sportsmanship, and (3) to control physical contact between opponents during dead ball periods.

Violations

Violations penalize illegal player movement and ball handling, and also discrepancies in specified restrictions regarding the basket and its upward cylinder, certain court areas, and certain time durations. The purpose of violation rules is to penalize unskilled or uncontrolled play which otherwise might result in (a) sloppy, uncontinuous, disrupted, or congested action and / or (b) placing one or the other team at an unfair disadvantage. Like personal fouls, violations may be called *only when the ball is alive.* Unlike personal fouls, violations *never involve physical contact* between opposing players.

Major violations categories include (1) causing the ball to go out-of-bounds, (2) traveling, (3) illegal dribbles, (4) intentionally kicking the ball, (5) violating the free throw, jump ball, or throw-in provisions, (6) basket interference, or goaltending, (7) returning the ball to the back court, and (8) three-second (in the "key") or ten-second (in the back court) violations. Over thirty violations are specified in high school rules (3:27–30). Considerable study and experience is necessary to learn and understand all of these rules.

The penalties for violations are relatively uncomplicated. For all violations except basket interference or goaltending at the opposing team's basket, the offended team is awarded the ball for a throw-in at the out-of-bounds spot nearest to the point of the violation. When there is basket interference, or goaltending at the opponent's basket, one point is awarded by the floor official on a free throw and two points on a field goal attempt.

Jump Balls

Jump balls are basically a thing of the past because of the adoption of the alternating team possession procedure for situations that had called for a jump ball. Jump balls are now limited to the start of the game and at the start of any extra period.

Summary

Complete mastery of basketball rules is problematic at best. First, there are countless infractions and definitions to learn. Second, some of the more important rules have been deliberately written in general terms rather than with precision, in order to leave room for a judgment of each separate circumstance by the official. Finally, different basketball rules overlap more than the rules of other sports. Officials attempting to find answers in the rule book are constantly required to cross-reference from rule-to-rule and from page-to-page. The official who knows the rules and the reasons for the rules is going to find his or her assignment an easier one.

Mechanics

When a basketball game is officiated by floor officials who know their mechanics and execute them without hestitation, the game runs its course like a well-tuned and lubricated engine. The officials are more likely to have the confidence of players, coaches, and spectators. Attention is directed to the players and the action, not to the officials.

BASIC COURT COVERAGE

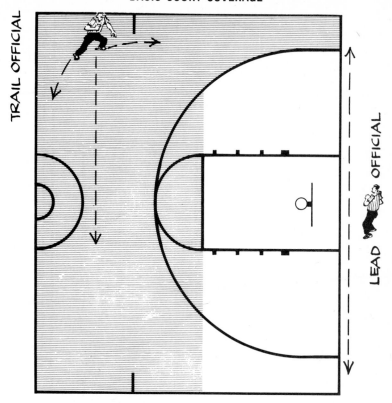

The front court is divided into two areas of primary responsibility. The lead official has primary responsibility for all action in the unshaded area. The trail official has primary responsibility for all action in the shaded area. A narrow band of transition area exists where the two primary areas meet and one official's primary responsibility ends while it begins for the other. Even though both officials have primary areas of responsibility, each shall call any infraction which is detected.

Figure 4.3 Basic court coverage. (By courtesy of the N.F.S.H.S.A.)

Positioning

Basketball officials must move constantly in order to observe the action from the most advantageous position. Stationary officials inevitably will find their vision screened by player movement. Playing experience helps an official to anticipate, then to move quickly and appropriately as play develops. The best position is where the official can *look through the action,* having the ball and adjacent opponents in view.

COVERAGE OFF THE BALL

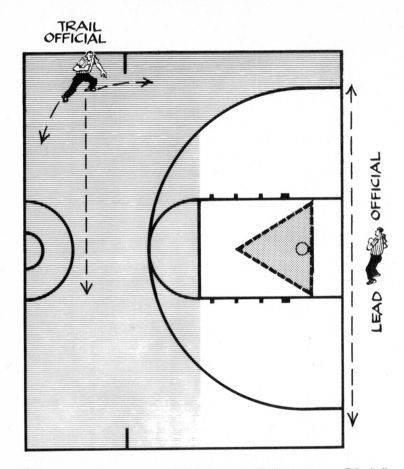

The triangle represents an area which is the most critical to coverage off the ball. While there are other responsibilities to coverage off the ball, the scope of the triangle represents a beginning focal point. The triangle will move as the ball and players move. The official who has coverage off the ball must concentrate and move to have a line of sight into the critical area away from the ball.

Figure 4.4 Coverage off the ball. (By courtesy of the N.F.S.H.S.A.)

Basketball mechanics designate a *lead* and a *trail* floor official. During court action near either basket the lead official is positioned out-of-bounds adjacent to the end line. The trail official is positioned in-bounds in the midcourt area closer to the side line to his or her left. The *primary* responsibility of each official is divided across the court basically by the free throw line extended and the three-point arc line.

Responsibility is shared in the center of the front court. Regardless of these guidelines, both officials are directed to *call every infraction they detect.*

When team possession changes and action moves to the other end of the court, the previous lead official automatically becomes the trail official, and vice versa. At all times when the ball is in play in-bounds, both officials are responsible for the *end line to the right and the sideline to the left.* Put in another way, when the ball is in the front court the lead official is responsible for the end line and the sideline to the left. The trail official is responsible for the division line and the sideline to the left. The subtle but fundamental notion of "end line right—sideline left" or "lead to your right, trail to your left" must be drummed into the official's consciousness until it becomes a reflex.

When "leading" a fast break, the official must avoid a natural tendency, while running at top speed, to take his or her eyes off the action. Seeing the play is more important than beating the players to the other end of the court. In many "controlled" fast break situations the lead official can "backpedal" most or all of the distance. Be sure to stay wide, near the sideline, in order to avoid obstructing play.

After any foul is called, the officials switch their respective end line and sideline responsibilities, or "change sides," before the ball is again put into play. This procedure balances area responsibilities throughout the game. Otherwise, each official would continuously be the lead official under the same basket, and thanklessly, one official would continuously be adjacent to the players' benches.

Basketball is a difficult game to officiate. It becomes virtually impossible for the official who is often out of position. Coaches and players know when an official is not in position to make a call. *Move. Never take your eyes off the action. Be at the right place at the right time. Look through the action. Lead right, trail left.*

Putting the Ball in Play

In basketball, the ball is put into play by three, and only three, procedures—a jump ball, a throw-in, or a free throw. Both floor officials must follow the correct mechanics for each procedure in order to provide a smooth and efficient game.

Jump balls. The official conducting the toss always faces the scorer's table sideline. The referee, rather than the umpire conducts the toss at the start of the game and each extra period.

The *free official* takes a position opposite the tosser six to eight feet in-bounds from the scorer's table sideline.

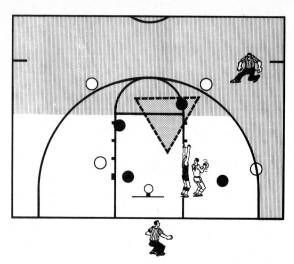

The lead official has the ball while the trail sights through the triangle for good coverage off the ball.

The lead moves to a position to get the 3-point line covered when the ball is in this area. The trail positions to cover the significant action off the ball through the triangle.

Figure 4.5 Shifting focus of the triangle. (By courtesy of the N.F.S.H.S.A.)

The toss must be vertical and should be thrown to a height slightly higher than the jumping ability of either player. The tosser should split his or her stance with the forward foot firmly planted. One or two hands may be used. Greater accuracy and consistency will usually result if the toss is started no lower than chest level, preferably at eye level. This is a skill that must be practiced. To avoid dental injuries, the whistle should not be in the mouth. The official must avoid a natural tendency to back off immediately after tossing for the jump. He or she should remain stationary until the players have made their moves following the jump.

During the jump, the tosser is responsible for illegal action by the jumpers. The free official is responsible for the eight nonjumpers. Either official may order a rejump if the toss is inaccurate; the free official can usually order a rejump more quickly and should not hesitate to do so.

Following a jump, the *free official goes with the ball and almost always takes the lead position* in either direction, especially on a fast break from the jump. The tosser accordingly fills in as trail official. Since quick changes in possession can occur at any time, the free official is the key to maintaining adequate coverage following a jump, because the administering official is momentarily "locked in" by player congestion.

Throw-ins. The throw-in is the most frequent method of putting the ball in play. It follows time-outs, all successful field goals and free throws, all violations, and those common personal fouls prior to the bonus penalty. When the ball goes out-of-bounds, it is essential that the officials make it very clear which team will take possession. The throw-in shall be made from where a ball went out-of-bounds or at the nearest out-of-bounds spot to the point of an infraction. (Exception: The designated throw-in spot along an end line shall never be within the free throw lanes extended.) The throw-in is administered by the official responsible for the given sideline or end line.

The mechanics for administering a throw-in are fairly routine and, following a violation, proceed in this order:

1. Stop the clock when the violation occurs, by sounding the whistle while vertically extending your right arm and hand.
2. Signal the type of violation (no signal for ball out-of-bounds).
3. Loudly call the jersey color and point the direction of the team gaining possession.
4. Using a sweeping arm gesture, point to the out-of-bounds spot of the throw-in.

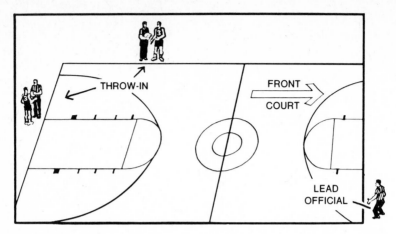

The trail official handles all back court throw-ins. The trail official holds the ball and does not hand it to the player until the lead official is down and across court. The official always takes a position so that both sidelines, the end line, and the division line can be covered.

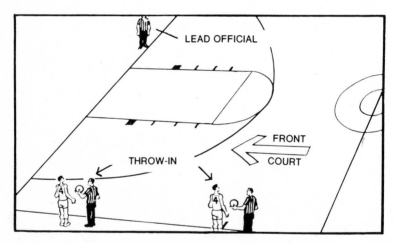

The trail official administers the throw-in on the sideline in the front court to the left. The officials are using the ''boxing-in'' method. One official is on each side of the thrower-in and they have both sidelines, end line, and division line covered.

Figure 4.6 The "Boxing-in" method for throw-ins. (By courtesy of the N.F.S.H.S.A.)

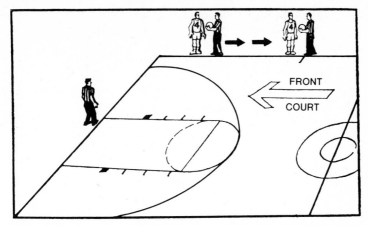

The lead official administers the throw-in on the sideline to the left and stands on the left of the thrower. The official administering the throw-in is now the trail official. The trail official moves to the end line and becomes the lead official. The officials are using the ''boxing-in'' method.

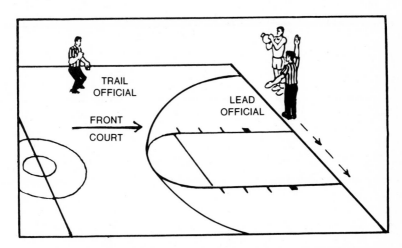

The lead official administers the throw-in on the end line and stands on the left of the thrower. After handing the ball to the player making the throw-in, the official will back up along the end line to get in proper coverage position.

Figure 4.6 *Continued*

5. Be sure that your fellow official is in position for the throw-in and that there are no substitutes waiting to enter the game; if waiting, wave them in. *

6. Take the proper "boxing-in" position (see later in this section) and hand, do not toss, the ball to the player who will make the throw-in.

7. The proper mechanical action is to maintain one open hand over the head because the clock is still stopped, a silent visible five-second count should be given by using the other hand.

8. Hold your position until the ball is in-bounded or five seconds expire.

9. When the ball is legally touched in-bounds, chop the time in with the extended arm.

The procedure for a throw-in *following a personal foul* is basically the same as above. After step 2 on the preceding page, however, the official calling the foul reports it to the scorer, and the officials switch their end line / sideline responsibilities. The throw-in should be administered (starting with step 3 above) by whichever official subsequently gains responsibility for the boundary line of the throw-in.

The position of the ball when a *time-out* is granted dictates the throw-in spot following the time-out. During the time-out period the official responsible for that throw-in boundary spot holds the ball there, and the other official takes a position at the division line away from the scorer's table.

Following a successful field goal or free throw, the team scored on proceeds with the throw-in without the official and *without a designated spot* for the throw-in. (A violation would be called against a player with the ball who moves from a *designated* throw-in spot.)

The idea of the "boxing-in" principle for throw-ins is to place the floor officials in advantageous starting positions. The floor officials should be positioned on each side of the action and each side of the player making the throw-in, "surrounding" the action.

Application of the "boxing-in" principle occasionally requires an official to "cross over" from one sideline to another following a throw-in. Crossing over is necessary only when the throw-in is made by a team from the *right sideline,* with reference to the team's direction. When made from the right sideline in either the back court or front court, the administering official becomes the trail official and the other official becomes the lead official following the throw-in. The two officials should time their "crossover" movements according to the developing play so that, as much as possible, both lines will remain covered.

In summary, the most important considerations in conducting a throw-in are to (1) apply the "boxing-in" principle, and (2) make definite

---

*A new mechanic being utilized is to "whistle" substitutes in also. This will keep your partner apprised that something is going on.

and deliberate signals prior to the throw-in to clearly emphasize possession and direction. In their pregame conference, the officials should agree on the procedures they will follow on throw-ins from any position on the court.

Fouls/Free throws. Basically, when a foul is called, the official making the decision designates the offender and reports the foul to the scorer. The other official "freezes" *while observing all players,* thinks out his or her next position, and secures the ball when convenient. The officials will switch positions, or "change sides," regardless of the type of foul called or its location on the court. In order to demonstrate smooth mechanics, both officials must anticipate their subsequent switched position after a foul has been called.

The procedure of the official calling a personal foul is, first, to stop the clock by sounding the whistle while vertically extending the right fist and pointing an extended left arm, palm down, at the offending player's hip. The official should "close-in" on the offender while signaling, stop, and verbally inform the player of the call by stating the player's number and jersey color. The designated foul signal, e.g., "charging," "blocking," etc., may then be executed and the foul reported to the official scorer. The reporting official should move at a good pace to a position near the division line and scorer's table to report the foul. If it is a free throw shooting situation, the ruling official should advise his/her partner of the number of the shooter before the foul is reported to the scorer. In reporting the offender to the scorer, the official may use fingers (one hand only) corresponding to the player's jersey number, but must be certain that the correct information has been communicated and understood.

If the foul results in a *throw-in,* the procedures specified in the previous section should be followed. Sufficient time should be allowed the official not administering the throw-in to secure the correct "boxing-in" position before the ball is handed to a player for the throw-in.

If a *technical foul* has been ruled, both officials should administer the free throws. The calling official handles the first free throw then moves to the division line opposite the scoring table prior to the second free throw, in preparation for the ensuing throw-in.

When a *false double* foul occurs, either official first administers the free throw(s) for the first foul called. The other official waits at the other free throw line with the second offended player, who will subsequently shoot there. After the second offended player shoots her/his free throw, the game progresses as if the first foul had not occurred. Technical and false double foul free throws occur infrequently.

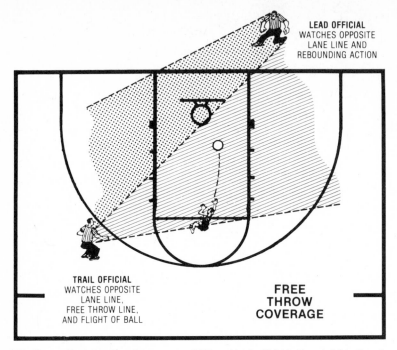

LEAD OFFICIAL
WATCHES OPPOSITE
LANE LINE AND
REBOUNDING ACTION

TRAIL OFFICIAL
WATCHES OPPOSITE
LANE LINE,
FREE THROW LINE,
AND FLIGHT OF BALL

FREE
THROW
COVERAGE

This diagram illustrates the primary responsibilities of each official in the administration of the free throw.

Figure 4.7 Coverage during free throws. (By courtesy of the N.F.S.H.S.A.)

For the bulk of all free throws attempted, the officials work as a team. The official who did not call the foul begins the teamwork by waiting with the ball within the free throw lanes of the *correct basket.* Both officials anticipate their new, switched positions.

The new *lead official* holds the ball under the basket while the administering *trail official* enters the lane from the left of the free throw shooter and takes charge—sees that the lane spaces are filled correctly and informs the players of the number of free throws. The lead official bounces the ball to the trail official and takes a position slightly out-of-bounds outside the lane extended and opposite the trail official. Before handing the ball to the shooter, the trail official checks the scorer's table for possible substitutes, waving them in if ready. After handing the ball to the shooter, he or she starts a silent, visible ten-second count and backs off to a position slightly behind and to the left of the free thrower, well out of the free throw circle. While backing off, the trail official then signals the number of free throws awarded. The opposite hand shall be extended over his/her head because the clock is stopped. If the throw is successful, signal the score. If it is unsuccessful, chop the time in when the ball is touched.

During a free throw, the lead official has one responsibility and the trail official several. The lead official watches for rebounding fouls and lane violations or fouls by players along the opposite lane. The trail official continues the ten-second count and watches for (1) lane violations or fouls along the opposite lane, (2) a free throw line violation by the shooter, and (3) basket interference or goaltending by either team.

If the shooter is entitled to additional free throws, the lead official quickly retrieves the ball after the first attempt and becomes the administering official. He/she steps into the lane, signifies one free throw and bounces the ball to the shooter. The trail official then assumes normal responsibilities as if he/she had handed the ball to the shooter.

Well administered free throws can do much to build communication and confidence between officials and players. The players can and should be cautioned to avoid needless lane violations. If the players of either or both teams are upset, the official can help by demonstrating calmness and by providing a little extra time for a "cooling off period." Generally, the actions and communications of the officials during free throws should be definite, brisk, and direct, featuring compatible mannerisms and good eye contact.

Signals

Twenty-five different officials' signals are specified and illustrated by the National Federation. With conscientious effort, the new official can master these signals during his or her first season of officiating. During the first game or two of that "rookie" season the official should be intelligently selective about which signals to learn and which can be executed. In the first game or scrimmage, the new official should be able to execute the following signals:

Blowing the whistle with authority.
Stopping the clock for a foul, violation, or jump ball.
Calling the jersey color and signalling the direction for a throw-in.
Signaling the number of free throws awarded.
Signaling whether an apparent free throw or field goal counts or is
    cancelled.
Signaling a player control foul.

Figure 4.8 Official basketball signals. (By courtesy of the N.F.S.H.S.A.)

Players and other officials need the above signals in order to continue the game without interruption or confusion. In subsequent assignments the official can progressively add new signals.

As in football, the basketball official must occasionally execute several signals following one decision. For example, when a player with the ball charges into a defensive player, the following signals would be given: (1) stop the clock for foul, point at offender, (2) player control foul, and (3) direction of offended team. If the offending player "scored" an apparent field goal on the play, the official would also signal "no score." In such a circumstance, the official should be deliberate in executing each separate signal. Otherwise, confusion will result.

Here are some suggestions:

1. Strong whistles only.
2. Be decisive and definite, but avoid "show-boating."
3. Don't rush the signals; the idea is to *communicate.*
4. Adjust your signaling mannerisms to the tempo and emotional level of the particular game; force yourself to act calmly and deliberately when the game's pace is hectic and/or one or both teams are upset.
5. When a field goal or free throw is scored, the trail official should immediately signal the number of points scored (one or two fingers) and the lead official then points down court, in the direction of the team gaining possession. On a three-point attempt the responsible official should signal by extending the right arm outwardly at head level with three fingers extended. If the try is successful, he or she then gives the football "touchdown" signal. The fellow official also gives the "touchdown" signal.
6. Immediately "back up" your partner's signal to *stop the clock* by executing the same vertical right hand or fist signal. Backing up other signals should be avoided unless (a) you are *certain* of the call and (b) a back up signal will help reduce confusion.
7. Practice the signals and common signal sequences.

Teamwork

Floor officials rely on each other for a smooth, well-officiated game. They must be on the same wavelength regarding all phases of mechanics. They must be receptive to and cooperative with each other. To a large degree, the floor officials will succeed or fail together.

Who calls what? Floor officials generally should call everything they see. Certain rulings however, are more clearly the responsibility of the trail official. The *trail official* is responsible for back court and free throw ten-second violations, midcourt five-second jump balls, and lack of sufficient action. The *trail official also has primary responsibility* for basket interference and ruling whether a field goal counts at the end of a period. Each official, lead and trail, is primarily responsible for ruling on possession when the ball goes out-of-bounds at his or her end or sidelines of responsibility. When a jump ball is tapped directly out-of-bounds without being touched by a nonjumper, the official who tossed for the jump has primary responsibility for awarding possession to the correct team, or ordering a rejump.

Either official may and should call three-second (in the key) violations. Either official may and should call *any foul anywhere on the court,* including fast break fouls when the lead official is obviously closer to the play but is screened out. (A better angle of vision is more reliable than closeness to the play.) Players and coaches may not understand or appreciate infractions called from a distance, but the officials' first obligation is to the game and to call every definite infraction of the rules.

Assisting each other on rulings. The most common situation where assistance is needed occurs when the ball goes out-of-bounds. If the official responsible for the given boundary line is in doubt or simply did not see who caused the ball to go out-of-bounds—he or she should stop the clock and quickly look to the other official. The other official should immediately signal the proper direction or, if also in doubt, immediately signal a jump ball and award according to the alternating possession rule. A brief delay is fairer to both teams than a guess.

Another situation where help is needed occurs when the *lead official calls a foul during a try for a field goal.* The trail official has primary responsibility for counting or cancelling field goals, but the lead official knows or should know whether the foul occurred before, during, or after the try. If the lead official knows the foul occurred *during the try,* he or she should ask the trail official if the try was successful and, if successful, immediately signal that the "basket counts." *If before or after the try,* the lead official can and should immediately cancel the "goal" without help and without even knowing whether the attempt went in the basket.

Mechanics for Three Floor Officials

A third floor official significantly increases officiating coverage of a basketball game. A referee and two umpires make up the team. These officials are designated as "center," "lead," and "trail" during game action, and prescribed mechanics are based upon these designations. A given official will rotate, as prescribed, from one designation to another throughout the game. The officials attempt to maintain triangular coverage, surrounding the action.

While play is in progress at either front court (1) the *lead* official is at the end line; (2) the *trail* official is always on the scorer's table side of the court at a distance similar to the trail official in two officials mechanics; (3) the *center* official is adjacent to the sideline away from the table, closer to the end line than the trail official. When possession changes and the ball moves to the other end of the court, the lead official becomes the trail official and the trail the lead; the center official remains center official at the other end of the court, away from the table.

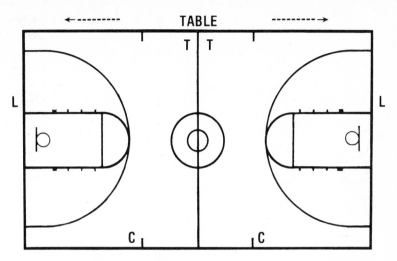

Figure 4.9 Front court coverage and movement by three floor officials.
Key: L—lead official
     T—trail official
     C—center official
(By courtesy of the N.F.S.H.S.A.)

Throw-ins are simplified by three officials mechanics, because it is almost always obvious which official is responsible for a given boundary line. The center official always has the sideline opposite the table. The lead or trail official will take the other sideline, depending on the ball's location. The remaining official will take the "relevant" end line. Crossing over is eliminated.

Jump ball mechanics are somewhat more complicated but, with experience, become more simple than in two officials mechanics. The *center official always makes the toss, facing the scorer's table. The free officials take positions adjacent to the two sidelines, each favoring the end line to his or her right* by six to ten feet. The free officials must be ready to react quickly to the direction following the jump. There is no immediate rush for the official making the toss.

When the direction of possession is known following the jump, the free officials know immediately which of them has become lead official. The other free official will become trail or center official, depending on the direction of the team gaining possession. If the direction is to the *right* of the tosser, the tosser remains center official and the other free official becomes the trail official. If to the *left,* the tosser moves towards the scorer's bench and becomes trail official; the other free official is in good position to become the center official, since he or she was already away from the scorer's table.

When there is a foul, the official calling the foul becomes (or remains) the center official and administers the free throws, if any, by the offended player. The other two officials rotate positions. Only the center and the lead officials are involved in supervising free throws. In free throw situations with three officials the positioning and orientation of the two officials supervising the free throws are the same as in two officials games at one end of the court—and *exactly the opposite at the other end.*

Problem Calls

Discussion of selected basketball problem calls in this book will provide a starting point and an analysis of components. There is no substitute, however, for individual study of basketball rules, comments on the rules, and the "Basketball Case Book"—supplemented by game experience and discussion.

Rebounding

Many coaches have said that "Games are won or lost on the boards." No one can dispute the fact that the dominant rebounding team will get more shots and thereby have a greater chance of winning. The official must prevent players of either team from gaining an unfair rebounding advantage through illegal contact. An added obligation is imposed by the potential for serious injuries from illegal rebounding contact. The word "rebounding," legal or illegal, is meant here to include (1) player attempts to "block out" their opponents in securing an advantageous position from which to gain possession, and (2) actually leaping for the ball.

Both lead and trail officials are responsible for calling rebounding fouls. Both are or should be in proper position to call illegal rebounding contact. The trail official's added responsibilites for the flight of the ball and basket interference need divert only momentarily his or her concentration on rebounding fouls. The lead official usually will disregard the flight of the ball.

The most common rebounding fouls involve illegal *blocking* during the shot, and an outside player "coming over the top" of (*charging*) the inside player. Comments in the "charging-blocking" and "screens" problem calls section also relate to rebounding fouls.

The basic principles of legal and illegal contact apply. Incidental contact will occur on almost every rebound and *should be disregarded.* Contact which affects the play *must be called.* A player may not interfere with an opponent's rebound opportunity by muscling that opponent from a legally earned position, pushing from the side, charging from behind, or impeding movement through holding or an unnaturally extended body position.

Here are some suggestions:

1. Be sure to call legitimate rebounding fouls early in the game. If players sense "loose" rebounding officiating, rougher play will surely follow.
2. The lead official will gain a better rebounding perspective if *not too close* to the action. Back off slightly on an outside shot.
3. Unnatural movements or positions in the air are usually the result of holding, pushing, or charging. Do not call a foul, however, unless *you know who caused the contact* in question. It might have been a teammate of the "offended" player.
4. To promote game continuity, do not call a foul on an outside player when the inside rebounder gains possession of the ball unless the contact is obvious or severe.

Charging or Blocking?
For decades basketball officials have been coping with this difficult, debatable contact situation. Charging/blocking decisions continue to cause problems despite gradual clarifications in official rule interpretations. When opponents run into each other, "charging" refers to illegal contact by the *offensive* player, and "blocking" to illegal contact by the *defensive* player.

One of the most common charging or blocking situations involves contact between a defensive player and an offensive player driving for the basket. If the defensive player has both feet down and takes a normal and stationary position in front of and facing the dribbler, *charging* should be called when significant contact occurs. If, on the other hand, the defensive player moves laterally into the path of the dribbler, especially after the dribbler has advanced his or her head and shoulders beyond the defensive player, *blocking* would be the correct ruling. Unfortunately, game situations are not always this clear-cut, and the official is left with the question: "Who had the greater responsibility for the contact?" If the dribbler and the defender are shoulder-to-shoulder, they must continue to move in a straight line. Any pressure contact exerted to crowd the dribbler to the outside should result in a blocking foul.

Another common and difficult charging/blocking situation occurs in pivot play. An offensive player with the ball and his or her back to the basket will turn or drive for the basket. In this situation, contact will often take place on the first move for the basket by the player with the ball. The player with the ball is responsible for illegal contact if he or

A defensive player may move into the path of a dribbler at any time, providing he is able to establish a legal position. To initially establish this position, he must be facing the dribbler with both feet on the floor. Subsequently, he may turn, crouch, or retreat in order to avoid injury if he is charged by the dribbler. Number 5 has established a legal position. If Number 5 maintains his legal position, the dribbler is responsible for any contact.

Figure 4.10 Charging or blocking? (By courtesy of N.F.S.H.S.A.)

she turns or backs into a defensive player who is in a normal and stationary defensive stance. * The defensive player is responsible if contact occurs after the offensive player has taken the first step past the defensive player and is then pressured from the side by the defensive player. The legalization of dunking increases the responsibilities of officials to penalize unfair advantages gained by illegal physical contact. Charging should be called if a player attempting a dunk "muscles" *through* a defensive player who has attained a legal position between the offensive player and the basket.

The practice of defensive players "acting as if charged" has been widespread and has had adverse effects on basketball. Coaches should discourage such histrionics, and officials should ignore them, attempting to rule only on the actual contact as it occurred. If a player persists in

---

*Contrary to mistaken belief, the player with the ball is not entitled to "one free step" prior to contact with a legally established defensive player. By rule, he/she must expect to be closely guarded when involved in pivot play action.

This is a player control foul on Number 4. Number 3 has legal position and does not have to move from it. The contact is caused by Number 4 getting into position for a shot. Number 3 is entitled to his vertical space.

Figure 4.11 (By courtesy of the N.F.S.H.S.A.)

acting as if charged and the official believes the game is being harmed, a technical foul for unsportsmanlike conduct may be called after first warning the player.

The reader is referred to the section on rebounding and screening problem calls for other examples of charging and blocking fouls.

Contact with the Shooter
The importance of thorough and consistent calls is obvious when contact involves a player trying for a field goal. Slight, almost invisible contact can significantly affect a shot. The same degree of contact on a nonshooter might be disregarded.

A flesh-striking-flesh slap sound may or may not involve illegal contact. A shooter's hand (not wrist) in contact with the ball is considered to be *a part of the ball*. To ignore a slap sound heard by everyone will surely cause criticism, especially by uninformed observers; nevertheless, the correct and fair ruling must be made.

Criticism will also occur when a foul is called on a defender who executes a "beautiful block" of a shot attempt but, in the process, charges or pushes the shooter. Body contact is illegal if it affects play and gives the defensive player an unfair advantage over the shooter.

Physical contact with the shooter occurring after a score should be disregarded unless flagrant. On the other hand, a foul should be called if the defender takes a position on the floor while the shooter is in the air in order to cause contact and, in so doing, places the shooter at a disadvantage. This circumstance may occur on jump shots, hook shots, or shots off a drive for the basket and should be ruled an intentional foul, with two free throws awarded to the offended player, even if the try is successful.

Traveling

This call should not be difficult for the official who is willing to study the rules thoroughly. The key is to be able to *identify the pivot foot* of the player with the ball. Some of the most common examples of traveling are:

1. When a player starting a dribble moves the pivot foot before dribbling.
2. When attempting to stop, a player is unable to establish the pivot foot and drags it or takes an extra step.
3. When a player attempting a jump shot slides both feet together just before the jump.
4. When a player with the ball either falls to the floor or attempts to get up after securing possession.

Each of the above must be called closely.

A missed or "broken" dribble is not illegal. By definition, a player cannot be called for traveling while dribbling. It may not be traveling when a player fakes the defender, takes a long step with the nonpivot foot and then leaps ten to fifteen feet before shooting or passing.

Legal and Illegal Screens

A screen can be defined as the act of taking a position to impede the movement of the opponent. Judging whether a screen is legal or illegal is complicated by the number of variables involved. The variables are (1) whether the screen is stationary or moving; (2) the distance from the player screened; (3) the screener's body position; and (4) whether or not the player screened can see the screen. As in all personal fouls, contact must take place for illegal contact to be ruled. Screening principles apply to offensive and defensive (e.g. rebound positioning) players alike, and to players with or without the ball.

A *stationary* screen is legal at any distance if the player screened can see it. A screen set behind an opponent, out of vision, must be set *one step* away from the opponent. A distance of one to two strides is required if the opponent is moving; judgment of the official should vary according to the opponent's speed and vision of the screen in this circumstance. A screener may face in any direction, but may not assume an unusual stance which extends a knee, hip, shoulder, or arm into an opponent's path.

The above guidelines assign responsibility for significant contact to the screener or to the player screened. A foul should be charged to the responsible player if significant contact occurs. In the case of a legal "blind" screen, however, no foul should be charged if the player screened stops on contact and proceeds around the screen. When two opponents are moving in the same direction along the same route, the player behind, as in the case of motor vehicles, is responsible for contact.

Considerable alertness and judgment are needed to rule on legal and illegal screens. Guidelines help, but the official must "put it all together" and attempt to come up with the right answer. The popularity of offenses featuring screens away from the ball does not make the official's job any easier.

Pressing Defenses

Pressing defenses apply pressure on the official, as well as on the team with the ball. Personal fouls, back court traveling, and illegal dribble violations are more likely to occur. Opposing coaches and followers want their teams, respectively, to be "protected" or "unhampered" by

Number 5 is blocking number 12 when he illegally contacts him with his arms in an effort to obstruct his movement. A player may not impede the progress of an opponent by extending an arm, shoulder, hip, or knee, or by bending the body into other than a normal position.

Figure 4.12 (By courtesy of the N.F.S.H.S.A.)

the officials. Pressing defenses may be categorized as full court, three-fourths court, or half court; the primary emphasis here is upon full court and three-fourths court pressing defenses.

The lead, as well as the trail official must take responsibility. Only the trail official calls a ten-second back court violation; otherwise, the load should be shared equally. The lead official's quandary is obvious. He or she must help in the midcourt area and also be ready to sprint to the front court end line if the ball is passed there. A helpful guideline calls for the lead official to help towards the midcourt area whenever *five or more* offensive and defensive players happen to be in the back court because of a pressing defense.

To be legal, a trap must conform to the guidelines for legal screens. A "trapper" may establish and maintain a position *within a step* of the player with the ball if the trapper can be seen by the player with the ball. A defensive player approaching from a blind side must initially provide a *full step.* If this defensive positioning conforms to legal screening guidelines, responsibility for any significant contact is with the player with the ball. Defensive players may not reach in from behind and contact a player with the ball. The player with the ball may pivot freely unless in so doing he or she significantly contacts a defensive player who has established a legal position.

Recent interpretations stress that defensive and offensive players should be penalized stringently for illegal use of the hands and arms. A dribbler commits a personal foul when he or she pushes a defensive player. A defensive player who "hand checks" an offensive player should be penalized. A pressing defense will produce more illegal hand and arm infractions than usual.

Lack of Sufficient Action

Lack of sufficient action rules place responsibility on one team or the other to "force action" and, thus, obviate gross stalling tactics. These rules apply to high school only, because the use of the shot clock in college games has eliminated its application. These rules relate only to the midcourt areas of the floor. If the score is tied, the *defensive team* is responsible; otherwise, the *team behind* is responsible. The leading team is never responsible. The penalty is a technical foul for each infraction—enforced by the trail official. Continued violations can lead to a forfeit.

Lack of sufficient action may be penalized only after a *warning* by the trail official. When the responsible team, whether on offense or defense, allows a lack of action in a midcourt area for *five seconds* the trail official should move to an easily seen position and call "play ball." The lead official will also give the signal. After being warned, the responsible team has only five seconds in which to force action. Failure to comply results in a technical foul. Each team is entitled to one warning for each period of play, which means that the officials must remember or record which team has been warned in a given period.

Fortunately, the rule and its severe penalty have largely eliminated lack of sufficient action infractions. Nevertheless, officials should occasionally review this rule and its rather complicated enforcement procedures.

Basket Interference

Dunking has been legalized, but other basket interference restrictions remain. It is not basket interference if a ball, in downward flight with a chance to go in, is touched when it had been previously touched away from the basket by an intervening player. If a player "pins" a shot against the backboard, basket interference may or may not be ruled depending on whether or not the ball was in its downward flight with a chance to go in.

A player may legally dunk and in so doing penetrate and touch the basket, but only after having gained control of the ball away from the basket and its cylinder. Dunking before the game and during intermissions remains prohibited and should be penalized by the officials.

The trail official has primary responsibility for calling basket interference. The ball is awarded to the offended team for a throw-in at the free throw line extended and no points are scored, when the violation occurs at the *offending team's basket.* If at the *offended team's basket,* two points are awarded on a field goal attempt and one point on a free throw.

Back Court Violations

It is difficult for an inexperienced official to apply the language of National Federation rule 9, section 9 (3:29), to real action. The intent of the rule is to penalize a team in control of the ball if that team returns the ball from the front court to the back court. The division line is a part of the back court for the team in control. In most cases the back court violations are obvious: a player standing in the front court with the ball pivots and steps on or over the division line; a bad pass is thrown from the front court to the back court and is first touched there by a player of the team which had been in control in the front court; etc.

This is basket interference by a Team B player at A's basket in both (1) and (2). Team A is awarded 2 points in each case when the interference occurs during a 2-point try. The official hands the ball to a Team B player for a throw-in anywhere along the end line nearest Team A's basket.

In (1), it is a basket interference violation for either the offense or defense to hit the net when the ball is on or within the basket. The violation causes the ball to become dead. If Team B interferes, Team A is awarded 1 point if it occurs during a free throw try and 2 points in the case of a 2-point try. If A interferes, no points can be scored, and the ball is awarded out-of-bounds to B at the nearest spot. In (2), a Team A player tips the ball into A's basket when the ball is on the ring. The violation causes the ball to become dead immediately. No score is allowed, and the ball is awarded to the opponents out-of-bounds at the nearest spot.

Figure 4.13 Basket interference. (By courtesy of the N.F.S.H.S.A.)

Following are two of the not-so-easy applications of the rule. It is a back court violation if a player on a team in control:

1. *When the ball is in the back court,* leaps from the front court, catches the ball in the air, and lands in the back court or on the division line; or
2. *When the ball is in the front court,* leaps from the back court, catches the ball in the air, and lands in the front court or on the division line.

If the ball is caused to go from the front court to the back court by (1) an uncontrolled rebound, (2) an uncontrolled jump ball tap, or (3) a deflection of the ball by a defensive player directly to the back court, there is no back court violation.

When an official understands the principles of (a) team control and (b) player location when in the air back court rules are not difficult to apply. A player in the air is "located" where he or she *last touched the floor.* The same principle is applied in determining whether a player is out-of-bounds when catching the ball in the air near a boundary line and landing in-bounds; it is a violation if the player jumped from an out-of-bounds spot.

In (1) number 4 causes the ball to be in the back court when he touches it before he touches the floor in the front court. While in the air number 4 is in the back court. In (2) this ball has not been to the back court since it has not touched the back court or anyone in it. While in the air number 4 is in the front court.

Figure 4.14 Backcourt violations. (By courtesy of N.F.S.H.S.A.)

Miscellaneous Considerations

Pregame Officials Conference
A thorough pregame conference is a must, especially if the officials have not worked together previously. The referee should take the lead, but the officials must treat each other as equals and speak candidly. Important topics should include pregame responsibilities, switching, throw-in coverage, pressing defense coverage, and backup signals. The officials should clarify which decision may or may not be called by the trail and by the lead official. A procedure should be established for the "off" official to assist with a ruling when the responsible official is screened out or otherwise unable to make the call. Questionable rules and recent rule changes may need discussion.

Postgame Procedure
Following the game, officials should refrain from conversation with either the winning or losing coach. The outcome of the game has been determined by numerous judgments. To defend any one call at this time would be neither feasible nor ethical. In the privacy of the dressing room, officials should take advantage of the opportunity to review specific game situations in an effort to become more proficient.

Officiating Evaluated by Coaches

What qualities do you appreciate in a basketball official?

1. Background
2. Knowledge of the rules
3. Humor
4. Confidence
5. Consistency
6. Hustle
7. Firmness
8. Conditioning
9. Receptiveness
10. Credibility under pressure
11. Courtesy
12. Dependability
13. Honesty
14. Judgment
15. Professional approach

Miscellaneous Comments

1. It is important that the official understands and appreciates the pressures of basketball on players and coaches in order to counteract occasional emotional outbursts.
2. The competent official fully understands the role of assuring that the game be conducted according to the rules.

Officiating Evaluated by Officials

What is the most difficult play to call in basketball?

1. Charging and blocking
2. Goaltending
3. Illegal screens
4. Double foul situations
5. A play away from the basket when a player is driving to the basket.

What is the most difficult phase of mechanics in officiating basketball?

1. Getting back to cover the fast break.
2. Lead official's view of the lane is often blocked by large players.

Miscellaneous Comments

1. There is no substitute for experience.
2. The level of officiating performance is directly related to individual's dedication and enjoyment of the game.

Play Rulings (1)

Situation: Both teams remain in their huddle following a time-out even though the official administering the throw-in has alerted them that play will resume. (a) Before; or (b) after the ball is placed at the spot, team A or B indicates it desires a time-out. *Ruling:* In (a) either team may request and be granted a time-out. In (b) only team A may be granted a time-out after the throw-in count has started.

Situation: What guidelines should be exercised by the officials when spectators' actions are such that they interfere with administration of the game? *Ruling:* The rule book states "the official may call fouls on either team if its supporters act in such a way as to interfere with the proper conduct of the game." It is significant to note the word used is "may." This gives permission, but does not in any way imply that the officials must call fouls on team followers or supporters. Thus, while officials do have the authority to penalize a team whose spectators interfere with the proper conduct of the game, this authority must be used with extreme caution and judiciousness. While the authority is there, an official will almost never use it, because experience has demonstrated that calling technical fouls on the crowd does not accomplish the purpose for which the call was intended. *Comment:* The behavior of spectators is that of the game committee or management. The rule book stipulates that insofar as the management can reasonably be expected to control the spectators, it is its responsibility to do so. Management has the responsibility of providing a site where the game can proceed in a sportsmanlike manner. If the conduct of spectators or a spectator prohibits the orderly continuance of a game, the officials will have a representative of game management take whatever action is advisable and necessary. This may require the removal of a team follower(s), or the clearing of the court of coins, debris, ice, or paper. If the disruption is not brought under control and the contest cannot safely continue, rather than assess technical fouls, the official is advised to suspend or forfeit the game. This action is taken only as a last resort.

Situation: The score is tied with one second remaining in the game. A1 is awarded a bonus free throw. After the ball had been placed at the disposal of A1, B1 disconcerts A1. The free throw attempt is missed. The timekeeper does not hear the official's whistle sound and permits the clock to start. May the referee put the second back on the clock? *Ruling:* Yes. This is authorized by the last sentence of Rule 2–14 which provides ". . . the referee may correct the mistake only when he or she has definite information relative to time involved." The referee not only orders the timer to put one second back on the clock but also awards A1 a substitute throw for the disconcertion by B1. In instances where the timer has not made a mistake, the referee is not authorized to either put time on the clock or to take time off the clock.

Situation: The visiting team has practiced on one end of the court prior to the jump to start the game, but the captain requests the other basket for first half of play. *Ruling:* The request is denied. The visiting team had the choice and exercised it when they warmed up on one end. If the visitors will be late arriving on the court they should notify the home team of their preference.

Situation: Does a player control foul count toward reaching the five personal fouls which puts the bonus in effect? *Ruling:* Yes.

Situation: The official is in team A's front court when he or she runs into a pass thrown by A1 from team A's back court. After touching the official, the ball: **(a)** goes out-of-bounds; or **(b)** rebounds to the back court where it is recovered by A2. *Ruling:* Touching the official is the same as touching the floor where the official is standing. In (a), the ball is awarded to B for a throw-in. In (b), the ball has been in the front court and then it has gone to the back court. Since A1 was the last player to touch it before it went to the back court, A1 caused it to go there. Consequently, this is a violation.

Situation: If a personal foul is flagrant, is the offending player always disqualified and is an additional free throw awarded? *Ruling:* The offending player is always disqualified. The extra free throw is awarded, provided such foul is not part of a double foul or a foul which otherwise carries a penalty of two free throws. In addition, the offended team is awarded the ball for a throw-in at the out-of-bounds spot nearest the foul.

Situation: Team B is using a pressing defense in an effort to gain control of the ball. Team B is trailing in the last part of the fourth quarter. What guidelines could an official use to judge whether a foul is intentional? *Ruling:* Some basic guidelines include: contact away from the ball; contact resulting when no attempt is made to play the ball; contact from behind or with no attempt to play the ball; grabbing a player around the waist; or simply pushing a player. These acts are not accidental, they are intentional. Usually contact in-bounds before the ball is released on a throw-in is intentional. The severity of the contact is not the basis for the call, it is whether or not the contact is designed or premeditated.

Situation: A1 catches the ball while both feet are off the floor, alights on one foot, jumps off that foot, and comes to a stop with both feet simultaneously hitting the floor. A1 then lifts one foot and throws for a goal or passes. *Ruling:* Legal. A1 may lift the foot in passing or throwing for a goal in this situation. However, A1 may not pivot, that is, A1 may not lift one foot from the floor and then step with that foot before the ball has left the hand or hands. By rule, a pivot means a player "steps once or more than once with the same foot. . . ."

Situation: A1 completes the throw-in to A2 to begin the second half. A2 is confused and dribbles toward the basket team A used during the first half and dunks the ball into the basket of team B. *Ruling:* Legal goal. Two points are awarded to team B. The ball is awarded to team A out-of-bounds at the basket of team B. Team A may put the ball in play from anywhere along the end line as after any score by B (earned or awarded).

Situation: Following the jump ball between A1 and B1 to start the first quarter, the tapped ball: (a) is touched by A2 and it then goes out-of-bounds; or (b) is touched simultaneously by A2 and B2 and it then goes directly out-of-bounds; or (c) is simultaneously controlled by A2 and B2. *Ruling:* In (a), team B will make the throw-in. The alternating possession procedure is established and the arrow is set toward A's basket when a player of team B is handed the ball for the throw-in. Team A will start the alternating procedure and will have the first opportunity to throw-in when the procedure is used. In (b) and (c), A2 and B2 will jump at the center circle regardless of where the ball went out or where the held ball occurred. The two free throw circles are no longer used for a jump ball.

Situation: Team A scores a field goal. Team B requests and is granted a charged time-out. Must the throw-in following the time-out be from a designated spot? *Ruling:* No. When the time-out is over, team B may make the throw-in from anywhere behind the end line. Team B is not required to make the throw-in from a designated spot. The same ruling applies to a time-out after a successful free throw attempt.

Situation: The bonus rule is in effect. While the ball is in flight during a try for field goal by A1, A2 fouls B1. B2 then commits a basket interference violation. *Ruling:* Both the violation and personal foul are penalized. Team A is awarded two points for the basket interference by B2 and then B1 is awarded a one-and-one attempt for the foul by A2.

Situation: B1 is standing behind the plane of the backboard before A1 jumps for a lay-up shot. The forward momentum of airborne shooter A1 causes a charge into B1. *Ruling:* B1 is entitled to the position provided there was no movement into that position after A1 left the floor. If the ball goes through the basket before or after the contact occurs it is a player control foul and the goal is canceled. If B1 moves into the path of A1 after A1 has left the floor, the foul is on B1. It is a two-shot blocking foul when the defensive player moves into the path of the airborne shooter with no intent to play the ball. If the defensive player moves under the airborne shooter and does not play the ball but rather takes away the landing spot it is a two-shot blocking foul. If a defensive player is trying to establish legal defensive position and makes a legitimate attempt to play the ball, it does not automatically constitute a two-shot foul.

Situation: A defensive player maneuvers to a position in front of the post-player A1 to prevent A1 from receiving the ball. A high pass is made over the head and out of reach of the defensive player. The post-player A1 moves toward the basket to catch the pass and try for goal. As the pass is made, a teammate of the defensive player moves into the path of A1 in a guarding position. Is this guarding or a screening situation, and what are the rights of the pivot player A1 and the defensive player who moves into A1's path? *Ruling:* This action constitutes a screening situation. The defensive player has switched to guard a player who does not have the ball. Therefore, the switching player must assume a position one or two strides in advance of the post player (depending upon the speed of movement of such player) to make the action legal. If the defensive player moves into the path of the post-player A1 after A1 has control of the ball (provided the post-player is not in the air at the time), the play becomes a guarding situation. If it is a guarding situation, no distance or time limit is involved.

BIBLIOGRAPHY

1. National Federation of State High School Associations, *1990–91 Basketball Case Book,* Kansas City, Missouri, 1990.
2. National Federation of State High School Associations, *1989–90 and 1990–91 Basketball Officials Manual,* Kansas City, Missouri, 1989.
3. National Federation of State High School Associations, *1990–91 High School Basketball Rules,* Kansas City, Missouri, 1990.
4. National Federation of State High School Associations, *1990–91 Official High School Basketball Rules, Simplified and Illustrated,* Kansas City, Missouri, 1990.

5

Football

The Game

Football is a physical semi-combative sport. Players collectively pit their physical attributes as well as skills against an opposing team. An emotional and uniquely intense atmosphere contributes to tremendous developmental benefits to players and strong spectator interest. Injuries, some of them very serious, are almost inevitable.

Football officials as well as coaches play an extremely important role in promoting maximum benefits and preventing unwanted harmful by-products. The officials are expected not only to assist in the orderly progress of the game but to keep it free from flagrant and uncontrolled violence. Injury prevention must be foremost in the minds of football officials.

The greatest difficulty in officiating football involves gaining and maintaining advantageous positioning without obstructing play. With twenty-two players in motion at the snap, officials are frequently screened out of the play. Consequently, they must be constantly moving and anticipating the movement of the ball and the players in order to establish or reestablish the best possible position to observe the action.

Despite the advent of instant replays the judgment and decisions of football officials are less subject to public scrutiny and criticism than in other sports. Football field and stadium dimensions place the action and the officials in positions more remote from the spectators. Player congestion at the scrimmage line obstructs vision from the bench areas and grandstands. The football official is thereby placed (advantageously) in a more independent position from which to exercise control. Remoteness and scrimmage-line congestion, on the other hand, impose an extra obligation on football officials to meet their responsibilities with integrity and unbiased objectivity. For the best interests of the players and the game, fouls must be called, control maintained, and injuries prevented.

Football officiating is enjoyable as well as challenging. The atmosphere is exciting. With more officials on the crew, feelings of "team spirit," morale, cooperation, and friendship are more likely to develop.

In the United States, "football is king" in terms of community interest, media emphasis, and economic factors. Football is as integral to the American culture as ham and eggs and hot dogs. Football officials can continue to make an important contribution toward maintaining and encouraging this great heritage.

Officials and Their Responsibilities

Depending upon the level of competition, the number of field officials varies from three to seven. The chart below shows a typical pattern for the number of officials assigned at different levels of competition in the United States:

Number in Crew	Designations	Common Level of Competition
Three	Referee, Linesman, and Umpire	High school, below varsity
Four	Referee, Linesman, Umpire, and Line Judge	High school varsity
Five	Referee, Linesman, Umpire, Line Judge, and Back Judge	High school varsity and playoffs, small college
Six	Referee, Linesman, Umpire, Line Judge, Back Judge, and Side Judge	College
Seven	Referee, Linesman, Umpire, Line Judge, Back Judge, Side Judge, and Field Judge	Professional

Most references in this section are to a crew of four officials unless otherwise noted.

Officials' Uniforms and Equipment

High school football officials' uniforms and equipment are prescribed in detail. Shirts are to be black-and-white one-inch vertically striped with a black knit cuff and Byron collar. They may be long- or short-sleeved, but the same for all members of a given crew. All-white tapered knickers should be worn, with a short overlap below the knee. High school and NCAA officials now wear identical stockings with a modified northwestern striping ($\frac{1}{2}''$ white, $\frac{1}{2}''$ black, $1''$ white, $\frac{1}{2}''$ black, $\frac{1}{2}''$ white). The shoes should be shined before each game and are solid black with black laces. The belt should be black, $1\frac{1}{4}$ to 2 inches wide with a plain buckle. The cap, other than the referee's cap, is to be a black baseball type with white pipings. Referee caps must be white regardless of the number of officials in the crew. If worn during the game, jackets must be black-and-white vertically striped. (2:7)

Prescribed equipment includes a whistle (an extra whistle is recommended), a $15'' \times 15''$ light gold flag penalty marker, game card, pencil, and two connected rubber bands with which to keep track of the correct down (one band around the wrist, tied to the second band which is stretched around one or more fingers, according to the down). (2:7) The referee needs a watch for regulating the twenty-five seconds before a down. It is recommended that the linesman use a clipping device, designed for that purpose, to attach to the line-to-gain chain at the yardline nearest the rear stake. All officials should have a white colored bean bag with which to spot the point where a kick is first touched or a ball is fumbled.

Pregame Responsibilities

Referee.

1. Visit team dressing rooms to provide each head coach with a list of the officials, discuss special situations, and verbally verify in the presence of the umpire that the players are legally equipped.
2. Conduct the pregame officials conference.
3. Approve the clock operator and review timing procedures.
4. Approve game ball(s) and give to umpire.
5. Conduct pregame toss and introduce team captains to each other.

Linesman.

1. Secure stakes, chain, and down marker.
2. With line-to-gain crew, review "do's" and "don'ts" of (a) moving the chains and down marker, (b) acting in a partisan manner, and (c) measuring for a first down.

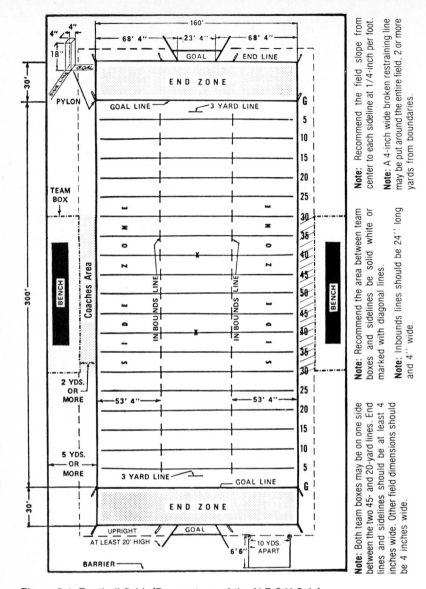

Figure 5.1 Football field. (By courtesy of the N.F.S.H.S.A.)

Umpire. Before the pregame conference the umpire should accompany the referee to locker room to check player equipment. Without exception, illegal equipment is to be disapproved. This will allow necessary adjustments to be accomplished with little disruption.

Line Judge.

1. Check proper working order of the clock and have an auxiliary timing device available.
2. Assist in starting the game on time.
3. Orient the ball boy(s).

The game responsibilities of each official are covered in the "mechanics" section of this chapter. The referee has final authority for resolving disagreements among officials and for decisions not specifically delegated to another official.

Timer. The timer, or electric game clock operator, is not designated in high school football rules as a member of the officiating crew. Nevertheless, the timer is essential to an efficient and smooth running game, as in all sports. If possible, the timer should be present at the pregame officials conference when procedures for starting and stopping the clock are reviewed. The clock operator should check the proper working order of the clock before the game.

The timer starts or stops the clock primarily as dictated by the signals of field officials. If the officials inadvertently fail to signal, or the timer does not see a signal, the timer should follow indicated timing procedures independently. No official's signal is given to start a stopped clock at the snap—the timer is responsible. Experienced timers respond semi-independently to obvious cues such as clearly incomplete passes. Nevertheless, timers should avoid a natural tendency to go on their own and neglect the signals of officials. Field officials have a far better position from which to rule on borderline timing-related decisions. Timing errors are correctable by the referee, but the process is judgmental and disruptive to game continuity.

Guidelines for starting and stopping the clock are described in the "Mechanics" section of this chapter on pages 113–32.

Basic Penalties and Rulings

The objectives of a football team are to advance the ball to the opponent's goal line and score, and to prevent the opposing team from advancing and scoring. Scoring results from *touchdowns* (six points), successful *tries-for-points* following touchdowns (one point if by kick, two if by run or pass), *field goals* (three points), or *safeties* (two points). Teams may advance the ball by kicking it (with the expectation of losing possession), running with it, or passing it. The ball may be passed forward from behind the scrimmage line and backwards from any point on the field. The team in possession of the ball has a series of four plays or "downs" in which to score, advance the distance-to-gain (ten yards), or surrender possession to the other team. A first down in a new series is awarded when the offensive team makes the distance-to-gain in four downs or less, or is awarded by a penalty.

Fouls and Penalties

Fouls may be called on teams, players, substitutes, coaches, or attendants, but not on followers, for acts which violate football rules. Penalties range from running off yardage to awarding scores or, ultimately, forfeiting the game. Players may be disqualified for flagrant personal fouls or flagrant unsportsmanlike conduct. Following "unfair acts" the referee may enforce any penalty he considers equitable, including yardage, awarding a score, or, in the case of repeatedly delaying the game, forfeiting the game.

　　All penalties are yardage penalties (see Table 5.1). A down during which a penalty occurred is replayed if the offended team accepts the penalty. (Exception: some fouls by offense contain a loss-of-down provision.) If a penalty is declined, the down counts. Some infractions by the defensive team result in an automatic first down.

Table 5.1   Summary of Penalties

	Rule Section Article	Signal
Loss of 5 Yards		
1. Failure to properly wear required equipment during down	1–5–6	23
2. Delay of game	3–6–2	7–21
3. Failure to properly wear required equipment just before snap	3–6–2d	7–21–23
4. Illegal substitution	3–7	22
5. Encroachment..	6–1–4 or 7–1–1	7–18
6. Free kick infraction	6–1–2, 3	7–19
7. Invalid or illegal fair catch signal	6–5–6, 7	32
8. False start or any illegal act by snapper	7–1–2, 3, 4 or 7–2–6	7–19
9. Less than 7 players on A's line or numbering violation.........	7–2–1	19
10. Illegal formation or procedure at snap	7–2–2, 3, 7	19
11. Illegal motion or shift...	7–2–4, 5	20
12. Illegally handing ball forward **(also loss of down)**........	7–3–2, 3, 4	35–9
13. Illegal forward pass **(if by A, also loss of down** in (a) and (c))**	7–5–2a, c, d	35–9

Table 5.1 *continued*

	Rule Section Article	Signal
Loss of 5 Yards		
14. Intentional grounding **(also loss of down)**	7–5–2b	36–9
15. Ineligible receiver illegally downfield **(also loss of down)**	7–5–7	37
16. Helping runner	9–1	44
17. Attendant illegally on field	9–8–2	19
18. Nonplayer outside of the team box but not on field	9–8–3	19
Loss of 10 Yards		
1. Illegal blocking technique	9–2–1a, 9–2–3a	43
2. Illegal use of hands	9–2–3b	43
3. Interlocked blocking	9–2–1b	44
4. Holding	9–2–1c, 9–2–3d	42
5. Runner grasping a teammate	9–2–2	43
6. Striking blocker's head with hand(s)	9–2–3c	43
Loss of 15 Yards		
1. Fair catch interference	6–5–5	33
2. Illegal block after valid or invalid fair catch signal	6–5–1, 9–3–2	40
3. Forward pass interference **(loss of down if by A**—give signal 33 and 9; **also 1st down if by B)**	7–5–6	33
If intentional or unsportsmanlike—an additional 15 yards	7–5–6	27
4. Illegal block below waist or on free kicker or holder	9–3–1, 3	40
5. Clipping	9–3–4	39
6. Chop block	9–3–5	41
7. Tripping	9–3–6	46
8. Charging into an opponent obviously out of the play	9–4–2b	38
9. Piling, hurdling, unnecessary roughness, etc., and other personal fouls	9–4–2	38
10. Grasping an opponent's face protector (or any helmet opening)	9–4–2h	45
11. Butt block, face tackle or spear	9–4–2i	24
12. Roughing passer **(also 1st down)**	9–4–3	34
13. Roughing kicker or holder **(also 1st down)**	9–4–4	30
14. Unsportsmanlike conduct by player or nonplayer	9–5, 9–8–1	27
15. Illegal participation	9–6	28
16. Illegally kicking or batting ball	9–7	31
17. Nonplayer illegally on field	9–8–3	27
Disqualification Associated with Certain 15-Yard Penalties		
1. Striking, kicking, kneeing	9–4–1	38–47
2. Any act if unduly rough or flagrant (give proper signal and follow with 47)	9–4–2, 3, 4	47

"A measurement cannot take the ball more than half the distance from the enforcement spot to the offending team's goal line. If the penalty would be greater than this, the ball is placed halfway from enforcement spot to the goal line." (3) For example, a ten-yard penalty measured from the 8-yard line would take the ball to the 4-yard line; a fifteen-yard penalty measured from the 26-yard line would take the ball to the 13-yard line, etc.

Penalty Enforcement

One of the important responsibilities of the referee is determining the spot on the field from which a yardage penalty should be measured. This spot is called the "spot of enforcement." Depending on the foul, the spot of enforcement may be the "previous spot" (where the ball was last put in play by a snap or free kick), the end of the run, the spot of the foul, or, in rare cases, the goal line.

The spot of enforcement is easily determined when a foul occurs simultaneously with the snap or between downs. ("Between downs" refers to the time period after the whistle ended the previous down until the ball is snapped on the next down.) When the foul is *simultaneous with the snap,* as in illegal motion, an accepted penalty would be measured from the *previous* spot (or the line of scrimmage). When the foul is *between downs,* as in dead ball fouls, or is a nonplayer foul, an unsportsmanlike foul, or a defensive foul during a successful try, field goal, or touchdown, the penalty would be measured from the *succeeding spot.*

Determining the correct enforcement spot for a foul occurring *during a down* is more complicated. First, officials must decide whether the foul occurred during a "loose ball play" or a "running play." A play must be categorized one way or the other whenever a foul occurs during a down.

The basic spot for a running-play foul is the *end of the run.* The basic spot for a loose-ball-play foul is the *previous* spot. For both types of play the penalty should be measured from the basic spot *unless* the foul was *by the offensive team behind the basic spot* ("all-but-one" enforcement principle). If by the offensive team behind the basic spot, an accepted penalty should be measured from the *spot of the foul.*

A down is categorized as a running-play down unless the down includes a legal forward pass, a scrimmage kick, a free kick, a backward pass, or a fumble made by the offense behind its scrimmage line, which are loose ball plays. *When a kick or pass is caught the play from that point on is a running play.*

Any live ball foul, other than a nonplayer or unsportsmanlike foul or a foul simultaneous with the snap, is penalized according to the all-but-one enforcement principle. All fouls are penalized from the basic spot, except the foul by the offense which occurs behind the spot. In that case the penalty is administered from the spot of the foul.

Figure 5.2 "All-but-one" enforcement principle. (By courtesy of the N.F.S.H.S.A.)

The correct enforcement spot for fouls during downs can usually be determined without difficulty if the officials carefully consider two types of questions:

1. Was the foul during a loose ball play or a running play?
2. Was the foul by the offense or the defense? If by the offense, was the foul behind the basic spot? ("All-but-one" enforcement principle.)

Mechanics

During a play, or down, the four officials jockey for position, attempting together to surround the action and keep all twenty-two players in view. A proper distance and angle must be maintained. A too-distant position weakens "presence" and control. A too-close position may blur vision and/or obstruct play. When a whistle ends a down, the officials near the ball should quickly close in on the action and help spot the ball for the next down. Decisive and efficient movements by the officials after a down help considerably to maintain a fast moving, organized, and disciplined game.

Starting Positions on Scrimmage Plays

Figure 5.3 shows where the officials are when the ball is snapped and basic coverage patterns following the snap.

The *referee* takes a position to one side and slightly behind the offensive team's backfield. He is to the *"wide side"* of the field, or, if the ball is in the middle of the field, as in the diagram, usually *away from the linesman*. The *umpire* is behind the interior of the defensive line clear of the linebacker's initial movements.

The *linesman's* starting position is outside the widest defensive and offensive players and *in the neutral zone*. (On a scrimmage play the neutral zone is the space established by running imaginary lines from the front and back tips of the ball directly to the sidelines.) The linesman, one of the two "flank" officials, is on the side of the field *opposite the press box*. The other flank official, the *line judge,* is opposite the linesman outside all offensive and defensive players to his side of the field. The line judge is usually positioned in the neutral zone; the only exception being a punt play when he is positioned near the punt returner(s) towards the sideline. On a given play the other officials check to see where the line judge is because their own play coverage responsibilities are affected if he is downfield.

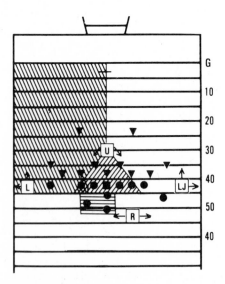

Figure 5.3 Running play from scrimmage. (By courtesy of the N.F.S.H.S.A.)

Scrimmage Play Coverage

Comprehensive coverage of a scrimmage play comes from a blend of fluctuating responsibilities and movement patterns as the play develops. Each official must know and cover his own responsibilities and also help with shared responsibilities.

Referee. The referee is responsible for fouls committed by or against a passer and against a punter. To fully protect a passer or punter, the referee should not immediately follow the flight of a pass or punt but watch for illegal contact after the ball is in the air. The referee rules on illegal passes and watches for illegal blocks behind the scrimmage line. He shares responsibility for any illegal motion other than when an offensive back is in lateral motion, which is the responsibility of a flank official.

On a running play the referee trails the ball carrier and frequently whistles the ball dead. Since the initial direction of offensive backs is sometimes deceptive, the referee should not immediately commit himself towards the scrimmage line, where he might hinder a reverse or screen pass. On wide running plays out-of-bounds the referee and umpire cover roughness and the flank official holds the out-of-bounds spot. When a flank official is far downfield the referee must cover that sideline as needed.

Following most downs either the referee or the umpire will spot the ball. The general guideline is for the referee to spot the ball when forward progress is behind or to the neutral zone, and for the umpire to do so if progress is beyond the neutral zone. Whoever spots the ball usually gets the correct forward progress from a flank official. After the ball is spotted, the referee announces the coming down and distance-to-gain and checks the down marker from a position adjacent to the ball. He steps away from the ball and executes the "ready for play" signal— a short blast of the whistle accompanied by a downward pump of the right arm. The twenty-five-second period between plays starts with the ready-for-play signal and is enforced by the referee.

Umpire. Fouls by interior linesmen are the chief responsibility of the umpire. Since it is impossible for him to see near-simultaneous contact involving nine or ten different players at the snap, the umpire should alternate his starting position from down to down, concentrating on different sets of opponents on each down. Even though he alternates his starting position and concentration, the umpire should be ready to call any foul he sees by any interior lineman on every down.

If the line judge is downfield the umpire should be positioned to that side of the field. The umpire shares responsibility for calling encroachment and false starts. The umpire rarely whistles a play dead—only if a fellow official is screened out or not in position. The umpire spots the ball more often than any other official.

On running plays to either side zone the umpire should go with the play and look for fouls adjacent to the ball carrier. On pass plays, the umpire is primarily responsible for ineligible receivers and determining whether a forward pass goes beyond the scrimmage line. *Move to the neutral zone* when the offense appears committed to a pass play. Follow the flight of a pass and help to rule whether it is legally caught. Being in the center of the action, the umpire cannot afford to worry about what happens behind him.

The umpire's movements and location can be likened to a "bullfighter in no-man's land." The umpire must utilize peripheral vision, experience, and instincts in order to avoid the obstruction of linebackers, pass receivers, downfield blockers, and ball carriers—and in order to avoid his own injury.

Linesman. The linesman is chiefly responsible for encroachment or false starts by any player. In addition, he calls illegal use of the hands on that side and improper direction by a man-in-motion towards the opposite sideline. On each down, the linesman must check and remember which players on his side of the field line up as eligible pass receivers. He must check for the number of players on the scrimmage line and for correct numbers.

On quick running plays up the middle the linesman, as a flank official, is responsible for determining the forward progress of the ball. When the ball is whistled dead the linesman points one foot (the foot towards the goal of the offense) slightly in front of the other to show the forwardmost progress to the official spotting the ball. If a running play comes to his side beyond the hash marks, he takes over as "referee" to cover the ball carrier and blow the ball dead. The linesman also gets the sideline spot and stops the clock if the ball carrier goes out-of-bounds. The referee and umpire will take primary responsibility for roughness out-of-bounds. If a running play comes right at the linesman, he must make his first move backward in order to stay clear, and to follow the play covering the sideline. The linesman *never turns his back to the play*.

On pass plays the linesman moves downfield and observes contact between pass receivers and defensive backs. The linesman should know whether a pass was in flight when a foul occurred, because penalties vary accordingly.

The linesman must maintain close communication with the line-to-gain crew, constantly reminding them not to move the down marker and chains or advance the down until instructed to do so by only the linesman. When the equipment is incorrectly moved following a play in which a foul occurred, the officials may be faced with a problem if the yards penalized should be from the previous line of scrimmage. The linesman, backed up by the referee, is responsible for having the correct down shown on the down marker.

Line judge. The responsibilities and general coverage of the line judge, *when on the line of scrimmage, are basically the same as those of the linesman.* The only differences are that the linesman is responsible for the line-to-gain crew and the *line judge* has *primary responsibility for covering the goal line and end line.* He also works with the ball boys.

When the line judge lines up *off the line of scrimmage,* overall coverage is weakened regarding the neutral zone, fouls prior to or at the snap, and illegal use of hands. Therefore, the line judge should line up *on* the line of scrimmage unless there is a strong possibility of a punt or pass play. When a punt is expected, the line judge should position himself slightly in front and to the side of the punt returner, alert to cover his sideline.

All officials.

1. Fumbles can create problems for the officials. Most fumbles occur when the ball carrier is tackled, frequently quite near the time when the official would normally sound the whistle to end the play. Withhold the whistle if a fumble occurs before the ball carrier has been downed. *Do not blow the whistle if away from the play.* Remember that a fumble after the ball carrier has been downed is irrelevant.

2. When the team on offense is in a spread formation, all officials should widen their starting position in order to gain a better view of all players.

3. *Hustle during and immediately after the down.* Active officials make their presence known to the players, which helps to reduce fouls.

Coverage of Special Plays

Approximately three out of four football plays are running or pass plays from scrimmage, to which the previous section applies. The football official must also be prepared to cover scrimmage kicks, plays near the goal line, tries-for-point, and kick-offs.

Scrimmage kicks. When the offensive team lines up for a scrimmage kick, the *referee* takes a position opposite the linesman, three or four yards in advance of and at least five yards to the side of the punter. This position will provide a good view of player contact with the punter. If it is possible that a rusher will contact the punter, do not initially watch the flight of the punt, but stay with the action near the punter. Be prepared to assist the umpire in ruling where and by whom the punt is first touched just *beyond the neutral zone*. A punt caught or recovered behind the neutral zone may be advanced by either team.

When a long punt goes out-of-bounds in flight, the referee should get a line on it, hold his position, and, through an arm signal, assist the linesman or line judge in locating the out-of-bounds spot. On short punts out-of-bounds to his side, whether in flight or not, the referee should run immediately to the out-of-bounds spot.

When a punt may go out-of-bounds, the referee must quickly adjust his position in order to get an accurate line on the path of the ball. The adjustment is much greater when a punt goes out-of-bounds on the line judge's side of the field, as is shown in Figure 5.4. Behind a punt in-bounds the referee moves slowly down the field, watching for fouls, and being ready to cover a long runback.

Before the snap the *umpire* should favor the line judge's side of the field. Following the snap, the umpire should watch for illegal contact in the line and *move to the neutral zone*. If the punt is blocked, assist the

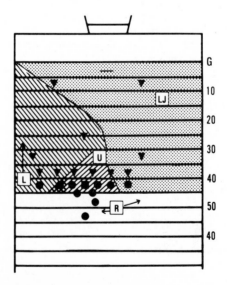

Figure 5.4 Scrimmage-kick.
(By courtesy of the N.F.S.H.S.A.)

referee in determining possession. Otherwise, move slowly downfield, observing contact away from the ball. The umpire is in an excellent position to rule on clipping and illegal blocks below the waist.

The *linesman* has challenging responsibilities on punt plays. He watches for encroachment and motion at the snap. Following the snap, he is responsible for determining whether a punt crosses the neutral zone. After that determination, he sprints downfield and takes punt return coverage responsibilities on his side of the field, whistling the ball dead following the return or stopping the clock if the punt goes out-of-bounds. If a punt *bounces* out-of-bounds downfield, the linesman holds the out-of-bounds spot or marks it with a bean bag and retrieves the ball. If the ball goes out-of-bounds *in flight,* the linesman moves gradually along the sideline until the referee signals the correct out-of-bounds spot. Before the play, caution the line-to-gain crew not to move until released.

On punt plays, the *line judge* takes a position about fifteen yards beyond the neutral zone, adjusting his distance according to the ability of the punter and the wind factor. The line judge enforces "fair catch" restrictions or "referees" a punt return up the middle or to his side of the field. His responsibilities are the same as the linesman's on punts that go out-of-bounds to his side of the field. If a player on the kicking team first touches the ball downfield, mark the yardline of the touch with a bean bag or your cap, and stay with the play.

The line judge is responsible for calling touchbacks on punt plays. The touchback signal should be executed immediately when a punt contacts anything on or beyond the goal line inbounds.

Scrimmage plays near the goal line. The intensity frequently found in a football goal line play is rarely, if ever, matched in other team sports. Twenty-two players "psych" themselves toward extra efforts. Emotion and violence levels are high. Fumbles and fouls of all kinds are more likely, especially by inexperienced teams. Pileups surround the ball carrier and obscure his penetration towards the goal line. Obviously, the officials must be certain of their respective responsibilities on goal line plays and carry them out without hesitation. Personal qualities such as poise, confidence, courage, and integrity become more critically important near the goal line.

The official's starting positions and responsibilities are basically the same as for other scrimmage plays, but, because forward progress is more crucial, the flank officials vary their mechanics slightly. When the ball is inside the 5-yard line they should be on the scrimmage line at the snap and move to the goal line following the snap. On a running play close to the goal line, both flank officials should be at the goal line in order to best determine whether a *live ball in possession of the offensive team has penetrated the plane of the goal line.* Because of their poor visual angles, the referee and umpire should avoid ruling a touchdown unless certain of proper possession and penetration of the plane.

The touchdown signal should be given immediately by an official certain of a touchdown. If no fouls have been called, the referee then signals to verify the touchdown. No signal other than the "ball is dead" signal is given if there is no touchdown. When, because of a pileup, flank officials are uncertain of a touchdown, they should close in on the action decisively and, when certain, signal either a touchdown or a dead ball.

Correct positioning by flank officials can also be of critical importance on pass plays near the goal line. Passes thrown near the intersection of a *boundary line* with (a) the goal line or (b) the end line require expert positioning. In such circumstances, it is difficult, without hindering players, to gain a good visual angle of both lines and the players' feet. You must not be too close to this play. If possible, take a position slightly out-of-bounds. The ruling is dictated by the feet of the receiver or interceptor and the position of the ball in possession relative to the plane of the goal line. The line judge has primary responsibility for the end line.

Try-for-point plays. If the team attempting the try lines up for a run or pass, the responsibilities of all officials are the same as for any goal line play. If the team shows a kicking formation, the line judge immediately runs to a position adjacent to the goalposts. The line judge signals

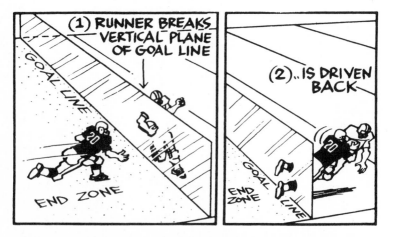

Figure 5.5 Penetrating the plane. Touchdown, ball has broken plane of the goal line. (By courtesy of the N.F.S.H.S.A.)

"thumbs up" if the kick is above the crossbar or "no score" if below crossbar. The referee then signals "touchdown" if the kick passed between the vertical uprights or "no score" if wide to either side.

Before the snap the referee takes a position five to seven yards behind the point where the holder will spot the ball and slightly to the side away from the holder. After the snap the referee moves more directly behind the kicker in order to secure a more accurate line on the kick in flight. The linesman assumes his normal position, observes the neutral zone and rules on roughing the kicker or holder after the kick is in flight. The umpire watches for illegal use of the hands or roughness in the line.

A generally accepted "new" mechanical action calls for the line judge to line up on the goalpost to his side of the field and the referee to line up towards the other post. The judge rules "no good," if outside his post or under the bar. The referee rules on his post and also picks up any signal by the judge.

Kick-offs. Figure 5.7 shows the official's starting positions and basic movements on a kick-off. The referee and linesman are positioned on opposite sides of the field near the 5- or 10-yard line of the receiving team, about ten yards inbounds. The linesman is opposite the press box near the sideline of the line-to-gain crew. The referee and linesman check to be sure there are eleven players on the receiving team.

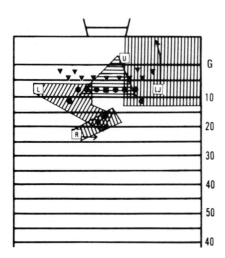

Figure 5.6 Positions for try-for-point or field-goal attempt. (By courtesy of the N.F.S.H.S.A.)

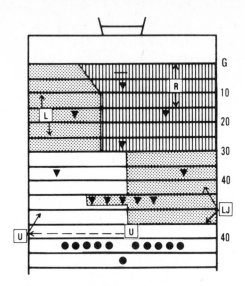

Figure 5.7 Kick-off. (By courtesy of
the N.F.S.H.S.A.)

The line judge is on the same side of the field as the referee, just out-of-bounds between the receiving team's 45- and 50-yard line. Five receiving-team players must be between the 45 and 50 when the ball is kicked. Be alert for an on-side kick.

The umpire hands the ball to the kicker and tells him to kick when the referee signals. He then counts for eleven kicking team players behind their 40-yard line. If either team has an incorrect number of players on the field or has players out of position, the *official responsible should call the error to the attention of a team captain so it can be corrected before the kick-off* is signalled by the referee. The umpire then runs to the intersection of the sideline and the 40-yard line. All officials raise their right arm to indicate readiness, and the referee then drops his arm and sounds his whistle for the kick-off.

The umpire and line judge check for encroachment in their respective zones before the ball is kicked. When the kick is first legally touched (by the receiving team in the field of play), the nearest official signals to start the clock. All other officials back up this signal. Kick-off penalties are enforced by the umpire if measured before a re-kick.

On runbacks to his side or up the middle, the referee stays with the ball carrier and the linesman moves upfield observing action away from the ball. If the runback is to the linesman's side of the field, these responsibilities are reversed. The umpire and the field judge stay wide as they go with the kick-off, looking for fouls away from the ball and alert for a kick out-of-bounds or a player running out-of-bounds. On long, break-away returns, the field judge or umpire, respectively, will usually pick up coverage of the ball carrier from the referee or linesman, who then concentrate on action away from the ball.

Important Routine Procedures

The prescribed mechanics regarding starting and stopping the clock, measurements for first down, relocating the ball and chains after the first and third periods and administering penalties should be followed closely. These situations occur regularly and are described below.

Starting and stopping the clock. Basically, the *clock starts* when:

1. A *free kick,* such as a kick-off, is *legally touched* by player (FK);
2. The *ball is snapped,* except on a try-for-point or for an untimed down (S); or
3. The referee signals to start the clock after *marking the ball ready-for-play* (RFP).

Football rules specify which of these three apply, *depending upon why the clock was stopped.* The following list shows the different circumstances which cause the clock to be stopped and, for each, the correct time to restart the clock. The *clock is stopped* when there is:

1. A *foul* (RFP), but the clock should not be stopped during a down for a foul.
2. A granted *team time-out* (S).
3. A *ball-out-of-bounds* (S).
4. An *incomplete pass* (S).
5. An *ended period* (S).
6. A *made or awarded fair catch* (S or FK).
7. A *score* (FK).
8. The ball became dead behind goal line (S).
9. A team attempts to consume time illegally (S).
10. The penalty for delay of game foul is accepted (S).
11. An official's time-out (RFP), unless the clock had been stopped for reasons other than the official's time-out or the foul, in which event it would be (S), some common reasons being: change in team possession; a first down; measurement of a possible first down; or an injury.

Key: RFP   Clock should be started when the ball is marked *ready-for-play.*

       S   Clock should be started on the *snap.*

      FK   Clock should be started when a *free kick* is legally touched.

The rule of thumb is that the clock starts (1) with the ready-for-play (RFP) signal if it were stopped because of activity involving the *officiating* crew (first down measurement, penalty, line-to-gain changed, etc.), and (2) with the snap (S) or the touching of a free kick (FK) if it were stopped because of player activity (team time-out, player out-of-bounds, incomplete pass, scoring play, illegal time consumption, etc.).

The referee and line judge have primary responsibility for being sure that the game clock starts and stops at the correct times. Nevertheless, all officials should back up another official's signal to start or stop the clock. The official closest to the play should signal first on a ball out-of-bounds, an incomplete pass, a made fair catch, or a score. The official calling the foul is responsible to stop the clock when the ball becomes dead.

Measurements for first downs. Measurements are usually made where the ball became dead at the out-of-bounds spot, in either side zone, or between the side zones. When a flank official marks forward progress with his foot, the referee may elect to place the ball for measurement either at that foot or where the ball became dead, whichever spot would seem to provide for a more accurate decision. The referee decides whether a measurement is required and if required beckons the linesman to bring in the chains. The linesman should see that the chain is tightened toward the backward stake. He should then grasp the chain at the center of the yardline nearest the rear stake, instructing the down-marker man to place the down marker at the point of the forward stake. The linesman and two stake men then run toward the position of the ball, and the linesman carefully places the chain in the center of the same yardline as close as possible to the position of the ball. The line judge should keep players from both teams back and away from the measurement. The umpire takes the forward stake and, when the linesman is ready, stretches the chain and places the stake near the ball.

The referee determines whether or not the first down has been made. Any part of the ball extending beyond or touching the inside surface of the stake indicates sufficient gain. The referee signals the first down or shows the distance needed with his hands.

If the first down was made, the linesman personally supervises the new positioning of the chain. If not made, the linesman *must retain his grasp* and relocate the chain by returning to the same sideline/yardline intersection. If the first down was not made and the measurement was taken at an out-of-bounds spot or in a side zone the referee grasps the chain at the forward point of the ball and, with the assistance of the linesman and the umpire, positions the ball at the inbounds line.

Most experienced linesmen make preparations in advance of measurements by securing a clip attachment to the chain where the sideline and chalkline nearest the rear stake intersect. This is done before the first down of each new series of downs. Use of a clip eliminates the danger of losing the grip on the chain and also speeds up the measurement procedure.

Relocating the ball and the chain at the ends of the first and third periods. The referee is responsible for relocating the ball when team directions change following the first and third quarters. All officials should record the yardline position of the ball, the down, and the distance-to-gain before moving to the other end of the field.

The referee measures the distance from the nearest yardline to the forward point of the ball, estimates the ball's distance, if any, from the inbounds line and runs *diagonally* to the corresponding position at the other end of the field, spotting the ball there.

The linesman grasps the chain at a convenient yardline, *noting which yardline it is,* and instructs the chain crew to *reverse their positions.* The linesman and chain crew then run to the corresponding yardline at the other end of the field. *After the referee has spotted the ball,* the stakes and chain are relocated and the down marker is placed opposite the forward point of the ball. When the first or third period ends with the forward point of the ball exactly on a yardline or the distance-to-gain is exactly ten yards, this entire chain crew procedure is not absolutely necessary.

Administering penalties. When a foul is detected *during a down,* note the spot of the foul, the number of the offending player, and the location of the ball at time of foul. Drop your penalty marker and *continue to officiate. Do not sound your whistle.* When the ball is dead, the time-out signal should be executed and *full information* given to the referee by each official who called a foul. The umpire secures the ball. An official must cover the dead ball spot.

The referee gives the preliminary signal for the foul, facing the press box. He should vocalize the foul as a first check for correctness. He then goes to the enforcement spot to present the options to the captain of the offended team. The options should be precise. "Captain, if you accept the penalty, you will have the ball second and six at the 15-yard line. If you decline, you will have the ball third and two at the eleven." If the captain's choice is obvious, quickly inform him what the obvious choice is, giving him a brief chance to disagree. If he says nothing, proceed with the obvious choice.

If the penalty is accepted, the umpire should visualize the distance and *run it off.* Do not step off the yards unless the field is poorly marked. Give the signal for the foul to both sidelines and check the down marker. Check the readiness of both captains and signal ready-for-play. If possible, give the offending player's number to the offending team captain. When a player is disqualified, the official calling the foul will report it to the referee and to the coach.

If the penalty is declined, the referee goes to the spot of the ball and signals the foul followed by the declination signal to both sidelines.

If double fouls cancel each other, the referee properly spots the ball, faces the proper directions while signaling each foul and then gives the declination signal.

When more than one foul is enforced, i.e., live ball/dead ball distance penalties for each, the referee shall place the ball and signal after each distance is run off. Note that a first down might be involved. If so, set the chains before measuring the next penalty if the first penalty gains a first down.

All officials should check the correctness of the enforcement spot and the distance of all penalties. Too frequently, football officials who seldom referee do not wish to "get involved" or do not know the correct enforcement spot.

Undoubtedly, more inadvertent mistakes are made by field officials when fouls are called and penalties administered than in any other phase of football officiating mechanics. Here is a list of some of the errors or omissions which can result in errors:

1. Sounding the whistle when the ball is in play;
2. Failing to note the spot of the foul, possession, and the offending player's number;
3. Failing to follow the play to its conclusion after dropping the penalty marker;
4. Moving the down marker and/or chains too soon;
5. Inadequate communication between the referee and the official(s) who called the foul;
6. Presenting inaccurate or unclear options; and
7. Penalizing from the wrong basic spot. (See "basic rules and penalties.")

Awareness of these common errors and omissions can help to prevent unnecessary and unwanted inequities.

Signals

Football officiating signals include the whistle, the penalty marker, and prescribed hand signals. The *whistle* is used for only three reasons: (1) to signal the end of the down and curtail further action when the ball becomes dead at the end of the play; (2) by the referee only, to call attention to the ready-for-play signal after a down or before a free kick; and (3) rarely, when necessary to gain the attention of another official. The whistle ending a down should always be blown with a sharp blast and only by the official or officials ruling that the ball became dead. Consecutive short blasts are occasionally needed when attention is not readily gained. *The whistle should not be blown* (1) when a foul is detected with the ball alive, (2) when a fumble has occurred with the ball alive, or (3) as a "back-up" whistle by an official away from the action. Many football officials prefer to carry the whistle in the hand rather than in the mouth in order to prevent inadvertent whistles. The umpire should hold the whistle in his hand.

When not in use, the *penalty marker* should be tucked into a hip pocket with a protruding corner providing an easy grasp. The spot of a foul can be better identified and retained if the marker is dropped or thrown to a spot. Nevertheless, the responsibility is greater to continue to cover the action than to get the marker to the exact point of the foul. The penalty marker should be thrown high in the air or aggressively towards the spot of the foul when the official detecting the foul is a distance from the center of the action. The bean bag or your hat, not the penalty marker, should be used to mark out-of-bounds spots and first-touch-of-kick spots.

Only the referee gives *signals* which designate the type of foul. (Exception: When the umpire runs off a penalty before a repeated kick-off.) This is done twice for each foul—once just before presenting options and again, to both sidelines, after the penalty has either been run off or declined. All officials may and should give signals regarding starting or stopping the clock, dead ball, incomplete pass, a score, or a touchback. (Touchbacks are rarely, if ever, signaled by the umpire.) Other signals given only by the referee are: first down, penalty declined, no score, ready-for-play, and official's or team time-out.

Signals should be given authoritatively and decisively, but not for the purpose of showmanship. In stopping the clock, the arms should be crossed back and forth two to four times; *all officials repeat this signal.* An incomplete pass signal is always followed by the stop-the-clock signal. The incomplete pass signal should be given instantly with only *one distinct* sweep of the arms, executed in a semi-crouched position. This is immediately followed by the stop-the-clock signal executed two to four times in an *upright position.*

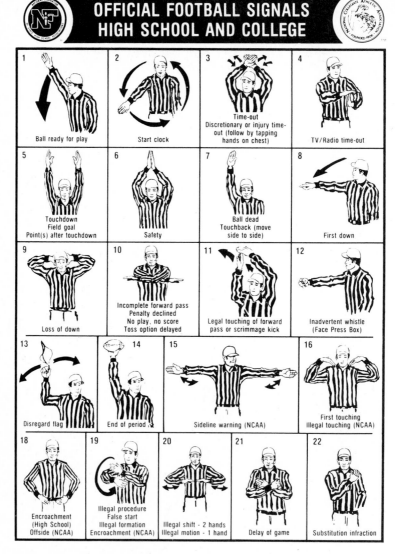

Figure 5.8 Officials' signals. (By courtesy of the N.F.S.H.S.A.)

Teamwork

It is essential that the football officiating crew work closely together as a unit. Football officials have twenty-two players to supervise on a playing area of 57,000-plus square feet on which a very physical and emotional game is played, and in which there are many different responsibilities to fill and procedures to follow. A football down cannot be run without several types of officiating teamwork being noticeable.

OFFICIAL FOOTBALL SIGNALS HIGH SCHOOL AND COLLEGE

23 Failure to wear required equipment	**24** Illegal helmet contact	**27** Unsportsmanlike conduct Noncontact foul	**28** Illegal participation
29 Sideline interference (NCAA)	**30** Running into (NCAA) or roughing kicker or holder	**31** Illegal batting Illegal kicking (Followed by pointing toward toe for kicking)	**32** Invalid fair catch signal (High School) Illegal fair catch signal
			33 Forward pass interference Kick catching interference
34 Roughing passer	**35** Illegal pass Illegal forward handing	**36** Intentional grounding	**37** Ineligible downfield on pass
			38 Personal foul
39 Clipping	**40** Blocking below waist Illegal block	**41** Chop block	**42** Holding or obstructing
			43 Illegal use of hands or arms
44 Helping runner Interlocked blocking	**45** Grasping face mask or helmet opening	**46** Tripping	**47** Player disqualification

NOTE: Signals number 25 and 26 are for future expansion.

Figure 5.8 *Continued*

Who calls what? As specified earlier, the referee protects the passer or punter and administers penalties; the umpire concentrates on interior linesmen; the linesman supervises the line-to-gain crew; the line judge is responsible for the end line and fair catches; and so forth. In other play situations responsibilities are shared by two or more different officials.

For example, any or all of the four officials may call a false start or encroachment; both flank officials look for forward progress; the referee and umpire share responsibilities regarding first touches of punts just beyond the neutral zone and ruling on possession following blocked punts.

The following guidelines are suggested:

1. Do not make a call if you know that it is the responsibility of another official. You must assume that the other official knows it is his responsibility and has a reason for not calling it, or for delaying momentarily before calling it.

2. If you have a total responsibility or a share in the responsibility for a call, rule on it without delay. If the responsibility is shared, do not wait for another official to do the job—he may not have seen the play or the foul, or he might even be waiting for you to rule on it.

3. Your main obligation is to the game. Therefore, *make your ruling without delay* if you are not certain who has responsibility but *know* that a foul has occurred, that the ball has become dead, etc.

Rotating coverage. At any given moment of live ball action one official will have responsibility for the ball carrier. As the play develops, this responsibility may rotate from one official to another. Such rotations almost always occur when a ball carrier breaks loose for a long gain. They are also common on scrimmage running plays to a side zone when responsibility shifts from the referee to one of the flank officials. The common sense guidelines for both officials involved are (1) to retain initial coverage responsibilities *until the rotation becomes obvious* and then (2) to accept the rotation as a fact and concentrate on the new responsibilities. *Observation of play away from the ball is important and should not be neglected.* When the ball is carried into a side zone and the flank official to that side had lined up on the scrimmage line before the play, the rotation usually occurs at the hash marks. Some officials use simple pointing signals to communicate the switch to the other official.

Communication. Football officials cannot afford to spend time in running conversations or "bull sessions" when on the field. They are officials with an important job to do. Nevertheless, brief and to-the-point communication can improve efficiency and performance and also help to develop a sense of teamwork and *esprit de corps* during a game.

Certain verbal and visual reminders are commonly used by experienced officials. *After every down* the officials should repeat to each other and to the players the *down* and *distance-to-gain,* showing the down with fingers (one, two, three, or a fist for fourth down). When the clock is started or stopped or the ball becomes dead, the officials can occasionally yell "wind it up," or "stop the clock," or "dead ball, dead ball." When a ball carrier is very close to a first down, flank officials can help the referee and umpire by yelling "close, close" as a reminder to spot the ball with care.

Relaying the ball. The officials *relay the ball* back to the proper inbounds spot when the ball is a distance from the spot following a down. This routine is common following incomplete passes, kicks or plays out-of-bounds, and touchbacks. One, two, or even three relays may be needed. Following a long incomplete pass the ball may be relayed from one flank official, to the other flank official, to the umpire and to the referee at the previous scrimmage line. While the ball is being retrieved, a chain should be formed and the ball relayed to the correct spot by short, underhand passes. Relay passes should be thrown no farther than ten to fifteen yards. If the distance is greater, the official should run the ball back before throwing it. The umpire is most frequently involved in relaying the ball, but all officials should be ready to help according to the particular circumstance. Accurate, hustling techniques in relaying the ball keep the game moving and show the officials in a good light.

Mechanics for Three Officials

The three officials are designated as referee, linesman, and umpire. On scrimmage plays the referee lines up in a normal position to the side of and slightly behind the offensive backs and to the opposite side from the linesman. The linesman is in the neutral zone facing the press box outside the widest offensive player. The umpire normally takes a position three to five yards behind the defensive line somewhat to the referee's side of the field. On expected passes the umpire moves further to the referee's side.

Positions and responsibilities on kick-offs differ from four-man coverage in that the linesman is responsible for the neutral zone of the receiving team.

On punts the positions and responsibilities of the linesman are the same as in four-man mechanics. The umpire takes a position about twenty yards downfield outside the widest defensive back opposite the linesman and becomes responsible for that sideline.

Coverage of pass plays by three field officials is somewhat awkward. As in four-man mechanics, the umpire moves to the neutral zone when the offense shows pass. This leaves the linesman with extensive responsibilities regarding illegal contact downfield. The referee must attempt to rule on such illegal contact in the side zone to his side of the field, but is hampered by his protect-the-passer/illegal passes responsibilities. The umpire can pick up some of the slack by (1) assuming primary responsibility for all illegal offensive or defensive contact during the pass rush and (2) when the pass is in flight, quickly shifting his vision in the direction of the pass downfield.

Coverage of scrimmage plays near the goal line is also awkward, in that forward progress away from the linesman may be difficult to determine.

On try-for-point plays when a kick is attempted, the umpire takes a position near the endline outside of the goal posts opposite the linesman, and rules whether or not the kick clears the crossbar.

Scrimmage play responsibilities. The referee must cover plays into his side zone. (Only on punts and kickoffs does the umpire have sideline responsibilities in three officials games.) The linesman marks all forward progress and the referee and umpire divide ball-spotting responsibilities the same as in four-man mechanics.

When two opposing eligible pass receivers are making a simultaneous and bona fide attempt to catch or bat the ball, and there is unavoidable contact, it is not a foul. The defender and receiver both have a right to attempt to gain possession of the pass.

Figure 5.9 Pass interference. (By courtesy of the N.F.S.H.S.A.)

Problem Calls

Pass Interference

More judgment is needed for pass interference calls than for any other football infraction. Furthermore, the judgments rendered are more subject to criticism because:

1. Borderline pass interference decisions are fairly common.
2. The success or failure of pass plays is usually considered more critical than running plays.
3. Pass interference situations are more likely to take place "out in the open" where everyone can evaluate the decision.
4. Many spectators and players and some coaches do not know the correct pass interference rule interpretations.

When a forward pass is in flight all defensive players and all eligible receivers have an *equal right to the ball.* The two key questions are:

1. Did a player interfere with an opponent's opportunity to play the ball?
2. Did either player play the man and not the ball?

A player of either team may not run through an opponent who has established an advantageous position before the ball arrives. By the same token, *no foul should be called* when opponents having an equally advantageous position contact each other while attempting to play the ball. Pass interference should be called *with or without contact* if a player "face guards" an opponent, or changes direction or stops with an obvious intention to impede his opponent. Under high school rules, pass interference can only occur on forward passes thrown *beyond the neutral zone.* Under college and pro rules (but not high school) interference can occur only when a pass is "catchable." What *should* the high school football official rule be when there is illegal contact downfield between receiver and defender while a forward pass is in the air, *but if the pass is not catchable?* High school rules seem to suggest that pass interference should be ruled. However, a case also might be made for ruling "holding," or "illegal use of hands," or "personal foul"—or, depending on the circumstances, "no foul" with a verbal warning since, conceivably, no unfair, advantage had really been attained.

A

It is illegal to "play through" a man in order to get to the ball during a forward pass. In this illustration, it will be interference if No. 20 contacts No. 85 before the ball reaches him.

B

Defensive pass interference. Number 18 has directed his attention to blocking the vision of the receiver which indicates an intent to hinder the receiver rather than catch or bat the ball and it is, therefore, interference even though there is no contact.

Figure 5.10A and B Pass interference. (By courtesy of the N.F.S.H.S.A.)

Here are some interpretations:

1. When a potential receiver for either team is tripped, it is not pass interference if both players were playing the ball.
2. Offensive players downfield may not block or use their hands to push off from an opponent.
3. Defensive backs may legally block a potential pass receiver before the pass is in flight, but may not impede the potential receiver after he makes his cut.

Restrictions on the *defense* relate only to the period when a *forward pass is in flight*. On the other hand, *offensive players* are restricted *from the time of the snap until the flight ends.* Offensive pass interference, therefore, is especially difficult to enforce when the initial play action appears to show a running play but suddenly becomes a pass play.

Pass interference cannot be ruled until a foward pass is thrown. For this reason, flank officials must *mentally record what happened after the snap and before the pass.* It helps to "think pass" if in doubt whether a play will become a run or a pass play.

Fouls Regarding the Passer and Punter

These are the primary responsibility of the referee. Alertness and accurate judgment are needed.

Roughing the passer or punter. A defensive player may not charge into the passer or punter clearly after the ball is in flight. No foul should be called if the rusher clearly attempts to avoid illegal contact and the contact is incidental. Roughing the passer should not be ruled if the defensive player is close to the passer and his momentum causes him to contact the passer just after the pass is in flight. Roughing the punter should not be called when contact seems unavoidable in these circumstances—(1) the punt is blocked and (2) the would-be punter has momentarily fumbled and/or is running with the ball. Almost all contact following an unblocked punt should be called.

Fumble or incomplete pass? When an offensive player is tackled while attempting a forward pass and the ball comes loose, the referee must decide whether or not the passing arm had started its forward motion. If so, signal an incomplete pass. If not, the ball is alive until whistled dead with either team in possession. The referee must make a decisive decision on this play, but also be careful not to blow his whistle too soon.

Intentional grounding. This infraction is officially designated "pass purposely incompleted." (3:42) The passer's intent may be to prevent a loss of yardage by throwing the ball out of the reach of any player. This is strictly a judgment call. A foul should be called only if the "circumstantial evidence" seems clear-cut, since judging a person's intentions is risky. Was the passer about to be tackled? Did the passer's grip on the ball slip? Was he off-balance? What was the intended direction of the throw?

Neutral Zone Fouls

A great number and variety of infractions may take place just before, during, and after the ball is snapped. All officials should be "super alert" when the teams line up for a down.

Just before the snap all officials should look for encroachment, false starts, illegal shifts of positions, the number of players on the scrimmage line, and incorrect numbering. Encroachment should be called when a *player of either team* other than the center *enters the neutral zone before the snap* and after the center has adjusted the ball. The first player who encroaches is called. If an offensive player *false starts first,* no encroachment would be called. A false start is any accidental or intentional movement by any offensive player which is similar to a starting movement. A personal foul may be called on a defensive player if he deliberately charges into an offensive player after a false start. The whistle should be *blown immediately* and the flag thrown when a player false starts or encroaches (even if he encroaches just at the snap).

At the moment of the snap, flank officials should look for illegal lateral motion and all officials should be alert for illegal snaps. If there is illegal lateral motion the penalty flag should be dropped, but the whistle should not be sounded; continue to officiate. In the case of an illegal snap, sound the whistle immediately.

After the ball is snapped, the umpire, linesman, and line judge should concentrate on initial contact along the line within their respective jurisdictions. Look for personal fouls such as striking an opponent with a fist, illegal use of hands or arms, and illegal "crack back" blocks. If any of these are detected, drop the flag and stay with the play.

In summary, the whistle should *always be sounded immediately* when there is:

1. Encroachment;
2. An illegal snap; or
3. A false start.

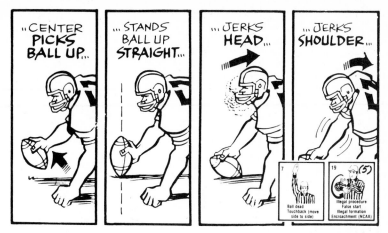

Each of these snap infractions causes the ball to remain dead and the down cannot be started. The penalty for a snap infraction is 5 yards measured from the succeeding spot.

Figure 5.11 Illegal snaps. (By courtesy of the N.F.S.H.S.A.)

Throw the flag but withhold the whistle and continue to officiate when there is:

1. An illegal shift before the snap;
2. An illegal motion at the snap;
3. An illegal position at the snap; or
4. Any other foul after the snap.

Thorough coverage of the neutral zone on every down is difficult but not impossible. Each official should be aware of his responsibilities and shift his concentration as the down progresses from illegal shifts, encroachment, or false starts to illegal motion, positions, or snaps to illegal blocks and personal fouls.

Butt-Blocking and Face-Tackling

The intent of butt-blocking and face-tackling rules is to prevent serious injuries. Prior to the inclusion of these rules, some players were being taught to aim their helmets or face masks directly at an opponent when forcefully blocking or tackling. The understandable results were head and neck injuries. Existing rules now require the blocker or tackler to shift his head to the side at the moment of contact in order to block or tackle with the shoulder rather than the head. *These rules must be strictly enforced.*

Butt-blocking is a personal foul and consists of driving the face mask, frontal area or top of the helmet directly into an opponent, as the primary point of contact, either in close line play or in the open field. The penalty is 15 yards. If the act is judged to be flagrant, the offender is disqualified.

Figure 5.12   Butt-blocking. (By courtesy of the N.F.S.H.S.A.)

Grasping the Face Mask

This rule now applies to all helmet openings (i.e. under the helmet opening, front or back) as well as the protective bar(s) on the helmet. For the infraction to be ruled, the bar(s) or helmet opening must be securely grasped. The infraction must be signalled without hesitation.

Clipping

The incidence of clipping infractions has been reduced in recent years, largely because of additions to football rules. Blocking below the waist is now illegal. Nevertheless, clipping has not been eliminated and must be called rigidly in order to prevent serious leg injuries.

A clipping infraction is defined as accidentally or intentionally charging into a player other than a ball carrier from the rear *above or below the waist.* The classic clip occurs when a player throws himself against the back of an opponent's knees. *Clipping and blocking below the waist are legal* (1) against a ball carrier, and (2) within the "free-blocking zone," an imaginary eight yards by six yards area for each separate down four yards to each side of the ball and three yards to each side of the scrimmage line. *Officials should not call clipping or blocking below the waist unless they see the initial contact.* Borderline clips or blocks below the waist should be judged according to whether or not the player blocked was able to see and evade the blocker.

Obviously, considerable judgment may be required in order to rule accurately on clipping. See the whole play!

Late Hitting

The officials' control of a football game can hinge largely on their ability to enforce the rules regarding late hitting. Unnecessary injuries and unwanted flareups may result from looseness or inconsistency in this area. The most important requirements are to hustle and be on top of the play—to whistle the play dead quickly and decisively—and then to close in on the action. Frequently, the officials can talk players out of late hitting—"GO EASY, THE BALL IS DEAD." "STAND UP, HE IS OUT-OF-BOUNDS."

Considerable alertness and judgment are needed. Players are expected to react to the whistle. A personal foul should be called when a player, clearly after the whistle, drives into or piles on an opponent. When such contact is flagrantly late and rough, the player should not only be penalized but warned or disqualified. If, on the other hand, the player clearly attempts to avoid and reduce the contact when he hears the whistle or sees the opponent out-of-bounds, no foul should be called. A comment such as "Good job," or "Way to avoid him," will be helpful. Officials away from the play occasionally have a better perspective for judging late hitting and should not hesitate to make the call.

Late hits out-of-bounds near a team bench can be particularly difficult. The flank official is busy determining the out-of-bounds spot. Players and coaches create congestion and confusion. In this situation, all officials must make an extra effort to provide coverage, especially the referee and umpire.

Inadvertent Whistle

Despite their determination to avoid it, officials do occasionally sound their whistles when they shouldn't. To do this is embarrassing as well as inevitably unfair to one or both teams. Converted basketball officials accustomed to sounding their whistles for every infraction must particularly take care to avoid inadvertent whistles. Football officials should consider carrying the whistle in the hand rather than in the mouth.

Inadvertent whistles most commonly occur in the following circumstances:

1. When a foul is detected, especially at or immediately after the snap; and
2. When a down is about to end, possibly just as a live ball is fumbled.

When an inadvertent whistle sounds, *it counts and should not be ignored.* The ball becomes dead. To ignore an inadvertent whistle would be unfair to those players who heard it and probably reacted to it.

The adjustment made depends on the location and possession of the ball when the inadvertent whistle sounded. The down may or may not count.

Flag/Touch Football

Flag/touch football has become one of the most popular team sports played in the United States. The game has the great popularity of tackle football, but without the injuries and high costs of equipment.

With a strong emphasis on safety and fun, the game is designed for all ages and skill levels with the excitement of kickoffs, punts, and a "wide open" style of play. Flag/touch football is currently enjoyed by physical education classes, intramural sport programs, community and industrial recreation leagues, YMCA/YWCAs, and the U.S. armed forces as well.

Officials are a very important part of the game. Training and constant evaluations are essential to a successful officiating program.

Officials and Their Responsibilities

In flag or touch football, assignments of two officials (referee and back judge) or three officials (referee, back judge, and line judge) are common. Due to the wide open style of flag and touch football play, the umpire position is not used or needed. Approximately 90 percent of the plays called are passes. Thus, the back judge is positioned fifteen yards deep in the secondary, behind the defensive backs.

Suggested equipment are two whistles (one extra), lanyard, two penalty flags, game card, bullet pencil, rubber band to count downs, watch, and a bean bag. The back judge will keep the official game time.

The official's uniform should include a black-and-white striped shirt, black coach's shorts, white socks, a black hat with white piping, and a pair of athletic shoes. Appearance is an important ingredient for a successful official.

NIRSA Contribution

Prior to the 1980s there had been a lack of standardization regarding flag/touch football playing rules and officiating mechanics. After years of research involving related literature, players, coaches, and administrators, the National Intramural-Recreational Sports Association (NIRSA) recently published the fifth edition of a standardized, complete set of flag/touch football rules which includes interpretations, and an official's mechanics book. The NIRSA Flag/Touch Rules Committee, (comprised of educators who are also NFL, major college, and high school officials) thus developed and promoted the first and only internationally recognized official flag/touch football rules and mechanics book. The rules and mechanics book plus additional training tools, a 20-minute video on the rules, a 22-minute strategy video, a 22-minute mechanics video, and a clinician's kit, are available through NIRSA.*

Basic Penalties and Rulings

The intent of this section is to highlight several of the special rule areas of flag/touch football. Complete rulings and interpretations can be found in the NIRSA flag/touch football rule book.

The Game

Teams are comprised of seven players in the men's and women's divisions. Eight players make up a co-recreational team. Defensive players must line up at least one yard and the quarterback at least two yards from the scrimmage line. A passer is "downed" and the ball is dead if his or her flag is removed before the pass is released. The flag of a pass receiver may not be removed before the pass arrives; if it is, the play continues as one-hand-touch and the defensive team is subject to a pass interference penalty.

Equipment. Each player must wear a one-piece belt at the waistline with three flags permanently attached: one flag on each side and one in the center of the back. A legal touch consists of one hand between the knees and shoulders.

The field and line-to-gain. The field is divided into four 20-yard zones. A first down is awarded when a team advances the ball to the next line on the playing field in the direction of the opponent's goal line.

Game time. The game is divided into two 20-minute halves. During the first eighteen minutes of each half the clock runs continuously unless stopped for a score, team time-out, or official's time-out. During the last two minutes of each half the clock will be stopped and started as in regular football rules.

---

*NIRSA Sports Officiating Development Center, 850 SW 15th St., Corvallis, Oregon 97333–4145, (503) 737–2088.

Dead ball. The ball is dead when it hits the ground by a snap, fumble, or backward pass. On free kicks and scrimmage kicks the ball may be picked up from the ground and advanced by the receiving team only. However, once the ball is touched and hits the ground, it is dead.

Protected scrimmage kick. The offensive team captain may request a protected scrimmage kick on any down. On a protected scrimmage kick both teams must stay behind their respective scrimmage lines until the ball is kicked.

Try-for-point. The team scoring a touchdown has the option of attempting a one- or two-point conversion by running or passing. One point is scored from the 3-yard line and two points from the 10-yard line.

Tie-breaker. If, after regulation time, the score is tied, each team will be given four downs from the same 10-yard line to score. If touchdowns are scored during the tie breaker, one- or two-point conversions are attempted.

Problem Calls

Guarding the flag. This is the most difficult call an official has to rule. A ball carrier may spin or jump to avoid being deflagged, but may not obstruct a defender from removing their flag belt. Flag guarding usually occurs when the hand or ball is on or around the area of the flag belt to gain an advantage.

Blocking. Safety and injury prevention are paramount in flag / touch football. Screen blocking is used and defined as legally obstructing an opponent without contacting an opponent with any part of the screen blocker's body. As in basketball, position and arms at one's side are essential elements in screen blocking.

Pass interference. This is a tough judgment call for an official to rule. Two key questions the official must ask himself: (1) Were the receivers making a simultaneous, bona fide attempt to reach, catch, or bat a pass?; and (2) Was there an obvious intent to impede? It is also pass interference if a receiver is deflagged prior to touching the ball.

Miscellaneous Considerations

Pregame Officials Conference
The conference should be held after the officials are dressed, approximately one hour before the game. Through advance planning the referee can zero in on important rule and mechanics matters and materially improve the officiating that day. The referee conducts the conference but should welcome the expression of suggestions, questions, and concerns from the other field officials. Here are some of the topics to be covered:

1. Coin-toss mechanics.
2. Free-kicks reviewing positions and responsibilities.
3. Preview of coverage during scrimmage plays.
   a. Running plays positions and coverage
   b. Forward passes, eligibility of receivers, and interference
   c. Illegal forward passes (from beyond line, purposeful incompletion, thrown to ineligible receivers, on or behind the scrimmage line)
4. Positions and coverage during scrimmage-kicks.
   a. No blocking below waist
   b. First touching by K
   c. Fair catch situations
   d. Kicks out-of-bounds
   e. Interference
5. Goal line plays and tries-for-point.
   a. Variation of positions near goal line
6. Substitution rule.
7. Stopping and starting the clock.
8. Procedures during measurement for possible first down.
9. Duties during time-outs and the intermission between periods.
10. Penalizing personal and unsportsmanlike fouls.
11. Penalty administration.

Following the conference all of the officials should enter the playing area at least fifteen minutes before the kick-off in order to accomplish their several important on-the-field pregame responsibilities.

Officiating Evaluated by Coaches
What qualities do you appreciate in a football official?

1. Integrity
2. Control

3. In good condition
4. Thorough knowledge of the rules
5. Poise
6. Willing to provide rule interpretations
7. Competed in the sport
8. Courage of convictions
9. Friendly
10. Efficient

Miscellaneous Comments
1. There is a definite need to provide more work for young officials to get the needed experience to move up the ladder.
2. A team should not be penalized because they are superior.
3. Complaints are more justified about what officials *do not call* than what they do call, especially when the call is obvious or a game is one-sided and the officials are in a hurry to end the game.
4. Officiating is a state of mind. Top officials show a positive attitude toward the game.

Officiating Evaluated by Officials
What is the most difficult play to call in football?

1. Pass interference
2. Deliberate grounding of the pass
3. Clipping; blocking below the waist
4. Quarterback being hit on the side and deciding whether the arm went forward for incomplete pass or if it was a fumble

What is the most difficult phase of mechanics in officiating football?

1. Being in the right place at the right time
2. Covering side zones and the deep pass play

Miscellaneous Comments
1. A large number of officials work only subordinate responsibilities while being "carried" by the referee.
2. Preventive officiating techniques must be learned quickly by the beginning official.
3. To fellow officials, good mechanics are just as important as knowledge of the rules.
4. The intent of each rule must be understood.
5. All positions in the crew are equally important.
6. To have played the game and to have had a desire to get back on the field is not enough. One must have a spirit for the work.

General Procedure for Becoming a Football Official

Interested individuals must first join their local officiating association. The association will make available, as a part of the membership dues, a kit of instructional materials which will include a study guide, rule books, mechanics book, and a case book. Association training programs feature required meetings, field work clinics, actual scrimmages, classification, and other written examinations. Successful candidates are then classified. A qualified list is forwarded to the area commissioner whose office is responsible for making the actual game assignments.

Play Rulings (1)

Situation: Near the end of the first period, A1 is discovered to be wearing: (a) a hard cast; or (b) shoes with cleat platforms which are more than 5/32 inch in height; or (c) a slippery substance on his uniform or hands; or (d) a knee brace which has an unpadded strip of metal across the front of the leg; or (e) a face protector which has a broken bar; or (f) a helmet without an exterior warning label. *Ruling:* A fifteen-yard penalty is assessed from the succeeding spot in (a), (b), (c), and (d) as the head coach has previously verified all players are legally equipped. The hard cast, cleat platforms, and the slippery subtance are all illegal and must be removed before further participation. In (e), the defective or illegal equipment must be repaired or replaced before A1 can continue to participate. No penalty is assessed in a case where the equipment becomes defective or illegal through game use. In (f) A1 will be given twenty-five seconds to comply. No penalty is assessed as it is assumed the label came off through game action.

Situation: After team A has set for more than one second, back A1 goes in motion. While he is in motion, back A2 takes one step forward. He then resets for more than one second, but A1 is still in motion at the snap. *Ruling:* Illegal shift. Movement by A2 constitutes a shift, and the failure of the entire team to set for one second after this shift is illegal.

Situation: With the ball at B's 1-yard line and twelve seconds remaining in the game, A1 advances to the ½-yard line. After the ball is dead, B1 fouls. The clock is stopped with five seconds remaining in the game. The foul was the only reason for the clock being stopped and it is restarted when the ball is declared ready-for-play. Before A can snap the ball, time expires. *Ruling:* The game is ended. There is no extension of the period for an untimed down unless there is acceptance of the penalty for a foul which occurred *during* the last timed down of the period. B1's foul did not occur during the down. However, if the referee judges B1 committed the foul to conserve time, he must delay starting the clock until the snap.

Situation: Substitute: (a) A1; or (b) B1, noticing his team has only ten players on the field, comes onto the field just as the ball is about to be snapped. *Ruling:* In (a), A1 must be on the field within fifteen yards of the ball and not violate the shift or man-in-motion provisions. Furthermore, the act of his coming onto the field must not deceive the defensive team. In (b), the substitution is legal as long as B1 is on the field on his side of the line of scrimmage prior to the snap.

Situation: A1 receives the snap behind his own goal line. A1 advances but is tackled and the ball becomes dead with its foremost point in the field of play. The remaining part of the ball is on the goal line. *Ruling:* Safety. To avoid a safety, the ball must be advanced completely out of the end zone with no part of the ball touching the goal line.

Situation: A scrimmage kick by K1 comes to rest on R's 6-yard line. R1 attempts to recover and advance but muffs the ball so that it rolls into the end zone where: (a) R2 downs the ball; or (b) R3 recovers and advances out of the end zone; or (c) K2 recovers and downs the ball in the end zone. *Ruling:* The ball became dead as soon as it touched the ground in the end zone. It is a touchback in (a), (b), and (c). The kick had not ended because muffing does not constitute possession; therefore, it is a kick into R's end zone which is a touchback. R will put the ball in play, first and ten, from its 20-yard line. The covering official should sound his whistle immediately when the ball becomes dead as a result of the touchback.

Situation: During a scrimmage kick beyond R's line R1 gives a fair catch signal. He muffs the kick and the ball bounces into the air, where: (a) R1 catches it five yards in advance of his muff; or (b) K2 pushes R1 in an attempt to reach the ball; or (c) K3 tackles R1 following the muff, preventing R1 from catching the kick; or (d) R1 is blocked below the waist by K4 and K5 "recovers." *Ruling:* In (a), R1 has made a fair catch and the ball will be put in play at the spot where the catch was completed. In (b), the contact with R1 by K2 is legal because K may retain possession following the muff by R1. In (c), it is a foul for K3 to tackle R1 following the muff, thus preventing him from reaching the ball. If the penalty for holding is accepted, it will be measured from the previous spot and the down replayed. The block by K4 is illegal in (d). This is a loose ball foul and the penalty, if accepted, will be measured from the previous spot and the down replayed.

Situation: Eligible receiver A1 blocks an opponent ten yards downfield while the pass is in flight. The pass is completed to A2 who is:
(a) beyond the line of scrimmage; or (b) behind the line of scrimmage

when he catches the ball. When the covering official observes the block by eligible receiver A1 during the forward pass, he immediately drops a penalty marker to indicate an infraction. *Ruling:* It is a foul for pass interference in (a), and a legal block in (b). It was proper for the covering official to indicate an infraction because he had no way of knowing whether the pass did or did not cross the line of scrimmage.

Situation: B1 intercepts a legal forward pass in his end zone. He then: (a) attempts to run with the ball but steps on the sideline in the end zone; or (b) runs with the ball and is tackled in his end zone; or (c) advances the length of the field to A's end zone, but during his run, B2 clips A1 on B's 6-yard line; or (d) same as (c) except B2 clips in his own end zone. *Ruling:* Touchback in both (a) and (b). Team A would accept the penalty for the foul in (c). Following enforcement, it is B's ball, first and ten on its 3-yard line. In (d), it will be a safety if A accepts the penalty.

Situation: Eligible receiver A1 is legally pushed out-of-bounds by B1. If he wishes to continue play, when does A1 have to return in-bounds? *Ruling:* Whenever a player is legally blocked or pushed out-of-bounds, he is expected to return to the field of play at the first opportunity if he wishes to continue his participation. A player who is forced out-of-bounds may return and participate legally if he does not intentionally delay his return. If A1 goes out-of-bounds voluntarily or accidentally, it is illegal participation if he touches the ball or hinders an opponent after returning to the field.

Situation: With fourth and 4 from R's 40-yard line, K1 punts. The kick is bounding near R's goal line and K2, in an attempt to keep it from penetrating the plane of the goal line, bats the ball at the 2-yard line back toward the field of play and: (a) it is recovered by R1 who advances to his 30; or (b) it is recovered by R2 who attempts to advance and is downed in the end zone. *Ruling:* The action by K2 is an illegal bat regardless of the purpose. It is a foul during a loose ball play and the basic spot is the previous spot. In (a), R would probably accept the result of the play and put the ball in play first and ten from its 30-yard line. In (b), R's most advantageous choice would be to accept the penalty, with a replay of fourth down from K's 45 with nineteen yards to go.

Situation: K1 is in illegal position and the scrimmage kick by K2 is caught by R1. During the return by R1, there is clipping by R2 and a subsequent fumble by R1 is recovered by K3. *Ruling:* Double foul. Even though there was a change of team possession during the down, the team gaining final possession had fouled before gaining possession. Both fouls occurred during the live ball period and the result is a double foul. The penalties cancel and the down will be replayed.

Situation: A1's pass is intercepted by B1 at B's 40-yard line. During B1's return, A1 and B2 begin fighting at A's 40-yard line. B1 returns the ball to A's 2-yard line. *Ruling:* If B accepts the penalty for A1's foul, it creates a double foul. B may retain possession by declining the penalty for A1's foul, in which case, it would be B's ball at its own 45-yard line. Both A1 and B2 will be disqualified regardless of whether or not B retains possession. *Comment:* Whenever both teams foul during a change of possession down and the team in final possession gets the ball free of a foul (with "clean hands") they will always have the opportunity to retain possession. The fact that their opponent's foul may have occured after change of possession has no bearing on the enforcement.

Situation: With first and ten from A's 30-yard line, A1 advances to B's 40 where he fumbles. A2 recovers and advances to B's 10 where he is downed. While the ball was loose following A1's fumble, B1 held A1, and during the advance by A2, B2 grabbed A2's face protector. *Ruling:* This is a multiple foul and the captain of A may accept either penalty or decline both and take the results of the play. If the penalty is accepted for B1's foul it will be enforced from the end of A1's run where he fumbled. It would be first and ten from B's 25. If the penalty for B2's foul is accepted it will be enforced from the end of A2's run. In this case it would be first and goal for A from B's 5-yard line.

Situation: During a scrimmage down, quarterback A1 throws a backward pass to A2 who runs about thirty yards behind the line and toward the sideline before throwing a forward pass downfield. There is holding by A3: (a) during the backward pass; or (b) during the run which preceded the forward pass; or (c) during the forward pass. *Ruling:* It is a loose ball play in (a), (b), and (c). The basic spot of A3's foul is behind the basic spot. *Comment:* All the action which preceded A2's forward pass is included in this single loose ball play. While it is possible to have several running plays during a down, with each one having its own basic spot of enforcement (where the related running play ended), there can only be one loose ball play during a down. Rule 10–3–1 (a3) states in part "also includes the run (or runs) which precedes such legal pass, kick or fumble" (from behind a scrimmage line). This means it includes all action from the time of the snap to the end of the "loose ball play." When any foul occurs during a free kick, scrimmage kick, legal forward pass, backward pass, or fumble made by A from behind the scrimmage line, even if several of these actions happen during the same down, the basic spot remains the same (the previous spot that is the spot of the snap or free kick).

Situation: R1 catches a punt on his 4-yard line and his momentum carries him behind his goal line where he is downed in the end zone. After the kick has ended, but before the ball becomes dead, K1 holds: (a) in R's end zone; or (b) at R's 5-yard line. *Ruling:* If R accepts the penalty in either (a) or (b), it will be R's ball first and ten from its 14-yard line. R will put the ball in play by a snap. If R declines the penalty in either (a) or (b), the ball will be put in play by R at the 4-yard line as the kick was caught there.

Situation: With third and goal from B's 2-yard line, A1's forward pass is intercepted by B1 in the end zone and advanced for an apparent touchdown. During B1's run, B2 clips at the 50, after which the coach of B comes on the field at A's 40 to criticize the official's call. *Ruling:* First and twenty-five for B on its 20-yard line. Since the foul by B's coach is a nonplayer foul, it is administered from the succeedinng spot after the penalty for B2's live ball foul is administered and the stakes have been set. This is not a multiple foul situation. If the foul by the coach was the only foul committed, the touchdown would stand and the penalty would be administered on the ensuing kickoff.

Situation: After A1 scores a touchdown, he is struck by B1. The coach of team A then insults an official; (a) before; or (b) after the ball is declared ready-for-play for the try-for-point. *Ruling:* In (a), the penalties for both the personal foul by B1 and the unsportsmanlike foul by the coach of team A will be enforced in the order of occurrence from the succeeding spot on the ensuing kickoff. In (b), the penalty against team A will be enforced as part of the try, resulting in A attempting the try from the 18-yard line, with the personal foul against team B assessed from the succeeding spot on the ensuing kickoff. In both cases, B1 will be disqualified.

BIBLIOGRAPHY

1. National Federation of State High School Associations, *1990 High School Football Case Book,* Kansas City, Missouri, 1990.
2. National Federation of State High School Associations, *1990 and 1991 Football Officials Manual,* Kansas City, Missouri, 1990.
3. National Federation of State High School Associations, *1990 Official Football Rules,* Kansas City, Missouri, 1990.
4. National Federation of State High School Associations, *Football Rules— Simplified and Illustrated,* Kansas City, Missouri, 1990.
5. National Intramural-Recreational Sports Association, *National Collegiate Flag and Touch Football Rules and Official's Manual,* Corvallis, Oregon, 1991, 1992.

6

Soccer

The Game

"The United States calls it soccer, Great Britain calls it association football. Soccer alias 'fuetbal, voetbal, calcio, fullback, podosphairo and fotbal' is the world's super sport. Soccer is the "granddaddy" of rugby and American football." (2:3)

It has been clearly established that more people play and watch soccer than any other game. World Cup television audiences have been estimated at 500 million. Soccer in the United States is progressing well after several attempts to establish a foothold on the American sports scene. Contributing factors to this phenomenal growth have been the exceptional junior programs for boys and girls and the participation of our college students in the 1990 World Cup in Europe. This gave American players the valuable experience of competing against the Europeans. Further attention to soccer is anticipated as the United States hosts the World Cup in 1994. Foreign superstar Franz Beckenbauer will head up the American effort. To fulfill FJFA requirements to host the World Cup, an indoor league has been proposed.

The popularity of the game can be attributed to its fitness benefits, low expense requirements, and the adaptability to all body types—the quick, agile, and wiry goalkeeper; the fast, aggressive, and proficient shooting forwards; a defense led by highly conditioned halfbacks with superior ball control skills; and finally, the balance, toughness, and

Photo by UPI/Bettmann Newsphotos

patience of the fullbacks. The continuous action, involvement of all players, and limited injuries also add to soccer's attractiveness. Soccer and basketball have many similarities—restrictions on body contact, penalty kicks/free throws, and the movement and positioning of officials. Hughes (4:12) adds that "It is a game where it is as important to be a quick thinker as it is to be a quick mover."

To sustain the growth of soccer, officiating must continue to improve. Officials are now required to belong to Associations. Officiating associations must meet the challenge through exacting rules training and practical field evaluation.

Officials and Their Responsibilities

The suggested officiating unit for interscholastic and intercollegiate soccer is the three-person, diagonal system of control. The dual officiating system is still utilized in some leagues at the various levels of play. The use of a single referee is common in international matches and often practiced in the United States to limit expenses. The three-person diagonal and dual systems will be discussed in detail in the mechanics section.

Officials' Uniforms and Equipment
The soccer official's shirt should be the solid black international shirt with white cuffs and collar. Black shorts with black footwear and black socks with white top complete the uniform. A possible exception would be made if one or both teams are wearing dark colors. The whistle should be mounted on the forefinger. The official should also be equipped with a pencil, notebook, yellow and red cards, and two watches.

Pregame Responsibilities
Officials should plan to arrive thirty minutes prior to game time. This will allow adequate time to check the field markings, goal nets, and game ball. A meeting with the coaches provides opportunities for introductions and rules coverage. A meeting with the captains for final instructions and the coin flip will precede a meeting with the two squads to clarify rules and to warn teams not to charge the goalkeeper. The official should assume the responsibility for checking the shoe cleats and shinguards, and answer any questions.

Game Responsibilities

Referee. "The referee's job demands a flawless knowledge of the laws of the game, coupled with sound judgment, the ability to handle people in stressful situations, and a high degree of physical fitness. He must keep up with the play, a particularly tough chore when the ball is booted fifty yards upfield." (3:25)

The referee makes all the calls, keeps time, and has complete control of the game. The referee will start and stop play according to the rules of the game, which include terminating the game in the event of extreme weather conditions, unruly spectators, or any other just cause. When a player is "cautioned," the clock will not be stopped but the coach will be notified. The referee shall enforce the rules and decide any disputed points. His or her duties include disqualifying a player for flagrant fouls or unsportsmanlike conduct, supervising all free-kicks and dropped balls, deciding whether or not a goal has been scored, supervising substitutions, stopping the game when a severe injury occurs, keeping non-players off the field, and deciding when and where the ball is out-of-bounds after conferring with a judge. (12:377)

The referee must signal all fouls. Officials should carry a yellow and red card for purposes of signaling the warning and disqualification of players. When a player is disqualified, that team will play one person short. Finally, the referee must signal the timekeeper for all time-outs and when the clock is to be started again.

Linesmen. If a single referee is used, two linesmen will be approved by the referee. They will assist the referee by indicating when and where the ball went out-of-bounds. They will indicate where the ball left the field by play by raising a flag and calling out which team is entitled to the throw-in. This must be confirmed by the referee by pointing to the designated throw-in spot. The linesmen will also assist the referee in determining whether a corner kick or goal kick should be awarded and whether an attacking player is offsides. It must be noted that linesmen's signals are NOT an indication of an award. The final decision must always be made by the referee. The linesmen will not have a whistle and must clearly understand their role of assisting the referee.

Ball holders. The home team should provide ball holders to carry extra game balls and act as retrievers to avoid unnecessary delays during the game. Another option might be to leave an extra ball behind each goal.

Scoring and timing. Most games are scored and timed by the referee on the field. The clock will be stopped only for serious injuries and necessary equipment repair. The clock does not stop for fouls. Teams may not call time-outs; all time-outs will be at the discretion of the referee.

Basic Penalties and Rulings

In determining fouls, the general rule dictates that the participants must *play the ball* and *not the opponent.* Deviations from this rule result in such violations as jumping, tripping, pushing, charging, high kicking, etc. It is critical to rule accurately whether a foul is intentional in order to avoid placing the opponent at a disadvantage and to keep the game under control. To minimize flagrant conduct, a warning system is practiced. A yellow card is flashed by the referee to denote a warning or "caution" and a red card disqualifies the offending player.

Penalties
For purpose of clarification, we will examine only the most critical personal, nonpersonal, and misconduct violations.

Major fouls. Direct free kick with opposing players at least ten yards from the kicker at the spot of the foul. (A goal may be scored directly off this kick.)

1. Kicking, Striking, Jumping and Tripping
   A player shall be penalized for kicking, striking or attempting to kick or strike an opponent. A player must be penalized for tripping—including throwing or attempting to throw an opponent by the use of the legs, or by low-bridging an opponent causing a fall or loss of control. The use of the knee in any way against an opponent is also a foul.
2. Holding and Pushing
   A player shall be penalized for holding or pushing an opponent with the hand(s) or with the arm(s) extended from the body and for impeding a player with the hand or any part of the arm extended from the body. Under no circumstances is a player permitted to push an opponent. (11:30)
3. Charging
   A player shall not intentionally charge an opponent unfairly. An unfair charge is one in which a player does not use shoulder-to-shoulder contact with an opponent and/or does not have arms and elbows close to his/her body, and/or does not have at least one foot on the ground, when the ball is not being played, and the charge is done in a dangerous manner. (9:30)

SOCCER FIELD

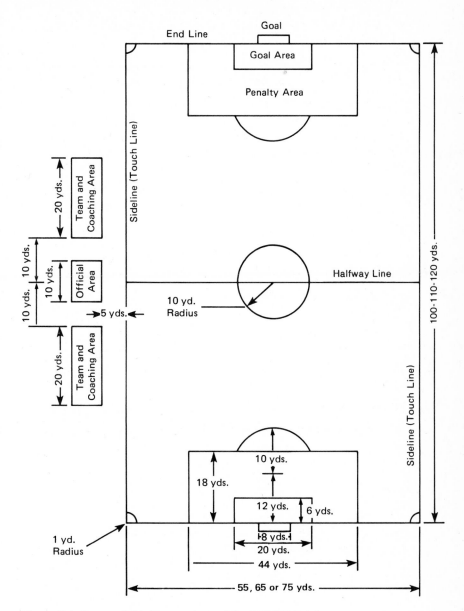

Figure 6.1 Soccer field. (By courtesy of the N.F.S.H.S.A.)

Minor fouls. Indirect free kick with opposing players at least ten yards from the kicker at the spot of the foul. (A goal may not be scored off this kick until another player touches the ball.)

1. Obstruction
   This is a non-contact intentional foul where a player not in possession of the ball, or not attempting to play the ball, runs between the opponent and the ball, using the body as an obstacle.
2. Dangerous Play
   Dangerous play is defined as play of such a nature as to be likely to cause injury. Three common types of dangerous plays are high kicking, double-kicking, and lowering the head.

Penalty kick. Direct free kick from the 12-yard penalty line awarded for a major foul committed by the defensive team in the penalty area. (A goal may be scored off this kick.) All other players must stand outside the penalty box and circle, ten yards away from the ball.

It should be noted that the ball must be kicked forward and the kicker cannot touch the ball again until another player touches or plays the ball. The goalkeeper must stand on the goal line without moving his or her feet until the ball is kicked.

Rulings

Kick-off. The game shall be started by a kick-off. The team winning the pregame coin toss shall choose one of the following two options while the loser has the remaining option:

1. To choose whether his or her team will kick off or go on defense.
2. To choose the goal that his or her team will defend.

Substitutions. Substitutes may enter the game on dead ball situations. If there is not a scorer, the player should request substitution to the referee. The player shall remain outside the boundary line until the referee beckons to have the player enter the game through the linesmen at the center of the field. The basic substitution rule and substitution rules for injured players vary widely within the various soccer associations.

The drop ball. The ball is put in play by being dropped by the referee between two opponents. The best example for using this might be a ball kicked out-of-bounds simultaneously by the opponents.

Ball in and out of play. The ball is out of play only when it has crossed completely over the goal or sideline on the ground or in the air and when play has been stopped by the referee.

Scoring. A goal is scored when the whole of the ball passes over the end line, between the goalposts and under the crossbar. This is the only means of scoring in soccer. One point is scored for a successful penalty kick from the penalty line or a successful kick from the field of play.

Handling. A player shall be penalized for intentionally handling the ball or touching the ball from shoulder to fingertips. Unintentionally handling the ball should not be penalized, but this varies with ruling associations.

Throw-in. A throw-in is performed by the player opposite the player who last touched the ball at the spot where the whole ball crossed the touch line. The ball must be delivered with both feet touching the ground on or behind the touch line. The release must be made with equal strength in both hands overhead and must be in a continuous motion. If throw-in is not taken from the designated spot, the opponent will take possession.

Goal kick. A free kick is made by the defending team from the goal area as a result of the attacking team causing the ball to go over the end line. The goalkeeper is limited to four steps before kicking the ball away.

Corner kick. A kick-in is made by the attacking team from the corner arc on the opponents' end of the field. A corner kick is the result of the defending team last touching a ball crossing the end line.

Tie-breaking procedure. Resolving tie games varies from league to league. The most common methods of resolution would be overtimes, sudden deaths, and, finally, penalty kicks. The team that wins the penalty kick tie-breaker shall be declared the winner. **(8:29)**

Mechanics

The comparative size of the soccer field and the nature of the game challenge the conditioning of officials. By comparison, one, two, or three soccer officials are responsible for field coverage up to 81,000 square feet while three to seven football officials are responsible for field coverage of 57,600 square feet, including end zones.

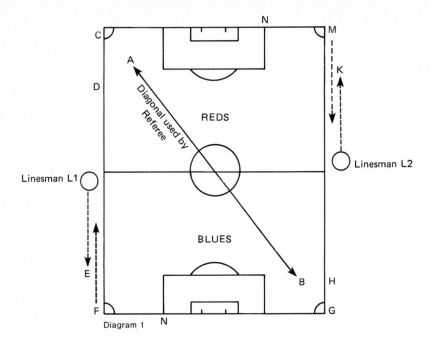

Figure 6.2 The relative positions of the lead and trail officials for specific game situations are as diagramed. (Permission has been authorized exceptionally by FIFA and is taken from the FIFA publication *Laws of the Game and Universal Guide for Referees.*)

The Diagonal System of Control

The most commonly used officiating system is referred to as the diagonal system. It is estimated that a referee working with two line judges may run from six to eight miles per game. This system guarantees good calls on out-of-bounds, offsides, goal kicks, goal scoring, and plays in the corners.

Figure 6.2, Diagram 1. The imaginary diagonal used by the referee is the line A-B.

The opposite diagonal used by the linesmen is adjusted to the position of the referee; if the referee is near A, linesman L2 will be at a point between M and K. When the referee is at B, linesman L1 will be between E and F; this gives two officials control of the respective "danger zones," one at each side of the field.

Linesman L1 adopts the *Reds* as his or her side; linesman L2 adopts the *Blues;* as *Red* forwards move toward Blue goal, linesman L1 keeps in line with second last *Blue* defender so in actual practice he or she will rarely get into Red's half of the field. Similarly, linesman L2 keeps in line with second last *Red* defender.

At corner kicks or penalty kicks the linesman in that half where the corner kick or penalty kick occurs is positioned at N and the referee takes position. (See Figure 6.3, Diagram 4—corner kick; Diagram 9—penalty kick.)

The diagonal system fails if linesman L2 gets between G and H when referee is at B, or when linesman L1 is near C or D when the referee is at A, because there are *two* officials at the same place. This should be avoided.

Figure 6.3, Diagram 2: Start of game. Position of referee at kick-off: R. Position of linesmen: L1 and L2; in position with second last defender players: O and ■. Diagonal followed by referee: A-B. Referee moves to diagonal along line → according to direction of attack. The ball is indicated by the Ball-●.

Figure 6.3, Diagram 4: Corner kick. Positions of officials the same no matter at which corner-area the kick is taken.

The referee (R) will work along line shown.

Linesman (L2), in accordance with the instructions from the referee, shall be near the corner flag or on the goal line near the corner flag to observe whether the ball is properly played; whether the opposing players are at proper distance (ten yards), whether the ball is behind the goal line, or whether incidents have happened possibly hidden from the referee.

Linesman (L1) will be in position at the halfway line for clearance and possible counterattack.

Figure 6.3, Diagram 6: Goal kick. The referee (R) will be in midfield adjacent to central point of diagonal.

Linesman (L1) is watching over the goal kick, positioned in line with the penalty area.

Linesman (L2) is in position in line with the second last defender pending a possible attack by the side taking the goal kick.

Figure 6.3, Diagram 9: Penalty kick. Players O and ■, with the exception of the goalkeeper and kicker, are shown outside the penalty area and at least ten yards from the ball. The goalkeeper stays on the goal line.

The referee (R) is in position to see that the kick is properly taken and that no encroachment takes place.

Linesman (L2) watches the goalkeeper to see that he or she does not advance illegally, and also acts as goal judge.

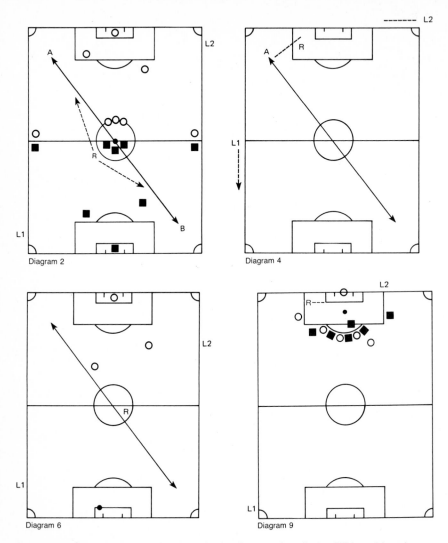

Diagram 2

Diagram 4

Diagram 6

Diagram 9

Figure 6.3 (Permission has been authorized exceptionally by FIFA and is taken from the FIFA publication *Laws of the Game and Universal Guide for Referees.*)

Linesman (L 1) is in position should the goalkeeper save a goal and start a counter-attack.

Two-Official System
The lead and trail method of field coverage is also effective. Depending on the position of the ball, referees move up and down the sidelines to afford maximum coverage.

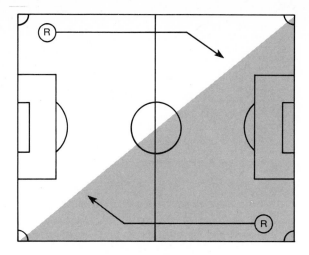

Figure 6.4 General field coverage.

The relative positions of the lead and trail officials for specific game situations are as diagramed in Figure 6.5.

**Responsibility for Declaring the Ball "Ready-For-Play"
When a Second Whistle is Required:**

Situation	Official
Start of each half	Trail
Kick-off after goal	Trail
Drop ball	Trail
Goal kick	Trail
Corner kick	Lead
Penalty kick	Lead
Free kick	Lead
Throw-in with no substitution	Neither—No second whistle is necessary.
Throw-in with substitution	Official responsible for ruling on the legality of the throw. (9:68)

Hand Signals
Hand signals are the simple gestures used by the referee to indicate the foul and to point out the direction of play. The most common calls are:

1. Throw-in: signal two hands overhead in throwing position and call out color.

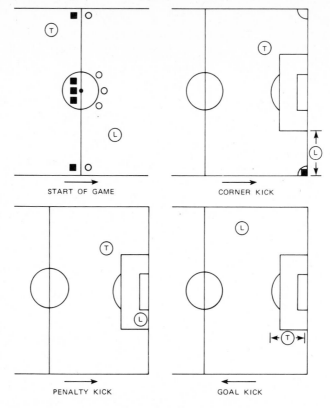

Figure 6.5 Positioning of lead and trail officials.

2. Corner kick: arm extended pointing toward corner.
3. Advantage clause (discussed in next section): opened hands, upward sweeping motion of the arms (no call on possible close call or violation to indicate debatable situation where offense might be placed at a disadvantage if called).
4. Direct kick: single forward underarm swing pointing to the direction of the kick.
5. Indirect kick: single raised arm with palm open in a forward direction.

Problem Calls

It should be noted that as players tire, fouls increase requiring even greater concentration by the officials.

Advantage Clause

Officials must guard against this violation by the defense wherein the offensive player breaks to the goal to gain the advantage, only to be fouled to offset that advantage. The infraction generally occurs when the offense is on attack. An example of such a situation would be intentionally holding an opponent from the rear in his or her solo move on the goalkeeper. The essence of the rule is to note the violation by the offending team without giving them any advantage by stopping the play immediately. It is imperative that the official enforce the penalty even if the ball is lost on the way in to the goal by the attacker. The foul should be indicated by hand signal and by calling out "advantage" or "play on." In addition to the foul call, the referee will issue a warning by flashing a yellow card. Intercollegiate rules call for the offender to be disqualified.

Playing the Ball

Often it is difficult to determine whether a player is legitimately playing the ball and not the opposing player. In the heat of the contest this judgment call may be of great consequence to the outcome of the contest. For example, charging is an illegal action of a player who violently contacts an opponent from a dangerous angle, while the opponent is off-balance or is not near the ball, or through the use of the hip or in any manner designed to prevent the opponent from reaching the ball. Pushing off is a very common infraction in "heading" plays in congested areas. A player must not use his or her hands or arms either to hold an opponent back or push him or her away from the ball. The violation often occurs when the arms of the players become interlocked and the referee must be watchful for such infringements which may appear "accidental." (12:29)

Offsides

The offsides rule was introduced to prevent uninteresting plays and methods of attack. The purpose of the game is to score but, if a player or players are allowed to wait in front of the opponent's goal without restrictions, the game becomes dull. Since the offsides rule provides for technical features of the game, it must be thoroughly understood, because when it is broken, attack stops immediately. (5:16)

Offsides occurs when:

1. There are not two defenders between the offensive player and the opponent's goal line at the time the ball is played to him or her; and
2. The offensive player is in his or her opponent's half of the field; and

Figure 6.6 (By courtesy of the N.C.A.A.)

3. The ball was last touched by a teammate; or
4. The offensive player is ahead of the ball when it was played to him or her. (6:12)

It is the position of the receiving player *when the ball was kicked* and not the position where he or she receives the ball that determines whether or not the receiver is offsides. A player in an offsides position shall not be penalized unless, in the opinion of the referee, he or she is interfering with the play or with an opponent, or is seeking to gain an advantage by being in an offsides position. (7:14) The most common offsides infraction occurs when there is a clear pass to a teammate who has assumed a position inside the second defender as illustrated in Figure 6.7. It must be reiterated that an offensive player assuming this position, but not receiving the ball, does not constitute offsides. This is illustrated in Figure 6.8.

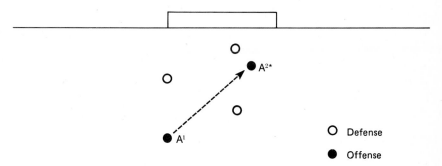

Figure 6.7 Offsides. *A^2 is not offsides until the ball is played by A^1 to A^2.

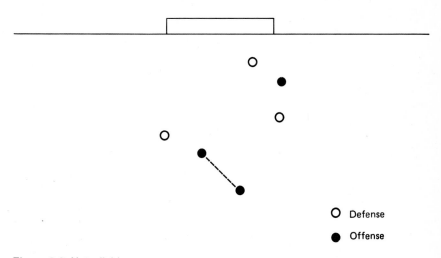

Figure 6.8 Not offsides.

Collision with the Goalkeeper

Whether the ball is loose or not, the goalkeeper may not be charged by an opposing player. "Blindsiding" the goalkeeper may result in serious injury to this key player. Both FIFA and NCAA rules classify this as a dangerous play which will result in removal without warning of the offending player who intentionally charges the goalkeeper. Incidental contact with the goalkeeper not affecting play should be ignored.

Miscellaneous Considerations

The referee must stay alert at all times as many soccer games are close and errors of omission can be consequential. An overrelaxed pattern of officiating in soccer can create these omissions. Other game concerns include substitutions and unnecessary conversation between opponents.

Delays on substitutions with the clock running can be used as a stalling tactic. Officials must be alert to offset this unfair advantage to the offending team.

There is considerable conversation between opponents during the course of a game. You should be on the lookout for what causes a sudden, unexplained flare-up. The retaliation may be easily seen, while the sly action that caused it escaped unnoticed. You cannot punish a player if you haven't seen the offense. If your suspicions are aroused, check with the linesmen. (10:21)

Officiating Evaluated by Coaches

What qualities do you appreciate in a soccer official?

1. Thorough knowledge of the rules with proper interpretations and intent
2. Punctuality
3. Consistency
4. Decisiveness
5. Always moving to get in the best possible position
6. Keeping the game under control

Miscellaneous Comments

1. Need for standard rules
2. Need for properly trained officials is critical to game's success in the United States

Officiating Evaluated by Officials

What is the most difficult play to call in soccer?

1. Offsides

2. Advantage clause
3. Scoring

What is the most difficult phase of mechanics in officiating soccer?

1. Position to make offsides call
2. In a two-official system, foul in partner's area when he or she is blocked out
3. Judging goal kick vs. corner kick on offensive side of the field in the two-official system
4. Actually seeing the ball cross the line for a score when the goalkeeper has possession of the ball

Miscellaneous Comments

1. The discipline of the coach has a strong bearing on the behavior of the players.
2. A team official is one who would rather "miss a call" than give a partner poor trail coverage. Making a call from the other area, lead or trail, in a two-official system, demeans the other official. The exception would be a major foul that was undetected by the other official.
3. Officials should not be called by the trailing official due to the distance away from the play.
4. Officials should take criticism without feeling personally maligned.
5. The game should be conducted with as little interference as possible. Constant whistling for questionable violations has a tendency to upset players, coaches, and fans, and cause the game to deteriorate.

Constructive Hints Summarized for Soccer Officials

- Control the game and be the boss. Show the players you mean what you say at all times.
- Know the rules, but don't be too technical.
- Be on top of all the plays. That's the only way the correct calls can be made.
- Don't anticipate or guess on any calls. If you are not in a position to see fouls plainly, and if there is any doubt in your mind whether they are fouls, don't call them.
- Every game is important to the player; he or she deserves a fairly officiated game.
- Never second-guess your partner. When he or she calls a play, that's just what it is. (Discuss problems at half time and after the game.)
- Make your decisions when at a dead stop. An official frequently loses his or her poise when calling and talking on the run.

SOUTHERN CALIFORNIA SOCCER OFFICIALS ASSOCIATION
1990–91 COACHES' EVALUATION OF REFEREES

GAME: .... ( ) vs. .... ( )

DATE: .... PLAYED AT ....

Name of Official	Preferred	Good	Satisfactory	Fair	Unsatisfactory
A.					
B.					

EXPLANATIONS ARE **REQUIRED** ON ALL UNSATISFACTORY RATINGS.

Please rate each referee below using the following scale:

   1—Outstanding   2—Satisfactory   3—Needs Improvement

A   B

.... Personal Appearance

.... Physical Condition

.... Knowledge of Rules

.... Ability to Keep up with Play

.... Understanding with Other Referee

A   B

.... Application of Advantage Clause

.... Clarity of Signals

.... Decisiveness

.... Impartiality

.... Attitude toward Players

.... Punctuality

CONSTRUCTIVE COMMENTS: _____

_____

_____

_____

_____

_____

Note: These reports will be used in the overall grading of referees, and it is important that they be RATED FAIRLY WITHOUT PREJUDICE, win or lose. Please mail reports back PROMPTLY.

PLEASE COMPLETE AND RETURN TO:

SCSOA—Referee Reports
531 11th Street
Santa Monica, CA 90402

SIGNED: ....

TITLE: ....

SCHOOL: ....

By Courtesy of the Southern California Soccer Officials Association.

- Never turn your head until the play is completed.
- Look directly at the offending player when you call a penalty on someone.
- Call your own plays. Never let the coaches or players call them for you.
- Never criticize any official. There will be days when you can't miss and there will be days when you can't seem to call them right.
- A smile and a pleasant manner will go a long way toward your success anywhere at any time.
- Do not let your voice or your tone be antagonistic.
- When the game is over, go up to your fellow official and walk off the field together. (7:6)

Play Rulings (9)
Situation: Team A arrives for the scheduled game to find that the scorers' and timers' table will be operating but no provision has been made to have both teams located on the same side of the field. *Ruling:* When a scorer and timer are used, both teams shall be on the same side of the field to facilitate substitution. (1–5–1)

Situation: The game ball is not satisfactory to the visiting team. The head referee's decision to use the visiting team's balls is protested by the home team. *Ruling:* The head referee shall choose three or more balls from those of both teams. (2–1–1)

Situation: The goalie goes down after making a save and remains motionless for a few seconds with the ball in his possession. *Ruling:* The official may stop play to determine if the goalie is injured. If, after examining the goalie, it is determined that the goalie is able to continue play immediately and no attendants have come on the field, replacement is not mandatory and play will start with an indirected free kick. (3–3–3)

Situation: A1 is discovered wearing illegal equipment during the game. The referee removes A1 from the field with instructions to correct the equipment. After the equipment has been corrected, A1 attempts to reenter when team B has possession of a throw-in. *Ruling:* A1 may reenter, but no substitutions may be made by team A. If team A had possession prior to the throw-in or the ball had gone over the goal line, A1 could reenter or the coach of A could substitute a new player. (3–3–4)

Situation: Player A1 is on the attack with the ball under control when fouled by B1. The ball moves sideways to player A2 who controls the ball immediately. *Ruling:* The official shall immediately either call the foul or signal "Play On," to indicate the foul was observed, but will not penalize team B because to do so would give an advantage to the offending team, Team B. (5–3–1)

Situation: A penalty kick has been awarded as time expires. The penalty kick is taken but is deflected by the goalkeeper and is shot back into the goal by a member of the kicking team. *Ruling:* No goal. When the ball is contacted by any player other than the goalkeeper after the penalty is taken, the ball immediately becomes dead because time has expired. (14–1–5)(7–1–4)

Situation: B1 moves over the halfway line prior to the kickoff. *Ruling:* The official shall verbally warn the player and play is restarted. A caution may be given if the action is repeated. (12–8–1)(8–1–2)

Situation: The ball is in the area of the field as follows: *Ruling:* In (a), the ball is out-of-bounds; in (b) and (c), the ball is still in play. A ball over any part of a line is considered to be on the playing field. (9–1–1)

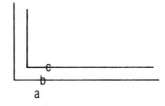

Situation: Player A shoots on the goal line and the (a) ball rolls along the goal line; (b) goalkeeper, in front of the goal, fists the ball out into the field of play; (c) ball goes through the goalkeeper's hands into the net. *Ruling:* In (a) and (b), no goal; in (c), goal. (10–1–2)

Situation: A defender on team B, with the goalkeeper out of position, heads the ball out, but in doing so falls into the goal. A2 gets the ball and passes it to A1 who has only the goalkeeper to beat. *Ruling:* The defender on team B left the field during the normal movement of play, and since no advantage is gained, A1 is not offsides. (11–1–2)

Situation: A1, who is in the air to head the ball, is approached by B1. (a) B1 goes up to head the ball simultaneously with A1; (b) B1 contacts A1 while A1 is in the air and B1 has both feet on the ground. *Ruling:* (a) Legal; (b) Illegal. Direct free kick. (12–4–2)

Situation: A1 takes a corner kick, which hits the goalpost and rebounds. A1 plays it again before it has been touched by another player. *Ruling:* Illegal: indirect free kick. (17–1–5)(13–3–2)

Situation: Extra time is allowed for a penalty kick to be taken. The goalkeeper deflects the ball to the goalpost, from which it rolls into the goal. *Ruling:* Goal, only the goalkeeper has played the ball and its hitting the post is incidental to the scoring of the goal. (14–1–6)

Situation: During the throw-in, the following happens: (a) A1 lifts the back foot from the ground while throwing the ball; (b) A1 takes a run up to the touchline and releases the ball with both feet on the ground; (c) A1 has one foot off the playing field and one foot on the touchline during the throw-in; (d) A1 throws to a teammate only three feet away. *Ruling:* (a) Illegal, award a throw-in to team B; (b) Legal; (c) Illegal because the feet must be outside the field of play; (d) Legal. (15–1–3)

Situation: The placing of the ball for a corner kick is: *Ruling:* (a) and (b) illegal; (c) and (d) legal. (17–1–3)

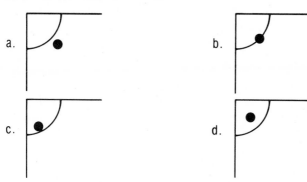

BIBLIOGRAPHY

1. *FIFA Laws of the Game and Universal Guide for Referees with USSF Supplement.* New York City, New York: United States Soccer Federation, 1977.
2. Frommer, Harvey. *The Great American Soccer Book.* New York City, New York: Athenum, 1980.
3. Herbst, Dan. *Sports Illustrated Soccer.* New York: Harper and Row, 1984.
4. Hughes, Charles. *Soccer Teamwork and Tactics.* South Yorkshire, England: EP Publishing Limited, 1979.
5. *Illustrated Soccer Rules Guide.* Chicago, Illinois: United States Soccer Federation, 1974. (By courtesy of D. J. Niotis)
6. Los Angeles Toros. *This is Soccer.* Atlanta, Georgia: General Lithographing Company, 1967.
7. Matthews, Dave, Ben McGuire and Jim Peterson, *Officials Manual: Soccer.* Champaign, Illinois: Stipes Publishing Company, 1972.
8. *NCAA Men's Soccer Rules.* Mission, Kansas: National Collegiate Athletic Association, 1990.

9. *Soccer Rules*. Kansas City, Missouri: National Federation of State High School Associations, 1990–91.
10. Taylor, Jack. *Soccer Refereeing*. London: Faber and Faber, 1978.
11. Wade, Allen. *Association Football*. London: Educational Productions Publishing Company, 1970.
12. White, Jess R. *Sports Rules Encyclopedia*. Palo Alto, California: The National Press, 1966.

7

Swimming and Diving

The Game

The advent of increased numbers of pools in schools and private homes, coupled with Olympic attention to the sport, has enhanced the prominance of swimming in the world. Few other sports afford such a wide diversification of events for so many contestants.

Much the same as in track and wrestling, the swimming official rules on the athlete's physical technique in the performance of an event. Improper stroke technique should disqualify the contestant. The starter may be required to perform more than one function.

The official should realize that serious competitive swimmers and their coaches are highly dedicated. This is evidenced by swimmers' commitments to long hours of practice for nine to ten months per year during a good portion of their youth. Even the youngest competitors seem to realize that whatever success they may earn depends directly on the work and effort they put into it. Regardless of whether the swimmer is of novice or Olympic caliber, the goals and rewards remain largely personal. (1:21) Consequently, these swimmers deserve a dedicated effort on the part of the officials.

There is a great need for competent officials. Officiating in swimming has been and is primarily conducted by coaches, former swimmers, and parents of swimmers. The quality and quantity of officials required demands that new "students" of swimming be developed to meet the needs of the sport.

Photo by Tony Duffy / All Sport

Officials and Their Responsibilities

The most common working unit is composed of a paid starter/referee supported by a corps of volunteer officials. Since many swimming officials have little or no competitive swimming or diving background, it is imperative that either a rules clinic and/or extensive premeet officials meetings be conducted to assure competent officiating. It may be necessary to assign more than one responsibility to each official in a dual meet. In a championship meet there should be only one responsibility assigned.

White clothing is recommended. This includes white slacks or shorts, shirt, and tennis shoes.

Meet Manager

The organizational and administrative details are the responsibility of the meet manager and are generally assumed by the host assistant coach in dual meets. In championship meets, this assignment is generally the function of the athletic director. He or she typically delegates it to the host swimming coach. A meet manager does not serve as an active official. Many schools now employ a meet manager with a computer for printouts in championship meets.

Referee

The referee has complete jurisdiction over the meet. This official must enforce the rules and assume the responsibility for making all official assignments. The referee has the responsibility and authority to expedite the meet by assuring a minimum of delays.

Before the meet the referee shall:

1. See that all equipment necessary for the proper conduct of the meet is in the proper place and condition;
2. See that the pool is properly marked;
3. Assign officials to particular duties, reviewing with them the positions and responsibilities of each; and
4. Before championship meets, conduct a premeet conference with the starter and a captain from each team to review meet procedures and special instructions. (5:14)

During the meet the referee shall:

1. Meet with the swimmers prior to each race to review lane assignments and starting instructions;
2. Check that each swimmer takes the proper lane, and signal the starter with a whistle that the starting commands may begin;

3. See that the meet progresses rapidly and that the results are announced properly; and
4. Assure that all competition is conducted according to rule. (5:14)

The referee is responsible for the recall function if there is also a starter.

Starter
The starter has control over the contestants after they have been assigned to him or her by the referee. Before starting each heat, the starter must explain to each competitor:

1. The starting signal (whistle, bell or gun);
2. The distance to be covered and where the race will terminate;
3. Stroke requirements; and
4. If necessary, call for "quiet at the start." (8:446)

In distance events, the starter shall signal by bell when the leading swimmer has two lengths remaining.

Stroke Inspectors/Turn Judges
In championship meets, inspectors will be positioned on either side of the pool, dividing the responsibility for half the lanes, in order to observe the strokes of the competitors. Turn judges shall rule on proper turn techniques. Two individuals generally work both strokes and turns. Violations in stroke or turn should be indicated by the official immediately raising his or her hand overhead with open palm. In dual meets, this responsibility is assumed by the starter.

Take-off Judges
A take-off judge is assigned to each relay team for the purpose of judging whether the second, third, or fourth swimmers are still in contact with the starting mark when the previous swimmer touches the end of the pool. A violation should be indicated by raising a hand when the last competitor in the water has finished.

Lane Judges and Timers
When automatic judging and timing equipment * is available, the results shown by such equipment will be considered primary and official. In case

---

*Automatic Judging and Timing Equipment. A completely automatic device is one which automatically starts with the starter's pistol and stops when a contestant touches the finish pad. A semiautomatic timing device automatically starts with the starter's pistol and stops when the lane judge presses a button when the swimmer in that lane finishes. Timing equipment must not interfere with the swimmer's starts, turns, or the function of the pool overflow system. (6:33)

of malfunction, secondary information from a semiautomatic timing and judging device with one or more officials per lane or the prescribed ballot system should be used. If neither the ballot system nor automatic timing and/or judging device is used, judges are designated to pick the places. In championship finals, two lane judges and three timers should be assigned to each lane. Many automatic timing systems are not sensitive on all surfaces. The swimmer must now touch the pad or the wall above the pad. Consequently, a hand may break the finish plane but not touch the finish pad. This necessitates backup watches on each lane in championship meets. Three timers are assigned to each lane.

In pools without automatic timing and judging devices the finish is determined by time—three watches per lane and the starter picks across the board to confirm places.

Clerk of the Course
This function, along with that of scorer and announcer, is generally assumed by a meet manager or secretary in a dual meet. The clerk should check each swimmer into his or her assigned lane. The effectiveness of the clerk of the course will determine how well a meet will run. The clerk should make arrangements to have the name of each contestant announced before the event, in time to enable the swimmer to get to the proper lane at the desired time in a relaxed manner. (3:38) In relays and championships, it may be advantageous to provide chairs for succeeding heats to avoid delays.

Diving Judges
For dual meets, two or three judges will evaluate each dive. The meet referee will serve as one judge. The home team is required to supply two judges if the visiting team does not exercise its option to supply one judge. The starter may also serve as a judge. Championship meets require a minimum of five judges. It is imperative that the judges assume a position that will afford them a profile view of the diver.

Scorer
In general practice this administrative responsibility is a function of the host school or club, regardless of the level of competition. The scorer is responsible for recording and scoring the meet. The starter is required to audit the score.

Announcer
The referee will assign the announcer, who usually doubles as clerk of the course, to announce each event, the swimmer in each lane, the results of each race, and the running score. If time permits, the pool and

conference records in that event should also be announced. The team manager of the home team often serves as the announcer. For championship meets, the clerk and announcer responsibility should be filled by two officials. The announcer must keep the meet moving and interesting, which can contribute to the success of the meet.

Runners

To coordinate the immediate scoring of each event, runners carry the results recorded by judges and timers to the scoring table. This function is usually performed by students or noncompetitors delegated by the team manager.

Basic Penalties and Rulings

Fouls

1. Interference will result in the disqualification of the contestant who interferes with another swimmer. The race may also be ordered swum over if conditions were unfair (e.g. lane line breaks apart).
2. Unsportsmanlike conduct will be penalized by the referee (disqualification). A prime example would be celebrating nonswimmers getting into the pool after a race without permission.

Stroke Requirements

Freestyle. Freestyle events allow the greatest freedom because any stroke or combination of strokes may be used. Any part of the body may touch the wall in executing a turn, and the finish may be made by touching the wall with any part of the body.

Breaststroke. "The body shall be kept perfectly on the breast and both shoulders shall be in line with the water surface. All movements of the arms shall be simultaneous and in the same horizontal plane without alternating movement. The hands shall be pushed forward together from the breast on or under the surface of the water and shall be brought back on or under the surface of the water. The hands can be brought beyond the hipline (waist), except on the first stroke after the start and each turn. During each stroke cycle, a part of the head shall break the general water level (the surface in a calm state), except that after the start and after each turn, the swimmer may take one arm stroke and one leg kick while wholly submerged. When the hands begin their sideward or downward press, a new stroke shall have been started. A wave passing over the head does not constitute a violation." The movements of the legs shall be simultaneous and in the same horizontal plane with feet turned outwards. The touch shall be made with both hands simultaneously but not necessarily level in high school. **(5:27)**

Butterfly. In the butterfly, the hands must be recovered and brought forward out of the water. The undulation of the legs and feet in the kick calls for simultaneous and symmetrical movements, as in a flutter kick. The touch is similar to that of the breaststroke. Infractions are most commonly called for breaking the legs apart in the dolphin kick.

Backstroke. The body shall remain on the back and the shoulders do not turn over beyond the vertical plane except while executing a turn. The turn requires that some part of the swimmer's body contact the end wall. After the final arm pull, the turn must be initiated in a continuous movement with the swimmer assuming a position on the back before a foot/feet leave the wall. The finish requires completion of the required distance and contact with the finish end, or the finish pad by any part of the swimmer. **(5:27)**

The penalty for improper stroke technique is disqualification from the given event.

Mechanics

In the congested area of the pool deck, mechanics become especially important. All officials must confine themselves to their respective working areas. The starter must keep the sides of the pool clear for officials observing strokes, turns, take-offs, and finishes. If possible, elevated stands should be situated on both sides of the finish to provide an unobstructed view for the judges. Timers should assume a position directly over their lanes at the finish. In many pools it is advisable to have the area around the starting blocks and in the proximity of the scoring table roped off and restricted to officials only. Bright colored caps are recommended as a means of identifying the officials.

Starting Procedure
The starter should come equipped with a .22 caliber starting gun. Other starting devices now include tones and beepers. Use whatever will assure a fair start.

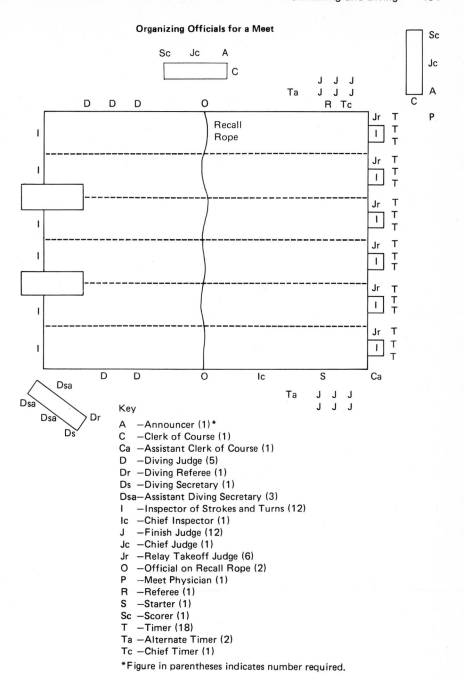

Figure 7.1 Organization chart for championship meet. (4:45)

Key

A —Announcer (1)*
C —Clerk of Course (1)
Ca —Assistant Clerk of Course (1)
D —Diving Judge (5)
Dr —Diving Referee (1)
Ds —Diving Secretary (1)
Dsa—Assistant Diving Secretary (3)
I —Inspector of Strokes and Turns (12)
Ic —Chief Inspector (1)
J —Finish Judge (12)
Jc —Chief Judge (1)
Jr —Relay Takeoff Judge (6)
O —Official on Recall Rope (2)
P —Meet Physician (1)
R —Referee (1)
S —Starter (1)
Sc —Scorer (1)
T —Timer (18)
Ta —Alternate Timer (2)
Tc —Chief Timer (1)

*Figure in parentheses indicates number required.

This official must strive for an equitable start for all competitors, or a position where the heads and backs and feet of all swimmers can be viewed to determine whether they are steady on the mark, or approximately 1–2 feet out in front of the swimmers. The starting sequence is as follows:

1. Sound whistle to alert timers and judges;
2. Command "take your marks";
3. Pistol shot or beeper if all swimmers are steady (no movement);
4. Second pistol shot or whistle if false start;
5. Signal to have the recall rope dropped to stop the swimmers; and
6. Restart race.

An experienced starter will repeat the command "quiet at the start" if there is undue noise and/or confusion before a race. The pistol should be cocked to reduce the chance of swimmers anticipating the starting gun. Furthermore, the starter should neither move the arm when firing the gun nor change facial expression. Finally, it is advisable to alter the timing of both the command "take your marks" and the pause between the command and the pistol shot. Veteran starters recommend dropping the inflection on the word "marks" and pausing at least one second between the command and the pistol shot. The cooperation of the swimmers coming down to their marks together by command is essential for a fair start. It is strongly suggested that the *swimmers* virtually "start the race" by their demonstration of readiness.

LANE NO. . . . .   VALUE . . . .

    OFFICIAL TIME . . . .

EVENT . . . .

HEAT NO. . . . .

SWIMMER . . . .

TEAM . . . .

TIMERS . . . .

TIMERS . . . .

TIMERS . . . .

ALTERNATE . . . .

HEAD TIMER . . . .

Figure 7.2 Timer's slip. (4:58)

Don't get the reputation of being a "fast" starter: the swimmers will be getting away from you. Don't be a "slow" starter: you will increase the number of disqualifications. (2:9)

Timing
Each watch should be tested prior to the race to determine its reliability. Watches off .2 seconds for the duration of the shortest race should not be used. A timer should familiarize himself or herself with the watch by starting, stopping, and resetting the watch. Cords for wearing the watches around the neck should be provided. Timers should be reminded to clear their watches before each race. This should be executed at the command of the head timer when he or she receives the ready signal from the starter. Each timer must start the watch at the flash of the gun, and stop the watch when the swimmer touches the wall. The index finger is faster than the thumb and its use is recommended. How precisely the watch is started and stopped may determine whether the swimmer will place. When three watches are utilized, the official time is determined as follows:

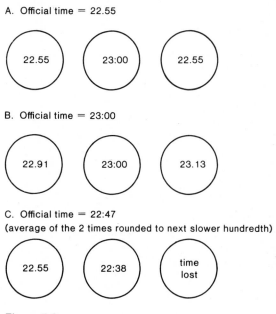

A. Official time = 22.55

22.55   23:00   22.55

B. Official time = 23:00

22.91   23:00   23.13

C. Official time = 22:47
(average of the 2 times rounded to next slower hundredth)

22.55   22:38   time lost

Figure 7.3

LANE NO. .... PLACE ....

EVENT ....

HEAT NO. ....

SWIMMER ....

TEAM ....

JUDGE ....

Figure 7.4 Judge's slip. (4:58)

Following a race, *watches should not be cleared until the head timer has had the opportunity to verify and record an official time.* Timers must be prepared to get wet as they should be positioned low and directly over or to the side of the starting block to closely observe the touch of the swimmer.

Other suggestions for improved timing include:

1. Checking the watch after the start to assure that it is functioning (if not, notify the head timer who will designate an alternative timer);
2. Avoiding unnecessary movement of the arm or hand when starting and stopping the watch to assure accuracy;
3. Not being fooled by a false finish (lunge, headlift, etc.); and
4. If the hand is not centered on a tenth-second mark, reading it at the next highest or slower tenth.

Relay Take-off Judging

The take-off judge should concentrate on observing the touch of the incoming swimmer by assuming the best possible view of the touch and the feet of the outgoing swimmer. If the outgoing swimmer leaves before the incoming swimmer touches, the judge's hand should be raised overhead to indicate the violation. When automatic equipment is used, back-up decisions are based on visual judgment.

Dive Judging

Preferably, one or more of the diving judges should have had diving experience. If this is not the case, the judges of the dive must take it upon themselves to study the scoring procedures diligently. Each dive is categorized by a predetermined degree of difficulty. Points are awarded from zero to ten.

The judges must consider the starting position, approach, hurdle, take-off, execution, and entry. Attention should be directed to the position announced for the dive-layout, pike, or tuck. Judges must be able to discern whether the diver has taken a minimum of three steps

DIVING SCORING

Very Good 8.5-10
Good 6.5- 8
Satisfactory 5.0- 6.0
Deficient 2.5- 4.5
Unsatisfactory 0.5- 2.0
Completely Failed   0

Figure 7.5

INTERSCHOLASTIC CHAMPIONSHIP DIVING

NAME ....   PLACE ....

DIVING

TEAM .... ORDER .... FINAL SCORE ....

Dive No.	Dive	Posi-tion	D. of Diff.	Judges' Awards 1	2	3	4	5	Total Award	Score
101	Forward Dive									
5111	Forward Dive 1/2 Twist									

Preliminary Total

201	Back Dive									
401	Inward Dive									

Semi-finals Total

301	Reverse Dive									

(Diver's Signature)

Figure 7.6 Diving score sheet for interscholastic championship meet. (4:57)

and has executed the dive in the air, not on the board. The degree of difficulty should not be given special attention by the judges. After each dive, the whistle is sounded by the diving referee. The judges simultaneously flash their scoring awards using flip-type score books. After all scores have been announced, the judges should close their score books in preparation for the next dive. The score is computed by multiplying the total score of the judges by the degree of difficulty.

Diving judges must continually guard against being swayed by mediocre dives with exceptional entries and against being overly concerned about "staying together" in awarding scores.

Problem Calls

Close Finishes

The common problems of lunging, splashing, and underwater touches emphasize the need for electronic devices, especially in the freestyle and backstroke finishes. Unfortunately, many coaches encourage their swimmers to raise their heads and make a splash prior to touching the wall in a close race.

Rolling Starts

A legal start requires all contestants to attain their starting positions, remain motionless, and wait for the starting gun. The starter should insist that swimmers assume the preferred position without delay. A rolling start is one where the swimmers persist in a slow downward movement in assuming their starting positions. For example, swimmers will begin to move with the "take your marks" command but will bend very slowly into the starting position, hoping they can be starting a recoil just as the gun is fired, gaining a split-second advantage. (2:9) Extra motion may occur in the normal hang starting position or in the grab starting cantilevered position. When a swimmer or swimmers are moving, the "stand up" command should be used to obviate the need for calling a false start. When this is not possible, a false start must be charged to the swimmer(s) committing the infraction(s). Collegiate rules disqualify contestants with one false start in dual meets and two false starts in championship meets.

Starters must be firm in their efforts to assure an equitable start for all contestants. From age-group swimming through university competition, starters must work for consistency. The command should be varied in timing and given in a calm, quiet voice to avoid exciting the swimmers and promoting false starts.

Effective starters will not hold swimmers if they go down to the starting position together.

Relay Take-offs

The most common infraction may be the relay take-off. Take-offs are difficult to judge since many touches are made underwater. If in doubt, don't call the infraction. There is an understandable but unjustified reluctance to make such a crucial call. If the starter is working the meet alone, the touch and take-off cannot be judged from a distance with any confidence. Adequately staffed championship meets have a take-off judge assigned to each lane. As in close finishes, implementation of automatic timing devices would minimize this problem. Regardless of age or experience a relay swimmer who "jumps" should be disqualified, since an advantage has thus been gained over those who have performed legally.

Stroke and Turn Infractions

Stroke infractions must be declared to the referee without delay. In keeping with the rules, the breaststroke is the most difficult to judge, with head position, shoulder position, and symmetrical movements all to be considered. Regardless of their age, swimmers who are shown leniency are granted an unfair advantage and will fail to develop a competitive skill. Stroke infractions should be strictly enforced in age group and interscholastic swimming; they are almost nonexistent in collegiate swimming. It is a good policy to develop uniform hand signals for stroke inspectors leading to disqualifications. Stroke technique is best observed from *behind* the swimmers. However, there are some situations where a side position is advised. If the inspector is not convinced that there is a stroke infraction, he or she should continue to watch the swimmer in question. When disqualifying a swimmer for a stroke infraction, it is important to explain the infraction to the swimmer in question after the race to avoid a reoccurrence. The swimmer is entitled to a tactful explanation by the starter or referee. Any attempt to coach should be avoided.

Miscellaneous Considerations

Volunteer Officials

In order to conduct an organized swimming meet, several officials are required. Championship meets require as many as thirty officials, a situation which presents a problem for small communities staging these events. An inadequate number of competent officials can result in inequities in judgment and the establishment of unreliable records. Due to financial circumstances, it is usually not feasible to provide a full complement of paid officials for dual or championship meets. Therefore, many responsibilities are assigned to volunteer officials. This creates a situation in which the host school or club must secure the services of interested individuals. Many leagues now require participating teams to staff one lane with timers and watches with the host team supplying all other officials. A clinic should be conducted prior to the meet date, or a premeet session should be conducted well before the scheduled hour of the meet. This meeting should instruct in how to use a stopwatch, proper positioning at the start and the finish of the race, correct recording procedures, and many other details. Successful meet directors recognize the importance of these volunteers and make it a point to keep them well informed on rule changes. Basic instructions should be attached to each official's clipboard. Volunteers should be treated with great respect, dignity and a sense of humor. If a banquet is customary at the conclusion of the season, it is beneficial to invite the volunteer officials in order to properly recognize them for their service to the program.

Training Officials

Ideally a clinic or clinics should be scheduled on nonmeet days to explain thoroughly the rules and to provide practice opportunities. Close (2:45) suggests three clinic phases: an hour and one-half lecture period, a one-hour pool demonstration and practice officiating session, and a final hour devoted to a written test on the material covered in the lecture and demonstration/practice. Torney (7:278) characterizes a good official as one who is "Well-informed, arrives early, has good rapport with competitors and coaches, and is properly attired, alert, decisive and fair."

Safety Issues

There is a great concern over warm-up policies. To avoid a loss of control, a lane must be set aside for lap sprints. Water depth at the start should be a minimum of 4 feet with 6 feet advised. Caution should be taken to have the diving area clear of swimmers. Finally, the clarity of the water should be checked for the purpose of providing favorable visual and sanitary conditions for the swimmers and divers. All of the above are the responsibility of the meet manager. The referee must confirm the pool dimensions for record purposes.

Age Group Swimming Programs

Many of the age group swimming program problems that develop could be circumvented by carefully developing a sound philosophy in the organization of an age group swimming program. Without a statement of objectives, it too often becomes one in which the adult coach, parents,

and *officials* have lost sight of the only justification for the program—
that it exists for the benefit of the children, not the glorification of
parents, coach, and swimming officials. (3:314)

Officiating Evaluated by Coaches

What qualities do you appreciate in a swimming official?

1. Completely familiar with the rules and applies them equally in all
   situations
2. Promptness
3. One who instills confidence in the athletes
4. Decisiveness
5. Willing to make the necessary disqualifications
6. Takes command of the contest without calling undue attention to
   himself/herself
7. Arrives equipped with guns, whistles, proper uniforms, rulebooks,
   etc.

Officiating Evaluated by Officials

What is the most difficult situation to call in swimming?

1. Relay without electronic timing devices
2. Stroke violations
3. Finishes of close races where timers and finish judges disagree

What is the most difficult phase of mechanics in officiating swimming?

1. Judging relay take-offs
2. High enough positioning to observe the entire field of competitors at
   the finish
3. Developing a starter's command that does not invite false starts

Sample Officials' Certification Test

Check or fill in one (or more if more than one is correct).

Timer

1. Which finger is suggested for starting and stopping a watch?
   a. forefinger
   b. middle finger
   c. thumb

PERFORMANCE RATING FORM FOR
SWIMMING AND DIVING OFFICIALS

Name of Official .... Capacity: .... Referee
                                                   .... Starter
Meet .... vs. .... Finish Judge
Date .... Place .... Inspector of
                                                  Strokes and Turns
Signature of Rater .... Diving Judge
Position of Rater: .... Timer
    (Encircle one) Referee — Coach — Observing Official   .... Other ....
                Other ....

Rating Scale for Duties Performed

Rating   Characteristic of Competency Desired for Officials at:
5—Superior   —National and regional level of championship competition
4—Good   —State championship and top-flight college meets
3—Average   —High school varsity, small college, and local championship meets
2—Fair   —High school junior varsity and junior high school meets
1—Poor   —Practice meets in schools and community organizations

Rating
(Encircle one)

Characteristic	Poor	Fair	Average	Good	Superior
Knowledge of the Rules	1	2	3	4	5
Displays accurate knowledge of the rules					
Renders proper interpretation of the rules					
Competency in Mechanics of Officiating	1	2	3	4	5
Assumes proper position and utilizes desirable movement patterns for specific duties					
Alert to total scene of contest and to cooperating and coordinating with other officials in performing duties					
Uses equipment properly, e.g., watch, gun					
Physical Attributes	1	2	3	4	5
Satisfactory physical condition					
Neat, tailored, and physically fit appearance					
Desirable Personal Qualities	1	2	3	4	5
Exerts positive control of responsibilities for supervising the contest					
Displays consistency and sound judgment in decisions					
Reflects confidence and poise, self-control, and calmness					

Total of
Key for Over-All Rating   Ratings ....
    18 and over — 5   OVER-ALL
    14-17   — 4   RATING ....
    10-13   — 3
    7- 9   — 2
    4- 6   — 1

Figure 7.7 Performance rating form—simplified version. (4:70)

2. If you did not start or stop the watch accurately or if it did not function properly for some reason, you should
   a. call for an alternate timer.
   b. record the same time as one of the other timers on your lane.
   c. report "no time."
   d. estimate the correct time.
3. What is the official time when three watches are used?
   a. the average of all three times
   b. the middle time if all differ
   c. two identical times

Finish Judge

4. In lane judging you pick the order of finish of:
   a. first place.
   b. the swimmer in your lane only.
   c. first, second, and third place.
5. Lane finish judges should stand
   a. at the end over the lane being judged.
   b. at the side several feet away from the end.
   c. at the side in a line with the end, preferably in a raised position.
6. If you know that a swimmer has been disqualified, what place do you award him?
   a. last place
   b. the same place as if he were not disqualified
   c. no place at all

Stroke and Turn Judge

7. A turn judge should be stationed
   a. on the deck in line with the end of the pool.
   b. at the end over the lane being inspected.
   c. in the stands at the side in a raised position.
8. In butterfly, which of the following are rules violations?
   a. more than one kick after the start and each turn before the first arm stroke
   b. recover the arms underwater
   c. use frog kick
   d. switch from dolphin to frog kick and back to dolphin kick
   e. use flutter kick after start and turns
   f. take underwater arm pull after start and turns but recover over surface
   g. touch below the water line
   h. somersault into the turn

9. Judges of strokes and turns report infractions to the
   a. chief judge.
   b. referee.
   c. recording desk.
   d. head lane timer.

Relay Take-off Judge

10. A relay take-off judge should watch
    a. both the touch and the take-off.
    b. only the touch.
    c. only the take-off.
11. When there has been a "break", the take-off judge should
    a. tell the other relay team members.
    b. not tell the other team members.
    c. raise his hand to indicate infraction.
    d. report the infraction to the referee.
12. Before the touch on a relay, the following swimmer
    a. may be in motion.
    b. may not be in motion.

Starter

13. What does the Starter say after "Take your marks"?
    a. "Get set"
    b. "Go"
    c. nothing
14. Before the gun, a swimmer
    a. may be in motion but not moving forward.
    b. must be perfectly steady.
15. Who may call a false start?
    a. referee
    b. starter
    c. chief judge
    d. clerk of the course
    e. stroke inspector

Answers to Sample Officials' Certification Test
1. a 2. a,c 3. b,c 4. b 5. c 6. b 7. b 8. b,c,d,e 9. b 10. b 11. c 12. a 13. c
14. b 15. a,b(2:60)

BIBLIOGRAPHY

1. Clark, Steve. *Competitive Swimming As I See It.* North Hollywood, California: Swimming World, 1967.
2. Close, Richard W. *Practical Swimming Officiating.* Stamford, Connecticut: Dolphin Aquatics, 1971.
3. Counsilman, James C.*Science of Swimming.* Englewood Cliffs, New Jersey: Prentice-Hall, Inc., 1968.
4. Meyers, Carlton R. and William H. Sanford. *Swimming and Diving Officiating.* Palo Alto, California: National Press Books, 1970.
5. *Swimming and Diving.* Kansas City, Missouri: National Federation of State High School Associations, 1990-91.
6. *1990 Men's and Women's Swimming and Diving Rules.* Mission, Kansas: National Collegiate Athletic Association, 1990.
7. Torney, John A. and Robert D. Clayton. *Aquatic Instruction, Coaching and Management.* Minneapolis, Minnesota: Burgess Publishing Company, 1970.
8. White, Jess R. *Sports Rules Encyclopedia.* Palo Alto, California: The National Press, 1966.

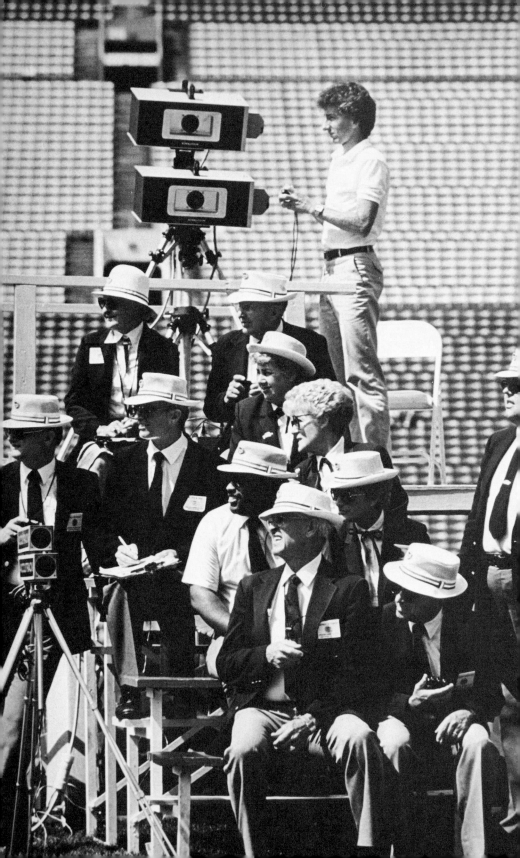

8

Track and Field

The Game

Man has been running from the beginning of time. "Running for fun" has evolved from an original context of running for survival. Track and field is considered an exacting sport full of challenges and a sport where the athlete must be self-reliant and absolutely on his or her own. The spectrum of competition ranges from children's match races to the Olympic Games.

Track and field is very satisfying to the individual as it is a natural activity and it provides a sense of achievement. (6:9) Ron Clarke (2:6) feels very strongly about the lasting benefits of track—the simple preparation, rigorous testing of one's own ability, friends made, and people met. Track and field undoubtedly contribute to the improvement of cardiovascular endurance which is a major component of physical fitness.

Track and field calls for a polished performance. The stopwatch and tape measure can produce precise information regarding improvement and positive results. The track and field athlete competes not only against the athlete in the next lane, but also against the standards of time, distance, and height. (3:10)

Track and field competition is unique in that several events progress concurrently. Due to the overlapping of events, there are understandable delays. Coupled with the challenge of individual effort,

Photo by Mike Powell / All Sport

the contestants exhibit considerable tenseness. The referee and starter must make a concerted effort to keep both the coaches and competitors calm throughout the meet.

Officials and Their Duties

As in swimming, the only paid official in most high school dual track meets is the starter/referee. The role of the referee is usually played by the host coach or athletic director. The numerous other volunteer officials required to conduct a meet are supervised by the starter/referee.

The recommended clothing for the starter is a distinguishable red jacket, black trousers, black socks, black shoes, white shirt with black tie and a red cap or hat.

Referee
The track referee has complete jurisdiction over the meet. The referee is responsible for ensuring fair competition for all contestants.

Before and during the meet the referee has specific responsibilities. The swimming and track referee have the same general responsibilities. Please view these responsibilities in chapter 7, Swimming and Diving.

The referee must be prepared to make decisions on any technical questions that arise during the meet. When there are no rules covering a dispute, the referee shall have the final judgment in the matter. (8:200)

Starter
The starter has control over the contestants after they have been assigned to him by the clerk of the course. The starter interprets the rules and makes judgements in the "spirit of the rules." Before starting each race, the starter should explain to each competitor:

1. The command and signal to be given to start the race;
2. The distance to be covered and where the race will terminate;
3. Relay exchange requirements; and
4. For races longer than one-quarter mile, signaling the last lap of the race.

The starter must have the ability to make fast, fair, and firm decisions.

"Premeet duties include: (1) inspect and test the gun(s); (2) inspect the starting and finishing lines, relay staggers, exchange zones, and cut-in flags; (3) confer with the meet announcer to familiarize him/her with the time schedule and plan for preliminary calls; (4) confer with the head finish judge to assure agreement and understanding of meet procedures; and (5) confer with the clerk of the course regarding prerace instructions to the contestants to avoid duplication of this information at the starting line."(12:72)

Inspectors

Spaced to best observe their assigned lanes, the inspectors should concentrate on runners changing course or impeding an opponent in an effort to pass. In relay races these officials must also determine whether the baton was passed in the prescribed passing zone. A violation is signaled by waving a red flag. The chief inspector is responsible for three assistant inspectors and for reporting violations to the starter. The starter/referee then rules on the disqualification. Inspectors will also be responsible for reporting hurdlers in violation of the rules. The most common violation would be the hurdler trailing a leg to the side and below the plane of the hurdle or pushing the hurdle over with the hands.

Clerk of the Course

The clerk of the course has the important task of seeing that the meet progresses according to the time schedule. This official is responsible for assigning contestants to their proper lane positions prior to each race and for placing all members of relay teams in their proper lanes. Before the start of each race it is recommended that the clerk of the course give the head finish judge a card with the names of the runners, their numbers, and the lanes in which they are running. The clerk should stay with the starter in dual meets and move to a designated check-in area for championship meets. In many dual meets the starter will assume the responsibilities of the clerk.

Finish Judges

The order of finish in all races is the responsibility of the head finish judge and the assistant judges. In dual meets there may only be three assistant judges, one assigned to pick each place. In championship meets at least two judges should be assigned to determine each place. When there is disagreement by the judges, the judge picking the highest place takes precedence. The head finish judge must view each finish and be prepared to resolve any conflicts in placing as determined by the judges.

Field Judges

Each field event has a judge and one or more assistants. Each judge is responsible for conducting his or her competition according to the rules governing that event. The judge at each event is also responsible for the activities of assistants in marking and measuring legal throws or jumps. The head field judge, in turn, supervises the overall conduct of the field events. This includes weighing, measuring, and inspecting all implements, checking the order of competition, and certifying any record made during the course of the meet.

Scorer
The primary responsibility of the scorer is to maintain running team scores as the results of the events become available. This should include a record of individual winners and their performances.

Announcer
Meet information should be provided to the contestants and spectators throughout the meet to maintain spectator interest. Announcements should be kept to a minimum in order to avoid interrupting and diverting attention from the competition. It is the responsibility of the announcer to give the ten-minute first call and the five-minute second call for each event.

Three warnings should be given for distance and hurdle events. There should be a fifteen-minute first call, a ten-minute second call and a five-minute third call.

Marshall
The marshall is responsible for keeping the competitive areas clear, and barring all unauthorized spectators and athletes not competing in the event in progress off the track and infield. This makes possible the steady progress of the meet. A special cap or ribbon worn on the jacket should be used to identify the marshall.

General Guidelines for Officials
Necessary items and rules for track and field officials:

1. A red flag and white flag (red to indicate fouls and white to indicate legal or successful attempt).
2. Stopwatch: Chronomix stopwatch and, if possible, an automatic photo-timer.
3. Clipboard, and pencils or pens.
4. Measuring tapes. Feet, and metric steel tapes (10, 25, 100, 150, and 300 feet).
5. Plastacene (horizontal jump officials). This is spread on the inner edge (toward the pit) of the board to check for faults in the long jump and the triple jump.
6. Report to the head official of your assigned event as soon as you arrive at the track site (thirty minutes before the event).

7. Do not leave the area of your assigned event unless you check with the head official of your event.
8. Prepare and be knowledgeable of the rules involving your assigned event.
9. Check the event recording sheet on how to record each trial.
10. When your event has been completed, check with the head official of your event before you leave the area. (11:4)

Basic Penalties and Rulings

Lane Violations
Inspectors should be cognizant of the importance of their responsibility. A competitor who steps on or over the lane to the inside in races around the curve should be disqualified. This can be interpreted as three consecutive steps with one or both feet. Runners may also be disqualified for jostling, cutting across, or obstructing another competitor. Runners should not be allowed to cross into the next lane in a straightaway race. If there is no contact or impedance, no foul should be called. The "two strides" rule or one full running stride must be enforced in races which permit the runners to cross in front of each other. (6:123) A major concern is to note any action that causes another runner to break stride or lose momentum.

Relay Passes
The most important considerations are that the pass be made within the allotted zone of twenty meters, and that, after making the pass, the runner does not veer out of the assigned lane, thus impeding an opponent's path. From a technical standpoint, the baton must be passed within the zone although the runner may be out of the passing zone. If the baton is dropped in the passing zone, either runner may pick it up.

Hurdle Clearance
A hurdler should be disqualified who advances or trails a leg or foot outside and below the plane of the hurdle. The rules make it very clear that the contestant's entire body must go over the hurdle. A hurdler may also be disqualified for running out of the assigned lane and obstructing another hurdler or deliberately knocking down hurdles. Accidentally knocking down hurdles will not be penalized.

Events Using Circles—Shot Put, Discus, Hammer
In the shot put event, the shot must land within a 45-degree sector extending from the center of the shot put circle. The shot must be put or pushed. Fouls should be called for throwing the shot and for letting the

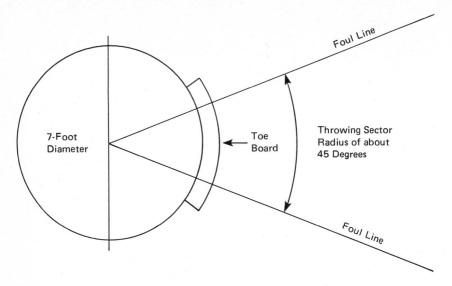

Figure 8.1 Shot put lay-out. (1:75)

shot pass behind or below the shoulder. Basic rules call for the competitor not to touch the top of the toe board or step out of the circle during the put. The contestant may touch the inside of the toe board. The competitor must leave the rear half of the circle after the attempt. The measurement is from the nearest mark made by the shot to the inside circumference of the restraining circle.

The basic in-the-circle rules governing a legal discus and hammer throw measurement are the same as those for the shot put. The hammer throwing sector is the same as the shot put (45 degrees) while the discus sector is 60 degrees. The discus and hammer events utilize a ring instead of the toe board used in the shot put.

High Jump
A missed jump is recorded when:

1. The crossbar is displaced in an attempt to clear it;
2. The jumper passes under crossbar or touches ground with any part of the body extended beyond the crossbar; or
3. The jumper approaches the crossbar and leaves the ground. (1:45)

A jumper is eliminated from competition when he or she misses three consecutive times at any height. If the event is tied, the winner will be determined by the fewest misses at the closing height or previous heights. A common misconception is that a jump is successful if the competitor leaves the pit before the crossbar falls off.

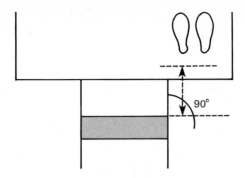

Figure 8.2 Long jump measurement.

Pole Vault

The pole vault is one of the most challenging of all field events. A combination of speed, strength, endurance, and coordination is required to succeed. A missed attempt is recorded when:

1. The bar is displaced by vaulter or pole;
2. The vaulter leaves the ground in an attempted vault and fails to clear bar;
3. Any part of the vaulter's body touches the ground beyond the plane of the stopboard; or pole touches pit.
4. During the vault, the vaulter displaces his upper hand higher on the pole or moves his lower hand above his upper hand. (1:70)
5. The vault is not completed in two minutes.

Long Jump and Triple Jump

Both events utilize a wooden take-off board with the edge of the board nearest the pit referred to as the scratch or foul line. The triple jump is a three-part action (7:231) that requires the competitor to make the first jump by landing on the same foot from which he or she took off, or hop; the second jump, or step, by landing on the opposite foot; and the third jump landing by preference. (9:75) The measurement in either event should be made at right angles to the foul line or from the closest point of entry to the front edge of the board. If necessary, to gain a right angle measurement, an extension of the scratch board may be made. A clipboard and a three-foot extension board should be provided.

Foul attempts should be recorded when contestants step over the scratch line before the jump, run beyond the foul line extended, or leave the pit out of control closer to the take-off board after landing in the pit.

Javelin

A legal javelin throw must be made from behind the arc, and the javelin must fall within the sector. Foul attempts will be recorded for throwing outside the sector, touching any surface of the foul board, the run-up lines, or the area outside the foul board or the run-up lines. (9:79)

Mechanics

Starting

A pistol of not less than .22 caliber that can be cocked and has a flash clearly visible to the timers must be used. The starter should repeat the race instructions to the participants and answer any questions that may be presented. Next, the head finish judge should be signaled that the race is about to begin. A flag-signal response, in lieu of whistles between the starter and the head finish judge, is suggested. After receiving a return signal from the head finish judge, the starter should take a position to the side away from the bleachers and ten to fifteen yards ahead of the competitors in straightaway races. In staggered races, the starter should be positioned on the inside of the track equidistant from all participants.

In a calm and relaxed voice, the starter should bring the runners to the starting line by giving the command, "On your marks!" while pointing the free hand to the ground. The starter should then allow ample time for the runners to assume a comfortable position in the starting blocks. When all runners are motionless and have their fingers in position behind the starting line the starter should raise the free hand overhead in the same position as the gun hand and give the command "Set," requesting that all contestants assume their final positions. After an interval of approximately two seconds and when all participants are motionless, the starter should discharge the pistol. As soon as the participants leave the starting line, the starter's assistants should move the starting blocks to the infield. In races of more than 800 meters the commands are "Runners, on your marks" followed by the gun (for college) and "Runners, set" and the gun (for high school).

Timing

Before the meet, the head timer should check the digital watches for accuracy. Before each event, the timer should complete the time slip, and then fill in the time immediately following the race. The slowest 1/10 second should be recorded on 1/100-digital watches. For example, 57.63 would be recorded 57.7.

In lap races, one timer should be designated to call split times for each runner.

The timer's slip should then be given directly to the head timekeeper, without discussion with the other timekeepers. The technique for timing is the same as that outlined in the chapter on swimming. A fully automatic timer utilizes a single electronic timer started automatically with the starter's gun and stopped by an electronic or optical device at the instant the first part of each runner's torso reaches the finish line. In the event of malfunction, this system is backed up with official timers. (9:61)

In championship meets, official pictures of all finishes may be taken. Utilizing the results of the automatic timer and the picture of the finish, the Chief Evaluator shall be responsible for the evaluation and interpretation of the finish place and time. (9:46)

"In order to help the judges when the finish is very close, photo-finish equipment has been devised which freezes the athletes on film as soon as the beam at the finish line has been broken; the athlete whose torso first crosses the line is the winner (the head and the arms do not count)." (4:8) Acutrack is highly recommended by track officials and coaches for this purpose.

Judging

Running events. Judges should be positioned in elevated stands approximately fifteen to twenty feet back from the finish line on either side of the track. After completing the prerace information on the finish slip, the judge should watch the race until the competitors are ten to fifteen yards from the finish line. The judge should then concentrate on the finish line and select his or her assigned place based on a torso finish. Even though the runners have been instructed to stay in their lanes and to turn around and face the judges at the end of the race, it is necessary for the judge to go immediately and obtain the name of the runner in question. The judge should then complete the slip and return it to the head finish judge who records the official results of the race.

Field events. The head field judge, event judges, and measurers should work together as a team to expedite the conduct of the field events. The head field judge must also ascertain whether the individual field judges have the necessary equipment to conduct the event. Along with the event scorecard, an instruction card that clearly outlines the basic rules of the event should be attached to the clipboard. An equipment list should be included on the instruction card. For example, the long jump

---

LONG JUMP/DUAL MEET

1. Six official entries (3 attempts)
2. Four advance to the finals (3 attempts) (one more than places)
3. Keep scratch line clean
4. Measure from point of entry to front edge of scratching line
5. Measure at right angles from the point of entry to the front edge of the scratch line extended (jumps entering extreme sides of the pit)
6. Falling back and out of the pit to gain balance is a foul jump (if behind feet in pit)

Figure 8.3 Long jump instruction card. (8:206)

list might include clipboard, pencils, tape, marking spike, shovel, rake, broom, leveler, red flag, traffic cones, ground markers for record efforts in the event, etc.

After each attempt, the judge should verify the measurement and instruct the event assistants to prepare the area for the next competitor. To expedite matters, it is suggested that the judge announce the "on deck" competitor well before each attempt. A rule of thumb in measurement calls for measuring to the lesser quarter-inch under 100 feet and to the lesser inch over 100 feet. To ensure accuracy, a steel tape is highly recommended. At the conclusion of the event, the field judge should record the place order, enter the distances, and turn in the results to the head judge and then to the scorer.

Meet Scoring (High School)
Dual meet scoring for individual events is 5–3–1 for the first three places. Relays in dual meets are scored 5 for first and 0 for second. In championship meets, scoring varies according to the number of teams entered.

Problem Calls

False Starts
False starts are sometimes the result of faulty starting techniques. Starters must be constantly aware that in short distance competition the runners are anxious and tend to anticipate the start. Regardless of the stature of the athlete, the false start must be called if there is a violation. Some starters have eliminated changes in body positions in

starting signals because runners often react to the hand being raised on the "Set" command. A quiet, confident manner helps to relax the competitors so that they will not try to second guess the starter. The starter must be cautious not to hurry the commands and thereby invite false starts. If the starter is not satisfied with the final starting positions of the competitors in the blocks, the runners should be requested to "stand up"; in such circumstances, a false start should not be assessed. To protect the interests of all contestants, the starter must allow ample time for all runners to prepare for the next start without undue hurrying. One false start will disqualify a contestant in college and high school competition.

Starters seem to prefer verbal commands over whistle commands. Whistle commands are recommended for curve starts. (One whistle: to marks; two whistles: set; and the gun.) In some situations, electronic signals are employed.

Event Delays
It was previously suggested that first and second and / or third calls for the running events be given and that in field events the "on deck" or next competitor be announced. Contestants participating in two or more events at the same time should be encouraged to return to an event as soon as possible in order to receive their allotments of attempts. If the contestant has just completed a running event, the field event judge will make it clear that the contestant must be ready to participate within 10 minutes. Ten minutes will then be allowed to complete the event. Regardless of the procedure adopted, a competitor should not delay the orderly progress of an event. The Track and Field Guide's statement on the subject is as follows:

> In all field events, except the pole vault, a competitor shall be charged with an unsuccessful attempt if he does not initiate his trial within 1½ minutes after being called by the event judge. (9:67)

For the same reason that one athlete can score in two or more events that are running simultaneously, he or she should be required to finish these events in the prescribed amount of time. This constitutes an integral part of the competition.

Long Jump and Triple Jump Judging
Careful scrutiny of the toe and the end of the board, or the scratch line, is an important part of judging these events. This is a judgment decision that must be made quickly. A good practice would be to clear the area immediately adjacent to the board and pit to eliminate the probability of contestants and spectators second-guessing the judge. Scratch line foul

Meet _____

Date _____

Place _____

Event _____

Competitors	Organization	Trials									Finals									Best Performance	Place
		1		2		3				1		2		3						
		ft.	in.	ft.	in.	ft.	in.			ft.	in.	ft.	in.	ft.	in.					

Place Winners

Head Field Judge _____

Field Referee _____

Official Scorer _____

Figure 8.4 Sample scorecard for discus, shot put, javelin, and long jump. (8:206)

calls should be made immediately after the contestant makes contact with the pit. If foul calls are made while the jumper is in the air, injury to the jumper may result. Contact with the surface in front of the board is not always visible. It is possible for the toe of the shoe to extend over the scratch line without marking the sand, dirt, or runway in front of the board. The judge must also be alert to protect the jumpers from nonjumpers who may be warming up near the runway.

Relay Exchanges
Too often this fact of meet officiating is overlooked. Since meets may not be decided at the time of the relay, indifference in judging relay exchanges can be critical. Inspectors must observe the passes and rule accordingly. With only one inspector at each exchange position, it is very difficult to observe the incoming and outgoing passes accurately. It should be emphasized that each team must wear identical uniforms.

Races 800 Meters and Up
Breaking to the inside at the 200-meter mark equalizes the competition for all lanes (on a one-turn stagger).

Blocks and Hurdles
In order to avoid delays following hurdle races and running events that require moving the hurdles and blocks respectively, the host coach must have reliable captains assigned to each responsibility.

Miscellaneous Considerations

Premeet Duties
The referee and starter should arrive early to inspect the track, starting line, finish lines, relay passing zones, and field event facilities and equipment. A meeting with both coaches should be conducted to clarify rules and answer any questions. The few minutes allotted for this meeting will usually pay dividends before the meet has ended.

Volunteer Officials
Finding reliable and capable volunteer officials, especially in youth meets, is a most difficult problem for track coaches. Time must be devoted to the active recruiting of these volunteer officials. Experienced volunteer officials should be solicited each year and commitments secured when possible. A personal contact should be made to assure them that their services are important to the continuance of the sport. On the day of the meet the coach should make every effort to

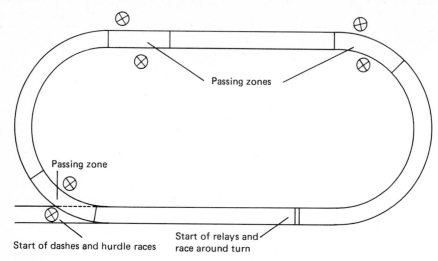

Figure 8.5 Suggested placement of inspectors. (8:207)

refamiliarize these individuals with their responsibilities. The coach should also take time to review with the volunteer officials the instruction cards attached to each field event scorecard. Take nothing for granted; if there are rule changes, clarify these before the meet. Don't assume that even experienced volunteers have kept current on rule changes in any given event. Make provisions for questions before the meet. It is the responsibility of the coach to support these volunteers by moving around during the meet and tactfully assisting them. It should be noted that most volunteers wish to be timers and tend to avoid the field events. The host coach should be alert to the fact that these volunteers would like to watch the running events. To accomplish this, it is recommended that they be relieved periodically. The coach should make it a point to thank all volunteer officials at the conclusion of the meet. Provisions should be made for refreshments/drinks for dual meets and food/drinks in large meets. A final touch should include a letter of appreciation and a complete summary of the meet results. (5:257)

Jury of Appeals
The coach has thirty minutes from the conclusion of the event to file a protest with the starter/referee who will make a ruling in a dual meet. A jury of appeals, usually consisting of the starter/referee, a representative of the host school, and conference representatives, will make the decision following the trials in preparation for the finals.

Trends
1. Interscholastic track adapting to metric races.
2. Development of club track programs.
3. Several states are considering the elimination of the pole vault event due to the increased number of injuries and law suits incurred.

Officiating Evaluated by Coaches

What qualities do you appreciate in a track and field official?

1. Punctuality
2. Willingness to accept responsibility
3. Hustle
4. Thorough knowledge of the rules
5. Fairness—all runners afforded an equal start
6. Personality—firm and exact but not harsh
7. Conscientious, calm, and relaxed

Miscellaneous Comments
1. Before accepting a volunteer officiating responsibility, individuals should study the rules and keep up-to-date on rule changes.
2. Officials should be on hand during the warm-up period to establish rapport with the competitors and ensure a prompt start of the event.

Officiating Evaluated by Officials

What is the most difficult situation to call in track and field?

1. Lane violations
2. Hurdle interference
3. Rolling starts

What is the most difficult phase of mechanics in officiating track and field?

1. Finish judging without adequate elevated finish line stands
2. Starter's position for staggered races (varies with recall method)

Track and Field Officials Training Sessions
Candidates should be well versed and trained in the following aspects and areas:

1. Thorough knowledge of fouls and infractions, duties, dress, and techniques.
2. Accuracy, quickness, and clearness in announcing fouls and the ability to make the correct decisions quickly and in an acceptable manner.

Pre-Meet Checklist

1. _____ CONFIRM DATE AND SITE OF MEET
      a. Check for conflicts of other local or regional events.
      b. Obtain necessary facility permits for location site.

2. _____ VERIFY INFORMATION TO BE INCLUDED ON OFFICIAL ENTRY
      FORM BROCHURE

3. _____ NOTIFY ARCO JESSE OWENS GAMES HEADQUARTERS OR
      REGIONAL COORDINATING AGENCY OF PARTICIPATION

4. _____ INFORM THE PUBLIC OF INTENT TO HOLD MEET

5. _____ DISTRIBUTE ENTRY FORMS—POST "SIGN-UP" POSTERS
      a. Develop system for receiving and recording entry forms.
      b. Notify participant when and where to report for registration
         day of meet.

6. _____ ASSIGN PERSONNEL TO WORK THE MEET
      a. Refer to "Statement of Duties."
      b. Send assignment letter.

7. _____ DEVELOP OPENING CEREMONY FORMAT
      a. Send letter of invitation to participating groups and
         participants.

8. _____ ORDER SUPPLIES FOR MEET
      a. Preliminary Meet
      b. Regional Championships

9. _____ SECURE NECESSARY EQUIPMENT FOR MEET

10. _____ PREPARE SCHEDULE OF EVENTS

11. _____ REVIEW FORMS

12. _____ CHECK AWARDS

13. _____ ARRANGE TO HAVE TRACK AND FIELD MARKED DAY BEFORE
      MEET

Figure 8.6 Pre-meet checklist. (1981 Guide for Conducting Arco Jesse
Owens Games. Los Angeles: Arco Jesse Owens Games, 1981.) (6:15)

3. Ability to start various races satisfactorily, both straight and
   staggered; to judge correctly and inspect the races; to time
   accurately; and to discern track infractions.
4. Ability to correctly judge and rule on fouls in the field.

Facility Checklist

_____ Availability—Restroom (male / female)

_____ Electrical Outlets _____ Power On _____

_____ High Jump Standards and Crossbars

_____ Grandstands

_____ Parking and Accessibility

_____ Maximum Number of Lanes

_____ Maintenance Personnel

_____ Lining of Track

_____ P.A. System

_____ Lighting (for Night Meets)

_____ Long Jump Pit(s)

The following Guidelines should also be kept in mind when selecting a site.

_____ The infield should be grass or tartan.

_____ If possible, track should be tartan or crushed brick (dust).

_____ The stands should be able to seat a minimum of 5,000 spectators and in many cases, more; and be separated by a barrier from the track.

_____ Concession facilities should be available for drinks and snacks (hot dogs, etc.).

_____ Night meets should have well-lighted facilities and good security.

_____ A portion of the stands should be able to be set aside as a "Bull Pen" or line-up area for participants. All participants will remain in this section until called by meet director or announcer for their event.

Figure 8.7 Facility checklist. (1981 Guide for Conducting Arco Jesse Owens Games. Los Angeles: Arco Jesse Owens Games, 1981.) (6:17)

5. Knowledge of correct positions to judge the events and the ability to give both good verbal instructions and correct arm and whistle signals.
6. Proper attitude and demeanor for making quick and accurate decisions and for carrying out officiating duties to the smooth and correct conclusion of the meet and events.
7. Thorough knowledge of the written rules of all events and the official's duties. (6:121)

Meet Director's Checklist

(For Use Day of Meet)

1. _____ Arrive 1-1/2 hours prior to start of meet
2. _____ Meet with facility coordinator; unlock gates, restrooms, etc. Have P.A. system turned on and test system
3. _____ Telephone numbers of scheduled personnel
4. _____ Forms:

   _____ Completed worksheets and event cards
   _____ Supply of blank forms:
   - Relay Event Cards
   - Qualifying Heat Cards
   - Master Heat Sheets
   - Final Heat Cards
   - Awards Cards
   - Other _____

5. _____ Check equipment and supplies (refer to your pre-established list)
6. _____ Set up Field: (See Sample Field Lay-Out Chart on next page)

   _____ Tie up banners
   _____ Arrange Nerve Center and awards area
   _____ Affix Victory Stand Cover to front of awards stand
   _____ Display awards on table on the infield

7. _____ Post Signs:

   _____ Registration Desk
   _____ Parade Line-Up Area
   _____ Bull Pen
   _____ Field Events (Long Jump-Pit 1; Long Jump-Pit 2, etc.)
   _____ First Aid Station
   _____ Media/VIP area
   _____ Nerve Center
   _____ Free T-shirts Distribution Center (Free iron-on decals)

8. _____ Hold Officials' Meeting
   - Distribute Officials' caps, visors and sport shirts
   - Tell Officials about Post-Game Reception

9. _____ Hold Coaches' meeting
   - Distribute T-shirts for participants
10. _____ Distribute Program containing Order and Schedule of Events
11. _____ Lineup teams/participants for "Parade of Athletes"
12. _____ Commence Opening Ceremonies (Refer to pre-established format)
13. _____ Announce that all participants must take their seats in the stands
14. _____ Have all officials take their stations
15. _____ Conduct Meet
16. _____ Closing remarks to participants and spectators
17. _____ Clean up field
18. _____ Move to Post-Game Reception

Figure 8.8 Meet director's checklist. (1981 Guide for Conducting Arco Jesse Owens Games. Los Angeles: Arco Jesse Owens Games, 1981.) (6:40)

Organization of Track and Field Area for Meets

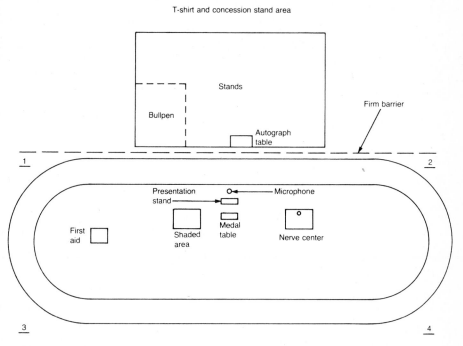

Figure 8.9 Organization of track and field area for meets. (1981 Guide for Conducting Arco Jesse Owens Games. Los Angeles: Arco Jesse Owens Games, 1981.) (6:41)

Play Rulings (12)

Situation: A1 establishes a record in a preliminary heat or in preliminary trials in a field event but does not equal it in the finals, or does not qualify for the finals. *Ruling:* The record is allowed. (3–3–6, 10–5–1)

Situation: A1 is competing in the high jump wearing only one shoe. When confronted by the high jump judge, A1 states an infected blister would be aggravated if he were to be required to wear the shoe, and the judge permits him to compete without the shoe. When the coach of B1 protests to the referee, the referee upholds the decision of the high jump judge. *Ruling:* The referee is in error. No official, including the referee (4–2–2) has the authority to set aside a rule. Contestants must wear shoes on both feet. (6–2–7, 2–3–1, 6–3–6)

Post-Meet Follow-Up

1. Prepare a Checklist:

   The following checklist will ensure for the Meet Director that all necessary follow-up items have been completed, participants have been notified of next step in program, and proper forms have been filed with Regional Coordinating Agency or National Meet Director. A brief description of these items follows the listing.

Post-Meet Checklist

1. _____ Prepare and distribute meet results to media outlets and participants.

2. _____ Send thank you letters to officials, track personnel, and others connected with the meet's function.

3. _____ Hold an evaluation meeting.

4. _____ Verify eligibility of winners and notify them of next level of competition and requirements.

5. _____ Complete and send in required forms to register your team for next level of competition.

6. _____ Assume responsibility for your team at next level of competition.

7. _____ Respond in timely manner to information requests from Regional Coordinating Agency, National Meet Director, or ARCO Jesse Owens Games Headquarters.

8. _____ Select chaperones to accompany Regional Team to Nationals.

9. _____ Accompany team to next level of competition. (4)

Figure 8.10 Post-meet follow-up. (1981 Guide for Conducting Arco Jesse Owens Games. Los Angeles: Arco Jesse Owens Games, 1981.) (6:47)

Situation: A1, A2, and A3 draw lanes 1, 2, and 3 and their competitors draw the outside lanes. Should the referee shift competitors? *Ruling:* If any school has more than one competitor in a race, it is best to draw by schools and to alternate teammates with competitors. However, if the draw is by individuals, each runner must start in the lane drawn. (4–3–2)

Situation: An inspector notes B1 impeding the progress of A1 by illegally crowding at the curve. *Ruling:* The inspector is required to signal the infraction by waving a red flag overhead. Following the race the inspector must report the infraction to the head inspector who will report to the referee. After hearing the evidence the referee shall make any decision regarding disqualification. (4–9–3)

Situation: The runners are in the "set" position and when the gun is fired, A1's starting block slips. *Ruling:* The start is considered to be unfair and the race is recalled. (7–1–2)

Situation: In one of the races, A1 is in forward motion after the "Set" position has been taken but the starter fires the gun. *Ruling:* The starter should recall the runners by firing the pistol a second time and disqualify A1 as a result of the false start. (7–7–6)

Situation: A1 and B1 reach the finish line at about the same time. A1 reaches forward to break the finish yarn with an extended hand or arm. *Ruling:* Under such circumstances, B1 should receive the benefit of any doubt as to who finished first. The referee has the authority to disqualify A1 if it is obvious the act was intentional. (7–2–2)

Situation: During the race, A1 accidentally uses one, or two, consecutive steps on or inside the curb. *Ruling:* No penalty should be enforced for such action, provided A1 promptly returns to the track. (8–7–7)

Situation: In a hurdle race, A1 loses his/her stride and runs around a hurdle or vaults in such a way that one leg trails to the side of a hurdle. *Ruling:* A1 should be disqualified. It is necessary that an attempt be made to clear each of the hurdles.

Situation: In the high jump, A1 hits the crossbar and it bounces on the supports but does not fall until after A1 has landed and has stepped out of the landing pit. *Ruling:* This is an unsuccessful trial. If a bar falls because of being hit by the jumper in his/her attempt, the position of the competitor at the time has no bearing. (70–4–3)

BIBLIOGRAPHY

1. Bowers, Richard. *Track and Field Events: Fundamentals.* Columbus, Ohio: Charles E. Merrill Publishing Company, 1974.
2. Clarke, Ron. *Ron Clarke Talks Track.* Los Altos, California: Tafnews Press, 1972.
3. Disley, John. *The Young Athlete's Companion.* Toronto, Ontario: The Ryerson Press, 1962.
4. *Encyclopedia of Track and Field.* New York City, New York: Prentice-Hall Press, 1986.
5. Foreman, Ken. *Coaching Track and Field Techniques.* Dubuque, Iowa: Wm. C. Brown Company Publishers, 1982.
6. *1981 Guide for Conducting Arco Jesse Owens Games.* Los Angeles, California: Arco Jesse Owens Games, 1981.

7. Harkins, Dorothy. *Selected Track and Field Articles*. Washington, D.C.: AAHPER, 1972.
8. Jordan, Payton and Bud Spencer. *Champions in the Making*. Englewood Cliffs, New Jersey: Prentice-Hall, Inc., 1968.
9. Thompson, Donnis H. *Modern Track and Field for Girls and Women*. Boston, Massachusetts: Allyn and Bacon, Inc., 1973.
10. *Track and Field Guide*. Shawnee Mission, Kansas: National Collegiate Athletic Association, 1991.
11. Track and Field News.
12. *Track and Field Rules*. Kansas City, Missouri: National Federation of State High School Associations, 1991.

9

Volleyball

The Game

During the past two decades, the growth of and interest in competitive volleyball in the United States has been remarkable. Particularly noteworthy is the fact that this growth has taken place at all levels of play—professional, Olympic, intercollegiate, interscholastic, recreational, and informal.

From the official's point of view there are three particularly important aspects of volleyball: (1) the pace of the game can be explosively fast; (2) judgment on ball handling is the most crucial officiating responsibility; and (3) the approach to volleyball, although highly competitive, is somewhat more sportsmanlike than any other popular American sport.

The volleyball official, therefore, must have lightning-quick reactions and very fine concentrative powers in order not to become absolutely overwhelmed by the speed of the action. The principles underlying ball handling decisions and volleyball in general must be fully understood. The fine spirit of this tremendous game must be exemplified at all times, which means being courteous but firm, being dedicated to the game, and officiating with an attitude of serving the players. The volleyball official must not be a tyrant nor a battle-hardened arbiter.

The upsurge of volleyball popularity in the United States has produced as a by-product a serious problem—a distinct shortage of qualified volleyball officials. As the quality of competition improves, the

Photo by Trevor Jones / All Sport

need for highly qualified officials is magnified. Players or ex-players frequently serve as the best officials, but many of them wish to preserve their amateur standing or are not interested in officiating.

If the great sport of volleyball is to develop to its fullest in the United States, as it should, adequate means of producing qualified officials must be developed. At the more advanced levels of play, good officiating is absolutely essential. The game cannot be played at its best without consistency in ball handling decisions and other difficult judgment areas, and without poised, intelligent, and courteous officiating.

Officials and Their Responsibilities

Volleyball officials include the referee, umpire, line judges, scorer, and timer. According to the level of play, volleyball matches are officiated by any number of officials from zero to ten. A full complement of ten officials would include a referee, umpire, scorer, assistant scorer, timer, assistant timer, and four line judges.

Officials' Uniforms and Equipment

National federation rules call for men and women to wear the traditional black-and-white vertically striped knit short-sleeve shirt along with black slacks. Athletic shoes and socks should be consistently black or white. College and U.S. Volleyball Association officials, on the other hand, wear an all-white or navy blue-and-white vertically striped shirt and navy blue slacks.

The referee and umpire should wear a whistle with a cord. The umpire should have a record of the team's lineups and service rotation. The referee should bring red and yellow cards if the red/yellow cards sanction system is in effect.*

Referee

The referee has final control and may overrule any other official, although considerable discretion is used in exercising this power. Only the referee is empowered to apply the red/yellow card sanction system. The referee takes a position on an elevated stand at one end of the net so that the line of vision is well above (two or three feet) the top of the net. One hand is placed on the net cable through the entire point to help detect illegal touches of the net. The referee may rule on any action that

---

*Beginning with the 1992–93 season, a red/yellow card system became a part of high school volleyball rules, with each state retaining the option of not using this system. (See page 230.)

occurs, but is particularly concerned with ball handling fouls, fouls at or above the net, player conduct fouls, and routine matters such as granting time-outs.

The referee routinely causes the game to progress by blowing the whistle and beckoning the server to put the ball in play. The whistle is again sounded to kill the play when a rally has ended or a foul occurred. A point is awarded, "side out" declared, or a replay ordered, as the case warrants.

Illegal alignment or overlapping should be called upon contact of the serve. Prior to every serve, scan the area—receiving team and coach; umpire, scorers, and timer; and the serving team, and coach. When all are in position and ready, then you signal and whistle for the serve.

Before the match the referee:

1. Examines the playing site, checking particularly the amount of clearance from boundary line to walls or obstructions and the height of the net.
2. Conducts a thorough prematch discussion with the umpire.
3. Conducts a prematch conference with the coaches and playing captains to cover pertinent rules and conduct the coin toss, * the winner having choice to serve or receive or to take either side of the net. (If teams split the first two games of a best-of-three match or the first four of a best-of-five match, the referee conducts another coin toss immediately after the second or fourth game.)

    During the match the referee communicates with the captains only. Any questions from other players must come from the captain. Coaches must call a time-out to review a decision. (Time-out is not charged only if the decision is reversed.)

Umpire

The umpire takes an out-of-bounds position near the end of the net opposite the referee and adjacent to the scorer's table. The umpire's chief responsibilities during play are to concentrate particularly on play between the spiking lines and to rule on situations which might be out of the referee's view. When the ball is served the umpire should view the entire receiving team from a position no farther down than the spiking line to check the serving order and for overlapping, and to observe ball handling. Ball handling fouls may be called by the umpire only when the referee's vision is blocked. This official controls the entry of substitutes into the playing area and repeats the referee's point and side out signals.

*The visiting team calls all tosses.

COURT DIAGRAM

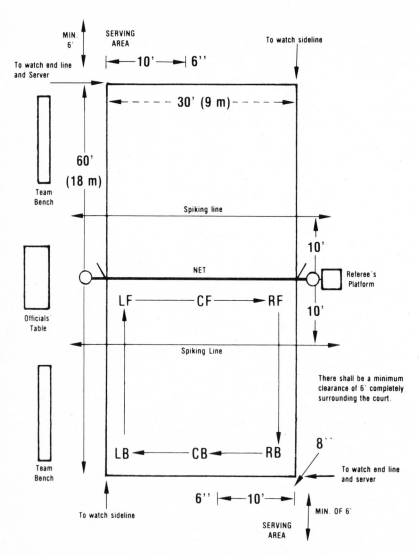

Figure 9.1 Volleyball court. (By courtesy of the N.F.S.H.S.A.)

The umpire has a wide range of responsibilities during dead-ball periods:

1. *Before the game,* to review the responsibilities of the scorer and timer and assist these officials as required; to check players' uniforms and equipment; and to check the correctness of each team's lineup.
2. *During time-outs,* to verify and place a check next to each team score; to communicate the number of time-outs remaining to the team calling the time-out; and, if either team delays following the time-out, to sound the whistle to hasten resumption of play.

When the ball is in play, the alert and competent umpire is mobile, constantly adjusting position as does the lead official in basketball. Mobility can improve the angle of vision and also remind the players of the umpire's presence. On the other hand, rapid action frequently frustrates effective movement. The intent of the umpire should be to emphasize mobility during the calmer moments of action and de-emphasize it when the action is explosive.

Here are some practical suggestions for the umpire:

1. Watch the bottom half of the net—concentrate on the defense on their way up to block.
2. Watch all follow-throughs of arms, hands, elbows, and bodies of defensive players and the spiker.
3. Watch all feet landing near or on the centerline.
4. Watch the turning of all bodies near the net as they move away from the net to continue play.
5. DO NOT FOLLOW THE BALL until all of the previous steps 1–4 are completed. Then you may pick up the play of the ball again.

Line Judges

There may be two or four line judges, usually two in high school volleyball. Where two line judges are used they stand near the intersection of the sideline with the end line opposite the serving area.

Line judges should be close enough to their corners to get a good, visual angle view of the boundary lines for which they are responsible— and far enough to allow free player movement. Like the umpire, the line judges should attempt to anticipate the movement of the ball and the players and vary their positioning accordingly, sometimes moving ten to fifteen feet. During game action they are concerned about three aspects of the playing rules: (1) Was the ball in- or out-of-bounds when it struck the court? (2) Who last touched a played ball or a block which landed out-of-bounds? (3) Was the entire ball in-bounds (within the net antenna

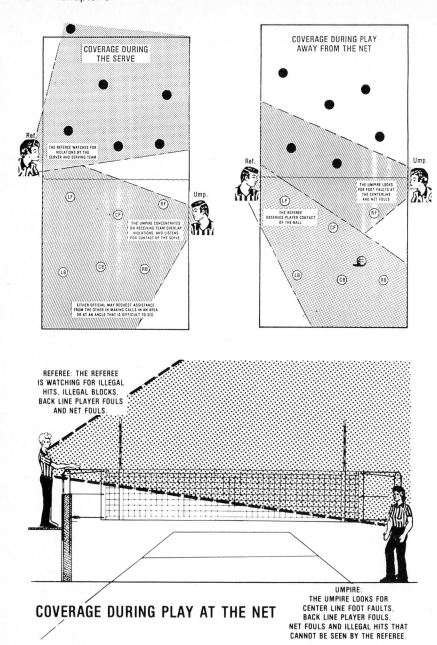

Figure 9.2 Coverage by the referee and umpire. (By courtesy of the N.F.S.H.S.A.)

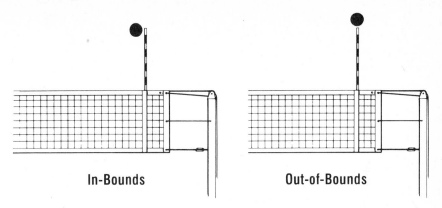

In-Bounds   Out-of-Bounds

Figure 9.3 (By courtesy of the N.F.S.H.S.A.)

extended) when it passed over the net? The line judges employ
prescribed hand signals (see Figure 9.5) and must hold their signal until
they are sure the referee has seen it.

Scorer and Timer
Volleyball rules place the scorer and timer opposite the referee and
near the umpire. They are seated at a table far enough from the court so
as not to impede the players' and umpire's movements.

The functions of the *scorer* are to record the score and operate
the scoring device, to record all time-outs and substitutions, and to
verify proper serving order to the referee prior to the start of and during
a game. When there is an improper serving order the scorer should
sound a signal at the time the serve is contacted.

As is the case in basketball, volleyball scoring is complicated and,
because of rapid-fire action, requires thorough training, alertness, and
reliability. Figure 9.4 shows a sample high school scoresheet.

The *timer* is seated next to the scorer and operates the game
timing device. Audio signals (usually a horn) are given to indicate
playing time, time-outs, or the end of intermissions. The complexities of
timing a volleyball match have been greatly reduced by the virtual
elimination in recent years of time-restricted games in high school and
college competition. At most levels of volleyball competition, however,
the rules permit the termination of a game following eight minutes of
ball-in-play action. This practice is common in intramural and community
recreation competition.

When the eight-minute game restriction is in effect, the timer starts
the timing device when each serve is contacted and stops it when a

SAMPLE GAME

DATE: _Sept. 6, 1989_   SITE: _Liberty_   •

GAME 1	TIME OUTS ☒ ☒ 3															First
Player No	Visitor: _Inde S_															Visitors
5	/ 2 3 – –															1̶ 1̶3̶
																2̶ 1̶4̶
6	R 4 5 ˢˣ 11/5 6 7 P– 15 16															3̶ 1̶5̶
																4̶ 1̶6̶
7 /3 7	S 7/13 –															5̶ 17
																6̶ 18
8	8 9 10 R –															7̶ 19
																8̶ 20
9	S 13/7 11 –															9̶ 21
																1̶0̶ 22
10 21	12 13 14 R R TX –															1̶1̶ 23
																1̶2̶ 24

Comments: Final Score | 16

Coin Toss: Visitors choose to serve first.   **Score**

                                                              V-H

    Visitors Serve: V 5 serves and scores first three regular points (1,2,3). Fourth
serve develops into side out.   3-0
    Home Serve: H 11 serves, side out.   3-0
    Visitors Serve: V 6 serves, replay called (no attempted serve). V 6 serves two
straight aces for points four and five. Next play is an opponent's substitution during
which H 11 is replaced by H 5 — (XS 11/5). **Note:** The number of the entering
player is written to the right. V 6 next two serves are for regular points (6,7) before
a penalty on the Visitors awards the serve to the Home team (P —).   7-0
    Home Serve: H 12 serves three straight points before Visitors (opponent) calls
time-out (XT). H 12 then scores points four, five, and six. Next serve is a side out. 7-6
    Visitors Serve: V 13 replaces V 7. V 13 serves, side out.   7-6
    Home Serve: H 13 serves two straight regular points (7,8). Next serve is called
a replay (R). Next play a penalty is called on Visitor (opponent), awarding point
to Home team (P 9). Visitors call time-out (XT). Home calls time-out (T). H 13 serves
one more regular point (10) before side out.   7-10
    Visitors Serve: V 8 serves three straight points (8,9,10). Next serve develops
into a replay. Next serve develops into side out.   10-10
    Note: The running score column is marked as the game progresses. When there is a
discrepancy between the running and individual scores, the individual score is considered
official. The shaded areas indicate a second service rotation.

Key: ⬚1 Point ⬚– Side Out ⬚PB Penalty Point Awarded ⬚P· Penalty Side Out ⬚R Replay

Figure 9.4A Scoresheet, visitor. (By courtesy of the N.F.S.H.S.A.)

whistle sounds and the ball becomes dead. If time runs out during ball-
in-play action, the timer withholds the audio signal until the ball
becomes dead. When, near the end of a period, a clock visible to the
players is not available, the timer periodically should call out the
remaining time in a loud voice during dead ball periods.

SAMPLE GAME

REFEREE *Linda Powell* UMPIRE *Jim Davies*

Serve	GAME 1	TIME OUTS ⊠ 3											
Home	Player No.	Home: *Liberty*											
X̶ X̶3	11 5 33	— 5/33 14 —											
X̶ X̶4													
X̶ 15	12	1 2 3 ᵀX 4 5 6 —											
X̶ 16													
X̶ 17	13	7 8 R P9 ᵀX T 10											
X̶ 18													
X̶ 19	14	—											
X̶ 20													
X̶ 21	15	11 12 13 SX/10/21 —											
X̶ 22													
X̶ 23	16	—											
X̶ 24													

14 Comments: P = Red Card #7 (7-0)   Official

Home Serve: H 14 serves, side out.	10-10
Visitors Serve: Visitors substitute V 7 back in for V 13 (S 13/7). V 9 serves point 11. Next serve, side out.	11-10
Home Serve: H 15 serves three straight points (11,12,13). Visitors substitute V 21 for V 10 (XS 10/21). Next serve, side out.	11-13
Visitors Serve: V 21 serves three straight points 12,13,14. Next two serves develop into replays (R,R). Home calls time-out (XT). Next serve, side-out.	14-13
Home Serve: H 16 serves, side out.	14-13
NOTE: With each complete service rotation (all six players serve) a different color pencil or ink should be used to begin the next rotation (i.e. first complete rotation — black; second complete rotation — red; third complete rotation — black). In sample game player V5 served points 1,2,3, and a side-out in the first rotation (black ink). Her first serve the second time around was a side out (red ink).	
Visitors Serve: V 5 serves, side out.	14-13
Home Serve: Home substitutes H 33 for H 5. H 33 serves one point (14). Next serve, side out.	14-14
Visitors Serve: V 6 serves two straight aces to win game. Record final score in appropriate boxes.	16-14

[X] Opponent   [S] Substitution   [XS/XT] Opponent Substitution

[T] Time-out   [TX] Opponent Time-out

Figure 9.4B Scoresheet, home. (By courtesy of the N.F.S.H.S.A.)

The practice of providing an assistant scorer and an assistant timer is specified in high school rules and is becoming more common. When present, these assistants are seated respectively next to and outside the official scorer and the official timer whom they are assisting. If a game is not determined by time, and no timer is provided, then the umpire should keep track of time-outs and time between games.

Basic Penalties and Rulings

The focus in this book is on high school (federation) volleyball rules, as contrasted with "international" rules. International rules form the basis in this country for the playing rules of (a) the United States Volleyball Association (USVBA) and (b) the National Association for Girls' and Women's Sports (NAGWS). Fortunately, the number of differences between high school and international rules have been significantly reduced over the past two decades.

A volleyball *game* is played to fifteen points, with a two-point margin needed to win. (Exception: games may be limited to eight minutes of ball-in-play action, but the game must still be won by two points.) A volleyball *match* consists of two out of three games in high school and three of five under NAGWS. The teams change sides of the net for each game. If the teams split and a final (third or fifth) game is necessary, a coin toss is conducted immediately after the second or fourth game in order to determine which team serves and the respective sides of the net for the final game. The teams remain on the same side of the net for the entire final game.

Only the serving team can score a point. If the servers' opponents win a given "point," it is termed "side out" and the serve goes to the opponents. When a serve touches the net, it is a side out. A ball in play, other than a served ball, remains a play if it touches the net. After the serve, each team may touch the ball no more than three times in returning the ball to their opponents. A single player may not play the ball twice consecutively, with the exceptions of (1) the block and (2) following simultaneous contact by teammates or opponents.

Service
The server must be behind and to the right ten feet of the end line when the ball is contacted. A depth of at least six feet should be provided for the server. The ball may be hit from the hand or from a toss.

The server may (within five seconds):

1. Bounce and hit the ball.
2. Toss the ball in the air, step onto the court (either catching the ball or retrieving the ball), step back and attempt to serve again.
3. Hit the ball directly off the hand.
4. Hit the ball overhand or underhand.
5. Have her or his body in the air over the end line at contact of the serve.

6. Step on but not over any of the lines that surround the service area except the end line.
7. Swing and miss the ball and attempt to serve again.

The server may not:

1. Serve prior to the referee's signal (replay).
2. Serve after five seconds have elapsed.

The served ball may not:

1. Touch anyone on server's side.
2. Touch the floor, net, net standards, net cables, net support cables, etc.
3. Touch the ceiling or any obstructions or obstacles on the ceiling or walls.
4. Pass under the net.
5. Cross outside or over the net antenna.

Fouls at the Net

At the moment the ball passes over the net, it must be entirely within the sidelines / net antenna.

Net fouls have been liberalized and now permit a player to cross the center line with the foot / feet as long as:

1. A part of the foot / feet remains on or above the center line;
2. The player does not touch the net (exception—no foul if touched only by the player's hair); and
3. The player does not interfere with the play of the opponent.

Ball Handling

The ball must be contacted cleanly and crisply by a body part or parts above and including the waist. With the exception of blocks and saves on hard-driven spikes, the ball may not be double-hit by a single player. Service returns *must* be cleanly hit, while a degree of discrepant leniency is granted on "sets," blocks at the net, and, more recently, spike returns.

When any of the above rules are violated, the penalty is either side out or point for the serving team. The volleyball official's job is simplified by this uniformity of penalties (either a point or side out).

Miscellaneous Rulings

1. *A game shall be forfeited* when (1) either team has fewer than six players before the match, or (2) a team refuses to play when directed to do so by the referee.

2. *A player, coach, or substitute may be warned, penalized,* (point or side out) *or disqualified for unsportsmanlike acts.* Only the referee may assess these penalties, although the umpire may advise the referee of such acts that the referee was not able to detect. Such measures may be taken for a number of reasons, such as attempting to influence an official's decision, disrespect, objecting to a decision, etc. Considerable discretion is required, since disqualification is never mandatory for any act. The red/yellow card sanction system is the formal means, originally under international rules, for dealing with unsportsmanlike acts in volleyball. A yellow card means a warning to a player or team. A red card means point or side out. Beyond these, a player or coach may be expelled from a game or disqualified from the match for specified infractions.

3. *The points made by a team should be cancelled* during the time of play when a player (a) was serving out of turn; (b) has entered a game for the fourth time (a player may enter a game only three times); or (c) has reentered a game in a position different from his or her first position in that game, relative to other players. Such violations also should be penalized when discovered via point or side out. Alertness to these violations will alleviate the need to cancel points.

4. *The referee should rule a replay* when the circumstances warrant. Such circumstances include: double fouls, an official's mistaken whistle, a foreign object entering the court, a ball "held" above the net by opponents, a player injury, or conflicting line calls which the referee cannot resolve.

Mechanics

Positioning

Placed on an elevated stand, the referee gains a greatly advantageous but largely immobile view of play. Prior to the serve, the umpire moves slightly along the sideline towards the receiving team to determine that no overlapping is occurring. At the moment of the serve and throughout the point, the umpire stays with the net (not behind the standards) to check on net fouls and foot faults while the referee goes visually with the ball.

The goals of the line judge(s) are to remain well away (three to ten feet) from the boundary lines and to anticipate the action and move quickly to the most advantageous position that will not interfere with player action. Given *two* line judges, these officials are constantly jockeying for a position to call either the end line or the sideline for which they are responsible. Given *four* line judges, each line judge is assigned one of the end lines or one of the sidelines and therefore needs to move only to avoid interfering with player action.

Use of the Whistle

The referee's whistle controls all volleyball action. It tells the server when to serve and sounds the end of a rally, killing the play. The umpire's whistle can also kill the play for cause. A well officiated volleyball match is characterized by frequent and definite hand signals and whistle soundings, *not* by verbal communication among officials, players, and coaches.

There is an art to the use of the whistle in volleyball. The experienced and capable volleyball referee varies use of the whistle according to the circumstances. When the action is fast and hectic before a large crowd, it is sometimes necessary to sound the whistle repeatedly with short, sharp blasts. When a ball is clearly out-of-bounds or a served ball hits the net only the mildest whistle is needed. The referee's whistle directing the server to serve should be of diminished intensity—loud enough to gain the attention of all players, but no louder. Use a double or multiple whistle for substitutions or time-outs so not to confuse the server. New officials are cautioned to hold their whistles out of their mouths when conversing with players, coaches, or other officials.

Hand Signals

Decisive and clear hand signals are very important to the success of a volleyball official. Good hand signals tend to eliminate the necessity for unneeded verbal communication and excessive use of the whistle. When conversation and whistling can be reduced, the game becomes more the *player's* game than the official's.

There are three requisites to effective hand signaling in volleyball. First, *know all the signals,* so that each can be used appropriately; second, execute the signals decisively, yet not dictatorially; and third, choose the right moment to use the signal, so that it need not be repeated or explained. There is an exact moment when all players and spectators normally look to the referee or umpire—whoever sounded the whistle.

Teamwork Among Officials

As mentioned before, the referee has the authority in volleyball to overrule another official. Obviously, this authority should be exercised with discretion. Players and coaches as well as the other officials become confused and irritated if the referee overrules fellow officials too frequently or without apparent reason.

Figure 9.5 Volleyball signals. (By courtesy of the N.F.S.H.S.A.)

The pregame discussion among members of a team of officials serves to establish the proper understanding for the particular match to be officiated. In a championship match where the umpire and line judges, as well as the referee, are experienced and knowledgeable, very few cases of overrulings by the referee would be expected. On the other hand, at lower levels of volleyball competition the referee is often the only member of the crew who really knows and understands volleyball rules and mechanics. In such circumstances, it may be necessary for the more experienced person not only to step in but to set the stage for doing so before the match. Generally, the referee should avoid overruling any decision by another official when the other official had a good view. The referee should use great discretion in overruling the umpire on ball handling decisions and net fouls.

Given an experienced referee/umpire crew, an observer would notice that the two would establish and maintain eye contact with each other whenever possible—that either would anticipate calls out of the view of the other and make the appropriate rulings. The referee controls the "flow" of the game. Neither official tries to over call the other. If during a match one official, either referee or umpire, feels her/his partner lost concentration or is not calling tightly enough, the partner can be brought fully back into the match by the one official making an obvious call that is normally the partner's call to make.

Beyond the "referee may overrule" aspect of volleyball officials' teamwork lies other normal aspects of officiating teamwork: a willingness to communicate with one another, a general attitude of support for one another, and a collective capability to rule and signal decisively. The relative lack of movement by volleyball officials, however, eliminates much of the necessity for teamwork found in such sports as basketball, football, baseball, and water polo. One other important aspect of volleyball officiating teamwork involves a close check between the umpire and the scorer and the timer to ascertain that no errors have been made in either scoring or timing.

Problem Calls

Ball handling decisions. The most difficult responsibility of volleyball officiating is to maintain consistency in decisions relative to ball handling fouls. The basic principle for ruling on borderline ball handling situations can be stated in the form of a question: "Did the ball *visibly come to rest* on the player's body part(s) at contact?" Experienced volleyball officials and observers have found that certain hand-ball contact positions often result in the ball coming visibly to rest at contact. Here are some suggestions regarding ball handling decisions:

1. Pay special attention to the team's setter(s). Have a definite criteria set in your mind that is so consistent that the setter(s) can adjust quickly and effectively.
2. Do *NOT* be influenced by the position of the player's body before, during, or after playing the ball.

3. Learn to momentarily transfer your vision from the ball as it travels towards the player who is about to make contact. Key in on the body part of this player, totally concentrating on the body part and not the flight of the ball. Thus, when the ball arrives you are able to see how the body part executes the contact and not the flight of the ball.

It is critical that a referee actually observe a ball handling foul rather than anticipating one as a result of a player's position. The principle of ball handling fouls must take precedence. Each ball handling decision made by the effective volleyball referee results from a judgment regarding whether or not the ball visibly came to rest.

The current trend in volleyball officiating, caused primarily by international volleyball influence, is for the referee to be less strict in whistling down improper ball handling used in (1) bumping spikes and (2) second touches. (The second touch is usually the "set-up" touch.) There is considerable worldwide disagreement regarding the strictness of interpretation on third, or "attacking" touches. No other single interpretation can influence the course of a volleyball match as will ball handling judgments.

Overlapping. Overlapping refers to an *improper petition, at the moment of contact on a serve,* by any player on either serving or receiving team except the server. If at that moment a player's position is improper—that is, if a back row player is closer to the net than the adjacent front row player, or if a center player is closer to either sideline than either adjacent side player—the referee shall sound the whistle and penalize the offending team by awarding, as warranted, a point or side out.

A player's position with respect to the overlapping rule is determined only by feet which are *touching the floor* at the moment of contact on a serve; an airborne foot does not count. Specifically, closeness to the net or to a sideline involving two adjacent players is to be determined based on which player's foot in contact with the floor was closer to the net or sideline at the moment of the serve. After the serve players may move to any position on the court on their side of the net.

In order to rule accurately and consistently on possible overlapping violations, the volleyball official should visualize imaginary lines from the floor-touching feet of adjacent players.

Here are a couple of tips that will help to improve your capability to rule effectively on overlapping calls:

1. Study the positioning strategies of different teams, both serving and receiving positions.
2. Before the match ask each coach independently if she/he uses any formations that you need to know about.

You are less likely to blow an inadvertent whistle if you are knowledgeable of various positioning strategies and you know the tendencies of each team.

Counting ball and player contacts. The basic rules on contacts or "touches" are that each team is entitled to just three (and no more) contacts of the ball each time a ball comes to their side of the net, and that one player may not touch or be touched by the ball twice in succession. These apparent straightforward rules frequently become complicated during the normal course of a match. For the players and coaches, ball and player contact rule interpretations provide a basis for fairness. For the officials, however, these interpretations require a thorough understanding of the rules, experience, concentration, and alertness—especially when the action is skilled and rapid.

The following questions and answers are posed for the purpose of introducing the prospective volleyball official to the complexities of counting ball/player contacts, but cannot substitute for a combination of exhaustive study of the relative playing rules and extensive officiating experience.

Question 1: *When is play on the ball NOT COUNTED as one of a team's three touches?*

Answer: When the play involves a *block* or *simultaneous touches by opponents.* The touch following the block of simultaneous contact counts as the first touch of three permissible touches.

Question 2: *When is it legal for a player to play the ball TWICE IN SUCCESSION?*

Answers:

1. Following *simultaneous contacts by opponents;* (The ball may next be legally played by a player involved in the simultaneous contact on whose side of the net the ball falls—and *counts as the first touch*.)
2. Following *simultaneous contacts by teammates;* (The ball may next be legally played by either teammate and *counts as the second touch*.)
3. Following a *block.* (A "block" by definition must be near the top of the net and not executed with a downward swing of the arm or hand. A player(s) involved in a block may legally play the ball next as a *first* touch.)

Question 3: *During a single attempt to play the ball, when is it legal for a player to be contacted by the ball twice in succession?*

Answers:

1. During a *block.* (The multiple-contact block does not count as a touch and may be followed by another touch by the same player, which would count as *a first touch.*)

2. On *one attempt to play a hard-driven spiked ball.* (This counts as *one touch*—the next touch must be by a different player.)

The referee who works advanced levels of volleyball competition is challenged by the fact that the above interpretations come into play frequently. Furthermore, they occasionally occur *in combination with each other* as a part of a single game action. Further complicating such situations are the possibilities of net violations or center line violations. These complications can cause the referee and umpire to divide their attention and perhaps to miss an action that calls for a decision. The referee should *concentrate primarily on the ball,* utilizing peripheral vision and feel of the net to determine whether or not other violations have occurred.

Reaching over the net to block. Players may reach over the net to their opponents' side while attempting to block so long as they wait for the team to complete their attack. A foul should be called if the ball is contacted by the blocker while moving parallel to or away from the net.

Determining Net Violations
It is frequently very difficult for the referee or umpire to determine whether or not the net has been touched while the ball is in play. When two to six opposing players are very close to the net and the action is explosive, net violations can easily be missed or ruled against the wrong team. No net violation may be called if the *force of the ball* causes the net to brush a player.

The well qualified volleyball official has the capability, developed through experience, of directing vision to the ball while applying discriminating peripheral vision to the net zone. The learning officials, on the other hand, must rely more on feel of the net supplemented by a constantly shifting direct observation until such time as his or her peripheral vision becomes more discriminating and reliable. The referee's hand-feel of the net cable can serve as a secondary check, but there is no substitute for actually seeing the contact with the net. Volleyball officials must avoid the temptation to ''guess'' on net contact fouls; they should call only those net fouls about which they are certain.

Balls Passing Over the Net Out of Bounds
Volleyball rules stipulate that the ball becomes dead and point or side out is ruled if the ball passes over the net from one side to the other *not entirely within* the net antennas (see Fig. 9.3). The addition of net antennas in recent years has helped the officials tremendously to make

this call accurately and consistently. Nevertheless, the prescribed positions of volleyball officials make this decision difficult, especially when there are only two line judges. Official rules imply that the line judges should call such fouls. In actual practice, the referee and umpire also call them even though their angle of vision is poor.

There is no problem when these shots are directed precisely at or away from a line judge behind one of the corners of the court. The best solution to this problem call is anticipation on the part of the line judges—a readiness to move to the precise spot where they will have a perfect angle of vision. A line judge is free to anticipate this call and to drastically alter court position when a second touch is misdirected out of bounds. The referee should instruct the judges about this difficult decision before the game, urging them to anticipate and to *move*. If, during the contest, the line judges *are* anticipating and gaining good position, the referee and umpire should leave this call to the line judges as much as possible.

Officials' View of Action is Screened by Players

Quite often the referee or umpire is unable to see the actual touch of the ball at the precise moment of the touch because an intervening player has screened the vision of the official. Fortunately, either the referee or the umpire usually has an unobstructed view when a fellow official is screened. Two guidelines apply to such situations: (1) the proven officiating maxim is that *you must call only what you see, not what you guessed to have happened,* and (2) the referee and the umpire should accept the fact that occasionally one of them will be screened out and the call must be made by the other. A predetermined gesture can be used whereby one official can communicate to the other, "I was screened out—that is your call to make."

Back Row Player Fouls

With the onset of greater mobility of players and teams executing multiple offenses, there are numerous opportunities for a back-row player to commit a back-row player contact foul.

A back-row player is not allowed to (a) block or attempt to block or (b) return a ball over the net that is *completely* above the top of the net while positioned (1) on or in front of the attack line or (2) having left the floor on or in front of the attack line.

The main responsibility for making this call lies with the referee because he or she can best see the bottom of the ball in relationship to the top of the net.

Miscellaneous Considerations

Pregame Conference

It is specified in the rules that the officials should discuss their particular approach to the match. At this meeting such items as signals, positioning, the authority limits of line judges, and helping each other when screened can be reviewed. Questions on particular rules and rule interpretations can be raised, analyzed, and agreed upon. The emphasis in these pregame officials' conferences is upon established teamwork and consistency within the officiating crew. The referee should take the lead, but according to the dictates of his or her personal approach, should involve each official in the discussion.

Officiating Evaluated by Coaches

What qualities do you appreciate in a volleyball official?

1. Confidence
2. Commanding presence
3. Consistency
4. Businesslike

Miscellaneous Comments

1. A coach looks for an official who possesses a high tolerance for stress and pressure.
2. A referee should be capable of making a quick and fair decision to prevent delays in the game.
3. Officials must be cognizant of current rule interpretations.
4. A good official with a degree of showmanship and fine personality can convey to the crowd moments of finesse, daring, and explosiveness.

Officiating Evaluted by Officials

What is the most difficult play to call in volleyball?

1. Observing a spiked ball touch blocker
2. Ball handling violations
3. Touching of the net or ball by spikers and blockers

What is the most difficult phase of mechanics in officiating volleyball?

1. Officiating stand not elevated enough to allow full view of the total play
2. Concentrating on top portion of net during a spike attempt
3. Player's back to officials when playing the ball, blocking the vision of the official

Miscellaneous Comments

1. A quick reaction time and keen sense of the game are required.
2. There is a definite need for formal volleyball officiating associations.
3. A good referee subtly controls the game, blends into the flow of the game.
4. Officials must make their rulings in a nonaccusing manner—be matter-of-fact rather than "HA! I caught you!"
5. Crucial is the ability to make a subjective call based on an accurate knowledge of the skill involved.

Play Rulings

Situation: Team A forfeits to team B with the score: (a) team A-13 and team B-14; or (b) team A-4 and team B-4. *Ruling:* In (a), team B wins 15–13; in (b), team B wins 15–0. (1–5–2)

Situation: A player enters the game wearing (a) a small stud earring; (b) a medical tag taped to the body under the shirt. *Ruling:* (a) Illegal equipment, unnecessary delay, earrings must be removed; (b) legal. *Comment:* If a player must wear a medical tag or religious medal, it is to be taken off the chain and taped to the body under the uniform. Chains, etc. shall not be worn. (4–1–6)

Situation: The referee notifies the coaches the prematch conference is to start. The coach of Team A: (a) sends a designated player but does not attend personally; (b) sends the assistant coach and designated player; (c) attends with the designated player but leaves before the coin toss is conducted; (d) sends the team manager and a designated player. *Ruling:* (b) and (c) Legal; (a) and (d) unsportsmanlike conduct, penalty assessed after the coin toss. *Comment:* The coach or assistant coach shall attend the prematch conference. (5–3–1)

Situation: A ball landing near an end line is called "in" by the line judge. The referee sees the ball land out-of-bounds. *Ruling:* Out-of-bounds. *Comment:* If the referee is unsure, the line judge's call stands. (5–3–3)

Situation: During a play at the net, the referee cannot determine whether a back-line player, who was in front of the spiking line, returned a ball higher than the top of the net. *Ruling:* No call shall be made unless the official can clearly determine a foul has been committed. (5–3–3)

Situation: Immediately after the referee gives a visual and audio signal for the serve, the umpire blows the whistle for a substitution. The server holds up on his or her serve hearing the second whistle. *Ruling:* Official's time-out. The referee informs the umpire the substitution was out-of-order and gives a new visual and audio signal for the serve. (5–3–3)

Situation: Prior to the game, the officials see a player wearing illegal equipment. They advise the coach/player how to make the equipment legal to avoid possible penalty and injury. *Ruling:* Correct procedure. *Comment:* Officials should routinely check players for illegal equipment or uniforms prior to the match. However, final responsibility for legality lies with the player and the coach. (4–1–1)

Situation: A team has only six players, one of which is injured during the first game and unable to play. *Ruling:* The team may play with five players, and the position of the injured player shall remain open throughout the game, which means the team shall rotate an extra position when it is the injured player's turn to serve. *Comment:* If able, the injured player could reenter the match during the second or third game. (6–1–2)

Situation: Team R is in one of the following positions at the instant of a legal serve:

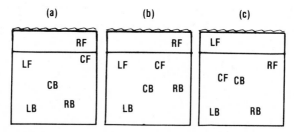

Ruling: (a) Illegal alignment, point; RF and CF are overlapping; (b) and (c) legal. (6–3–2)

Situation: Team R is moving in one of the following ways at the moment of contact on a legal serve:

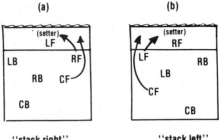

Ruling: (a) and (b) Legal. *Comment:* Player movement is legal provided the players are in proper alignment at the moment of serve. (6–3–2)

Situation: The center forward on the receiving team claims right forward on the serving team, who is standing close to the net but not jumping or waving, is screening his or her view of the server. *Ruling:* This is not screening. *Comment:* No player on the receiving team is entitled to a specific position on the floor. If a player on the receiving team cannot see the server, that player should move. If, after that player moves, the serving team's player moves to take another position which blocks that player's view of the server, the referee shall call screening. (6–4–1)

Situation: Three minutes before the scheduled starting time of a match, Team A (the serving team) presents its roster and lineup to the scorer. Then 30 seconds before the match, Team A presents 2 additional names for the roster. *Ruling:* Late roster, side out. Then names are added to roster; change of roster past deadline, point to Team B. *Comment:* The two violations occurred at different times, therefore, each is penalized. Team B will serve first, leading 1–0. (7–1–2; 9–7–PEN #3)

Situation: The left forward on Team A steps completely across the out-of-bounds extension of the centerline: (a) to hit the ball to teammates; (b) as a result of momentum from the play of the ball on team A's side of the centerline; or (c) in order to get out of the way of a play by a teammate. *Ruling:* In each case, it is a foot fault, and a point or side out is awarded to Team B. (9–5–2) (9–5–6)

Situation: A back-line player jumps from behind the spiking line, contacts the ball above the top of the net and in front of the spiking line, and lands in front of the spiking line. The ball is returned. *Ruling:* Legal. (9–5–5)

Situation: The right forward on Team A spikes the ball for a point after which he or she: (a) steps over the centerline; (b) touches the net. *Ruling:* No foul in (a) or (b). *Comment:* The ball must be in play for a net foul or foot fault to occur. (9–5–2)

Situation: LF on Team R contacts the ball at the sideline and returns it to the middle of the playing area by turning his or her wrist during contact. *Ruling:* Legal. *Comment:* If prolonged contact occurs while the hand is turning, an illegal hit is called. (9–4–5)

Situation: CF on Team R blocks a spike sending the ball straight into the air over Team R's court. The CF plays the ball next. *Ruling:* Legal; Team R has 2 hits remaining. (9–4–7)

Situation: The left back on Team A saves a hard-driven spiked ball so it deflects off his or her hand to: (a) the shoulder; (b) the biceps; (c) the other hand; (d) a forearm. *Ruling:* All are legal. (9–4–8)

Situation: There is simultaneous contact by Team S's spiker and Team R's blocker on a ball which is (a) directly above the net; (b) completely on Team R's side of the net; (c) completely on Team S's side of the net. *Ruling:* (a) Legal; (b) over-the-net foul on Team S, side out to Team B; (c) over-the-net foul on Team R, point. *Comment:* In (b), the offensive team must have the first opportunity to contact the ball. In (c), it is illegal to contact a ball which is completely on the opponent's side of the net. (9–6–4)

Situation: The left forward on team A spikes the ball, but at the instant the ball hits the floor on Team B's side of the court, the spiker contacts the net. *Ruling:* Double foul. *Comment:* Team B's failure to return the ball is a foul, as is the net foul by the left forward. Because they occur at the same instant, the proper call is double foul and a replay. (9–7–2)

BIBLIOGRAPHY

1. National Federation of State High School Associations. *1990–91 and 1991–92 Volleyball Casebook and Official's Manual.* Kansas City, Missouri, 1990.
2. National Federation of State High School Associations. *1990–91 Volleyball Rule Book.* Kansas City, Missouri, 1990.

Wrestling

The Game

Wrestling is one of the oldest forms of sport and combat dating back to 300 B.C. and the Stone Age Man. (4:3) Prehistoric man relied on strength and endurance to provide for himself when at peace and in combat. In 1927 the NCAA organized the Wrestling Rules Committee, which proved to be the greatest step ever taken toward developing amateur wrestling in America. (8:4)

The sport of wrestling is distinct in that it pits man against man in physical combat. Wrestling, one of the most strenuous sports, involves six to eight minutes of consistent action testing the contestant's speed, agility, balance, skill, endurance, strength, timing, and conditioning. In contrast to other sports where individuals of greater height and weight have an advantage, a young man of any body type can participate in wrestling with good results. (8:8)

Wrestling is one of the most difficult sports to officiate because the actions of the wrestlers are quick and are accompanied by constantly changing positions. In wrestling, an official may warn a contestant visually or verbally of a potential injury situation if his whistle is not readily available. The judgment of the referee could have a profound influence on the outcome of the match and the meet.

"Four things belong to a judge: to hear courteously, to answer wisely, to consider soberly, and to decide impartially."

Socrates

Finally, there is a trend that emphasizes dual meet competition to provide maximum opportunities for competitive experiences.

Officials and Their Responsibilities

Wrestling is somewhat unique, in that the referee works alone in most dual meets. Assistant referees are generally provided for elimination tournaments.

Officials' Uniforms and Equipment
The wrestling referee should wear a short-sleeved, knit shirt with black-and-white one-inch stripes, full length black trousers with black belt, black gym shoes, and black socks. The referee should also have a colored disc and a whistle.

Referee
The referee has full control of the meet and his decisions are final. The referee's primary responsibilities include checking the wrestlers to avoid health and safety hazards, clarifying the rules, awarding points for competitive maneuvers, penalizing for infractions of the rules, and finally, declaring a winner. The referee has an extremely challenging task as the spectators witness the match clearly from close proximity, and judgment must be exercised continuously. (6:104)

To minimize injuries, the referee should be constantly alert to detect illegal holds. Since a wrestler has only six to eight minutes to prove his superiority over his opponent, the referee must dedicate himself to the orderly progress of each match.

Requirements for being a good referee.
1. Thorough knowledge of the existing rules;
2. Knowledge of wrestling from personal experience in order to apply the rules effectively;
3. Accuracy in interpretation of the rules; and
4. Consistency in rule interpretations. (6:104)

Other procedures for qualifying officials should include attendance at clinics, a written test, a practical examination, and membership in the local officials' association. (1:196)

Premeet responsibilities. The referee should arrive 30 minutes before the meet, dressed in official attire, and ready to officiate.

Before the dual meet begins, the referee shall: (a) visit each team dressing room to inspect contestants for presence of oils or greasy substances on the body or uniform, rosin, objectionable pads, improper clothing, all jewelry, long fingernails and improper grooming; (b) clarify the rules with coaches and contestants upon request; and (c) review with the scorers and timekeeper signals and procedures to be used. (10:10) Just before the meet, the referee should call the two captains to the center of the mat to conduct the coin toss for choice of position in split or tie matches and remind the wrestlers of new rules he intends to enforce. When a match is to start, the referee should call the first two contestants to the center of the mat, where they shake hands and are given brief instructions:

1. They are to stop wrestling when the referee blows his whistle.
2. They are to attempt wrestling near the center circle of the mat. (8:249)

After the match. As in other sports, the referee should make it a point to leave immediately after the final match. The referee should not comment on the meet to spectators, press, coaches, or athletes.

Assistant Referees

The assistant referees' main function is to assist the referee on any action on the mat. This could include stalling, illegal holds, technical violations, and even disagreeing with a fall called by the referee. (10:11)

Match Timekeeper

The timekeeper is responsible for keeping the overall time of each match, time-out for injury, calling out the time remaining, and for signaling the referee, contestants, and spectators at the end of each period. The end of the period should be signaled by tapping the referee's shoulder or sounding a buzzer. The practice of throwing in a towel to signify the end of the period should be strongly discouraged. When no visual clock is provided, visual cards will be used to show fifteen-second intervals starting with one minute remaining in the match.

Scorer

The scorer should work closely with the timekeeper and record the points scored as signaled by the referee. The scorer is also responsible for recording the choice of positions (neutral, defer to opponent, up or down) during course of the match. The individual match score and team score is the scorer's responsibility.

Basic Infractions, Penalties and Rulings

Illegal and Potentially Dangerous Holds
The referee must be alert and in position in order to stop an illegal hold or potentially dangerous hold. He should anticipate the injury potential of these holds and attempt to prevent or block them before they reach the danger point. Whenever possible, an illegal hold should be prevented rather than called.

Unnecessary Roughness
Intentional striking, gouging, kicking, hair pulling, butting, elbowing, or an intentional act which endangers life or limb should be penalized. A wrestler lifting his opponent off the mat is responsible for his safe return to the mat. If he drops his opponent forcefully, he should be penalized.

Table 10.1

Illegal Holds

slam	full straight-back suplay
chokeholds	intentional drill or a forceful fallback
pulling back the thumb on 1, 2 or 3 fingers of an opponent's hand	
hammerlock above the right angle	twisting hammerlock
front headlock without the arm	full nelson
headlock without the arm	straight scissors and over-scissors
strangle holds	leg block
twisting knee lock	key lock
overhead double arm bar	full back suplay from a rear standing position
bending, twisting or forcing the head, or any limb beyond its normal limits of movement	locking the hands behind the back in a double arm bar from the front
	any hold used for punishment only (10:23)

Potentially Dangerous Holds

double wristlock	headlock with an arm or leg encircled
chicken wing	
guillotine, when being applied with the limb forced beyond normal range of movement	toe holds
	split scissors (10:24)

Conduct of Contestants
Penalties will be administered for:

1. Unsportsmanlike conduct;
2. Flagrant misconduct; and
3. Unnecessary roughness. (10:25)

Conduct of the Coaches, Team Personnel, and Others
Unsportsmanlike conduct by the wrestlers, coaches, and spectators will result in the removal of the offenders from the wrestling area at the request of the referee. Coaches are restricted to the bench while the match is in progress. If not curtailed, such action could provide an unfair advantage to a contestant. In addition, it disrupts the orderly progress of the match.

Technical Violations
Penalties will be administered for the following:

1. Assuming an incorrect starting position;
2. Going out of the wrestling area;
3. Grasping of clothing;
4. Interlocking or overlapping the hands, fingers, or arms around the opponent's body while in control down on the mat;
5. The figure 4 scissors around body and both legs; and
6. Leaving the wrestling area. (10:25)

The collegiate infraction penalty table is essentially the same as the interscholastic penalty chart. The college summary of technical violations is increased to include stalling, holding legs, false starts and starting positions, and coaching an injured contestant. It should be noted that officials must curtail any attempts by coaches to instruct their wrestlers during the recovery time.

Mechanics

The most important concern for the referee is to move constantly to secure the best possible position to observe and protect the wrestler in dangerous situations. Good positioning determines the effectiveness of the referee. It discourages illegal holds and minimizes possible injury to the competitors. It must be remembered that wrestlers may change positions so fast that several points may be awarded in a few seconds. The "away" position of the referee affords the best possible position to see both men and also the off-mat limits. The referee must stay far enough away from the wrestlers to avoid interference and close enough to the action to stop wrestling if necessary. This position also allows the referee sufficient area to avoid exposing himself to wrestlers coming over on top of him.

Wrestling Area
The wrestling area should be no less than 24' square in high school and 32' square for college with a 10' diameter circle. An alternate wrestling area should be a circular area of not less than 28' in high school and 32' in college with the same 10' diameter circle. A 5' protective mat around the perimeter of the wrestling mat is essential for the safety of the wrestlers.

Weigh-In Procedure
Unless administration weigh-in procedures are adopted by the state high school association, contestants shall have the opportunity to weigh in, shoulder-to-shoulder, a maximum of one hour and a minimum of one-half hour before the time a dual meet is scheduled to begin. When a preliminary meet is followed by a varsity meet, the 30-minute weigh-in period for the second meet may, by mutual consent, precede the preliminary meet. The weigh-in period shall extend no longer than 30 minutes and shall be conducted at the dual meet site. (10:14)

Failure to make weight will render a given wrestler ineligible to wrestle in that weight class. A contestant not able to make weight may enter the weight class next highest. Both interscholastic and intercollegiate rules allow for weight allowance provisions for dual and tournament competition. Interscholastic wrestling is considering new weight classifications with no weight allowances. They are maximums of 103, 112, 119, 125, 130, 135, 140, 145, 152, 160, 171, 189, and 275 pounds. "In a sport such as wrestling, athletes frequently place themselves on 'crash diets' combined with dehydration to make lower weight classifications. Such a practice haş received widespread condemnation from various sources including the American Medical Association." (2:126)

While Wrestlers Are On Their Feet
The referee sounds a whistle to start the match. He should face the scoring table with the contestants, scorers, and timers in full view. The referee should keep moving from one side to the other to get a clear view of both sides of the action, keeping a safe distance to avoid interfering with the progress of the match. The referee should watch for wrestlers intentionally backing off the mat and for stalling techniques; he should be alert to the enforcement of illegal starting position and action in collegiate competition.

PENALTY CHART

Infractions	Warn-ing	First Penalty	Second Penalty	Third Penalty	Fourth Penalty	Rule
Illegal Holds	No	1 Pt.	1 Pt.	2 Pts.	Disqualify	7-1
Technical Violations	No	1 Pt.	1 Pt.	2 Pts.	Disqualify	7-3
False start or incorrect starting position		Following two cautions there is a 1-point penalty for each infraction. (Does not count toward disqualification.)				
Stalling	Yes	1 Pt.	1 Pt.	2 Pts.	Disqualify	7-6
Unnecessary Roughness	No	1 Pt.	1 Pt.	2 Pts.	Disqualify	7-4-1
Unsportsmanlike Conduct During a Match	No	1 Pt.	1 Pt.	2 Pts.	Disqualify	7-4-2
Misconduct of Coaches	Yes	Deduct 1 Team Point	Removal of head coach from premises on second penalty and deduct 1 team point. Removal is for duration of dual meet or tournament session only.			6-6-5 7-5-4 8-1-5
Unsportsmanlike Conduct— Contestants (not during the match). Coaches and Non-participating Personnel	No	Deduct 1 Team Point	Remove from premises on second penalty and deduct 1 team point. Removal is for duration of dual meet or tournament session only.			7-4-2 7-5-3 8-1-4
Flagrant Misconduct— Contestants	No	Disqualify on first offense and deduct 2 team points. Remove from premises for dual meet or tournament session. Contestant is eliminated from further competition in dual meet or tournament.				7-4-3 8-1-6
Flagrant Misconduct— Coaches and Non-participating Personnel	No	Remove from premises on first offense and deduct 1 team point. Removal is for the duration of the dual meet or tournament.				7-5-5 8-1-5
Greasy Substance on Body or Uniform, Improper Grooming, Objectionable Pads and Braces, Illegal Equipment or Uniform.		Disqualify if not removed or corrected in allotted time (2 min.).				8-1-1

Summary of Technical Violations

Assuming Incorrect Starting Position and False Start (7-3-1)

Going Off Wrestling Area (7-3-2)

Grasping Clothing, Etc. (7-3-3)

Interlocking Hands (7-3-4)

Figure 4 Body Scissors (7-3-5)

Leaving Mat Without Permission (7-3-6)

Note 1—Disqualification due to technical violation, illegal hold, stalling, unsportsmanlike conduct during a match, or unnecessary roughness does not eliminate a contestant from further competition in tournaments. Disqualification for unsportsmanlike conduct not during the match eliminates a contestant or coach from the tournament session only. Disqualification for flagrant misconduct eliminates a contestant from further competition in the tournament and a coach is removed for the duration of the tournament.

Note 2—Points for unnecessary roughness, grasping clothing or locking hands, are awarded in addition to points earned.

EXAMPLE OF INFRACTIONS—Wrestler A in the first period locks his hands—penalty, 1 point. Shortly thereafter he is called for a false start and is cautioned. In the second period, he applies an illegal hold and is penalized one point. He is then called for stalling and given a warning. In the third period, he is called for an incorrect starting position and is again cautioned. He is later called for stalling and is penalized two points. Later in the period, he is called for a false start and is penalized one point. Later in the period, he locks his hands and is disqualified.

Figure 10.1 Wrestling penalties. (By courtesy of the N.F.S.H.S.A.)

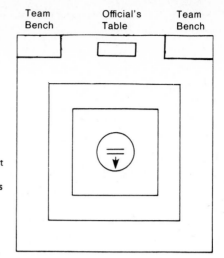

| Team Bench | Official's Table | Team Bench |

The MAT AREA includes the mat and a space 10 feet wide surrounding the mat including the team benches and the officials' table.

Figure 10.2 Wrestling mat area/dual meet. (10:9)

When Wrestlers Are On The Mat

The referee must be alert while the wrestlers are down on the mat, since positions are subject to quick changes. When the wrestlers become entangled, it is difficult to tell who has the advantage, especially along the edge of the mat. The referee should continue the match in the referee's position when the contestants go off the mat with one wrestler having the advantage, and if the match is stopped because of an injury or an illegal hold when one wrestler has the advantage. In high school wrestling the official should assume a position in front of the wrestlers, facing the scoring table, when continuing the match from the referee's position or on the mat. The referee should enforce the following requirements for the man in the down position:

1. Are his hands, knees, and feet parallel to each other?
2. Are his hands at least one foot in front of his knees?
3. Are his hands flat on the mat?
4. Is he sitting still?

A brief description of the referee's position by Hopke and Kidder (1:43) is as follows: The wrestler must be on both hands and knees with hands at least 12 inches in front of knees. The weight of the wrestler's body should be back with the hands touching the mat lightly, fingers pointing ahead and elbows slightly bent. This position will allow for a fast reaction of the bottom man. The referee should encourage a head-up position prior to the signal to begin wrestling. The referee should enforce the following requirements regarding the top man's position:

1. Is his hand flat on the stomach of the opponent?
2. Is his hand in the position on his opponent's elbow?
3. Does his leg touch the opponent's leg?
4. Is his head in a legal position?
5. Is his knee, outside of the parallel line of the hand, knee, or foot? (8:250)

It should be noted that current rules call for the knee on the nearest side to be down on the mat in high school rules and one knee to be down on the mat in college rules.

When the referee is satisfied that the contestants have assumed their proper position, he should raise his hand to indicate to the wrestlers and the timer that the match is ready to begin. The referee continues the match by sounding his whistle and bringing his arm down sharply. The referee should remain close to the contestants at all times to block illegal holds, to determine when the wrestlers go off the mat, and to award points for takedowns, escapes, near falls, and falls. Most important, the referee should be in a position to prevent possible bodily injury to competitors.

The offensive wrestler's starting position is one in which he is at the right or left side of his opponent with *at least one knee on the mat* on the near side of his opponent. The near side is the one on which the offensive wrestler places the palm of his hand on or over the back of the elbow. The offensive man's head shall be above the spinal column of his opponent's back. The other arm (right or left) is placed loosely around the defensive wrestler's body, perpendicular to the long axis of the body, with the palm of the hand placed loosely over the defensive wrestler's navel. A knee or foot may be placed behind the defensive wrestler's feet. The offensive wrestler's legs or feet may not be in contact with the defensive wrestler. (10:16)

Assistant Referees

Assistant referees are normally employed during semi-final and final championship matches. The assistant referees should sit or kneel outside the wrestling area and observe the action from that vantage point. When an assistant referee has an opinion different from the referee, he should raise his hand to gain the attention of the referee. When both assistant referees disagree with the referee, the referee will stop the match and conduct a conference with the assistant referees. This conference will be held on the edge of the mat in front of the timers-scorers table. The assistant referees' function is to keep score, time the matches and advise the referee. The referee has the power to deny the assistant referees.

Whistle Use
The whistle should be in good working order and available for immediate use. The whistle should be used only when required to start and stop the action, and then forcibly.

Hand Signals and Awarding Points
Hand signals are important to convey decisions to the scoring table, coaches, and spectators, such as points scored, illegal holds, and time-outs. Effective use of signals can alleviate the need for discussions during the match. The referee should point to the wrestler who has gained the advantage and, at the same time, holding his other hand above his head, indicate the number of points to be awarded with his fingers extended upward. Verbal statements should accompany hand signals for clarification. This aids in keeping the wrestlers, scoring table, and spectators informed as to what has happened and when. Referees should not assume that the points signalled are recorded. They should follow up by checking the scoreboard. If not thus recorded, the match should be stopped immediately and the scoring rectified.

Problem Calls

Calling Near Falls and Falls
Two point "near fall" requirements are satisfied if both shoulders or scapula of the defensive wrestler are held momentarily within four inches of the mat or less, when one shoulder or scapula is touching the mat and the other shoulder is held at an angle of 45 degrees or less from the mat, or when the defensive wrestler is held in a high bridge or on both elbows for 2 seconds. A three-point near fall is awarded if these requirements have been held continuously for five seconds.

Novice officials are too anxious to award points for near falls before the defensive wrestler escapes or time expires. Don't confuse pauses as new starts on move for new point awards. (An exception would be if opponent stops motion—then a new point award is possible.) Premature awarding of points could lead to duplication of awards. Each situation must be continuous and taken to its conclusion before the points are awarded.

The fall is the final outcome of a well-wrestled chain of maneuvers. (7:69)

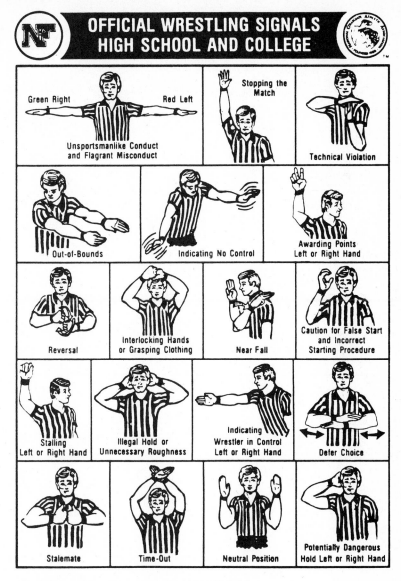

OFFICIAL WRESTLING SIGNALS HIGH SCHOOL AND COLLEGE

Green Right — Red Left — Unsportsmanlike Conduct and Flagrant Misconduct

Stopping the Match

Technical Violation

Out-of-Bounds

Indicating No Control

Awarding Points Left or Right Hand

Reversal

Interlocking Hands or Grasping Clothing

Near Fall

Caution for False Start and Incorrect Starting Procedure

Stalling Left or Right Hand

Illegal Hold or Unnecessary Roughness

Indicating Wrestler in Control Left or Right Hand

Defer Choice

Stalemate

Time-Out

Neutral Position

Potentially Dangerous Hold Left or Right Hand

Figure 10.3 (By courtesy of the N.F.S.H.S.A.)

In order to call a fall, the referee should be down on the mat "in the middle of the action" where he can see the scapulae in contact with the mat. When blocked out by the entangled wrestlers, it is permissible to feel under the shoulders of the wrestler on your blind side to determine contact with the mat. A one-second count by the referee is

SUMMARY OF SCORING

Dual Meet		Tournament	
Fall	6 pts.	Fall	1 pt.
Technical Fall	6 pts.	Technical Fall	1 pt.
Forfeit	6 pts.	Default	1 pt.
Default	6 pts.	Forfeit	1 pt.
Disqualification	6 pts.	Disqualification	1 pt.
Decision		Advancement	
(by 12 or more pts.)	5 pts.	Championship Bracket	1 pt.
(by 8 thru 11 pts.)	4 pts.	Consolation Bracket	½ pt.
(by less than 8 pts.)	3 pts.	Decision	
Draw	2 pts.	(by 12 or more pts.)	¾ pt.
		(by 8 or more pts.)	½ pt.
		Bye followed by a win	
		Championship Bracket	1 pt.
		Consolation Bracket	½ pt.
Individual Match			
Takedown	2 pts.	Near Fall	2 or 3 pts.
Escape	1 pt.	Time Advantage	1 pt.
Reversal	2 pts.	(Maximum for 1 full minute)	

Figure 10.4 (By courtesy of the N.F.S.H.S.A.)

required for a fall in college and a two-second count in high school. As soon as the fall requirements are satisfied, the referee should raise one hand and quickly strike the mat with his palm. There is a tendency to lean towards the near fall call. The one-second college fall requirement implies anticipation of this call. If injury occurs or the defensive wrestler indicates he is injured after near fall criteria has been met, the match will be stopped and a 3-point near fall will be earned. (10:18)

Edge-of-the-Mat Calls

If one wrestler has an "advantage" position, the match should continue as long as the supporting parts of either wrestler remain within the boundary lines of the wrestling area. Wrestling should continue if a *fall is imminent,* as long as both shoulders of the defensive wrestler are within the boundary lines. Consistency in judgment on the part of the referee is imperative. Vacillation in this situation may destroy the confidence of the wrestlers and coaches. "When there is fast action near the edge of the mat, the referee must decide which man, if either, had control when out-of-bounds was declared." (1:196)

Interlocking Hands

The detection of which wrestler's hand is interlocked is sometimes difficult to determine when the wrestlers are down on the mat. Too often a wrestler is penalized for interlocking hands when he actually has his

WRESTLING MEET

Date .... vs. .... Place ....

Won by .... Score .... to ....

Weight Class	Contestants	Neutral Up or Down	Man'ver Points	First Period	Second Period	Third Period	Time Adv.	Match Points	Team Score	Meet Our	Score Their
118		N U D	Man'ver Points								
		U N D	Man'ver Points								
126		N U D	Man'ver Points								
		U N D	Man'ver Points								
134		N U D	Man'ver Points								
		U N D	Man'ver Points								
142		N U D	Man'ver Points								
		U N D	Man'ver Points								
150		N U D	Man'ver Points								
		U N D	Man'ver Points								
158		N U D	Man'ver Points								
		U N D	Man'ver Points								
167		N U D	Man'ver Points								
		U N D	Man'ver Points								
177		N U D	Man'ver Points								
		U N D	Man'ver Points								
190		N U D	Man'ver Points								
		U N D	Man'ver Points								
H.W.		N U D	Man'ver Points								
		U N D	Man'ver Points								

Figure 10.5 Sample wrestling scoresheet. (8:216)

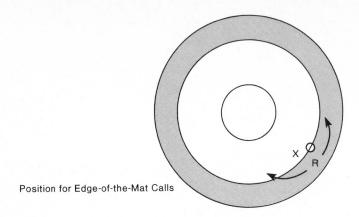

Position for Edge-of-the-Mat Calls

Figure 10.6 Position for edge-of-the-mat calls.

opponent's hand. The referee should be certain before making this call. The situation is most common when the wrestlers are executing the standup maneuver. Interlocking hands or gripping the clothing also occurs frequently during an escape or reverse maneuver.

Stalling

Stalling determinants should be clearly understood. Each wrestler must be working to improve his position or pin his opponent. The bottom man must make a legitimate attempt to gain control. Stalling on the top man is more difficult to call. Stalling penalties should be preceded by a warning and strictly enforced. Since the stalling rule presents a judgment problem, the rule has been minimized in importance through the years. Consistency is the key in this ruling.

   Common examples would include the following:

1. When one wrestler is ahead by one point with both wrestlers on their feet. Invariably the wrestler ahead will be penalized for stalling.
2. The bottom wrestler bracing, or "pitching a tent," to hold the lead for the duration of the match.

Miscellaneous Considerations

Tournament Seeding

In order to balance competition, two outstanding wrestlers in a weight class should be placed in the upper and the lower half of the tournament bracket. When numerous contestants are of equal ability, a draw for bracket position should be conducted. Criteria for selecting seeding includes defending champion status, an exceptional dual meet record, and won-loss record against common opponents.

Overtime Procedure
In tournament competition, if the match ends in a tie, three extra periods of one minute will be conducted to determine the winner. There is no carryover of penalties and warnings from the match to the overtime session. In the event of a tie in the overtime, each contestant will be evaluated using an established list of wrestling techniques criteria to determine a winner.

Injury Circumstances
An injured contestant may be awarded up to maximum time-out of two minutes, which is cumulative throughout the match, including the overtime. There shall be no limit to the number of time-out periods which may be taken in any match, but the total time-out shall not exceed two minutes. If, at the expiration of the time-out, the injured wrestler is able to continue wrestling, the match shall be resumed as if the contestants had gone out-of-bounds. Only the referee may call such time-outs. (10:28)

High School and Intercollegiate Officiating
Due to the exacting nature of intercollegiate wrestling, a minimum of two years' high school wrestling officiating experience is strongly recommended before moving up to intercollegiate officiating.

International Rules
There is a strong trend toward international rules adoption in which there is a strong emphasis on takedowns with declining emphasis on escapes.

Officiating Evaluated by Coaches

What qualities do you appreciate in a wrestling official?

1. Takes full authority (but not arrogant about it).
2. Sticks with calls, does not back down or change rulings (calm and deliberate).
3. In control of match at all times.
4. Hustle—was in best possible position to make the correct calls and protect wrestlers.
5. Alertness.
6. Consistency in enforcing rules, making calls, and utilizing proper mechanics.

7. Was reserved in making quick decisions.
8. Talked to wrestlers to prevent injuries and penalties.
9. Firm, knowledgeable answers to questions on rules and has concern for the safety of the wrestlers—not confusing interscholastic with intercollegiate rules.
10. Inconspicuous during the match.
11. Willingness to work all weight classes when an exhibition match is included.

Miscellaneous Comments

1. Referee must gain the respect of the wrestlers during the prematch conference.
2. Outstanding official was a former wrestler and is presently a coach with a good understanding of wrestling techniques, strategy, and rules.
3. Many ex-wrestlers are poor mechanically due to "old-hat" attitude and tendency to be overly friendly with wrestlers before the match.

Officiating Evaluated by Officials

What is the most difficult situation to call in wrestling?

1. Subjective calls which often bring disputes
2. Takedown without control
3. Edge-of-mat calls
4. Change of position or control as time expires

What is the most difficult phase of mechanics in officiating wrestling?

1. Scoring points while continuing to observe the action
2. See a pin in a cradle situation
3. Calling falls in fast-changing situations (half nelson with bridging and twisting)
4. Falls when the shoulders are covered "front and back" and reversals on the edge of the mat

Miscellaneous Comments

1. Many coaches are lacking in rules knowledge making it difficult for them to accept the rulings of the referee.
2. Wrestling is one of the most difficult sports to officiate because you are on your own to make all decisions.
3. Officials working both high school and college meets must be cognizant of the constantly changing rules.

Play Rulings (11)

Situation: During a tournament match, wrestler A had three penalties called on him. The match goes into overtime and A uses an illegal hammerlock. The referee disqualifies him and awards the match to B. *Ruling:* This is incorrect procedure. The overtime is a completely new match which is separate from the competition which resulted in the tie, with all the scoring, penalties, and warnings which occurred during the regular match cancelled. Consequently, one point is awarded to B.

Situation: At the weigh-in prior to a dual meet, Team A's 145-pounder is ½ pound overweight. Team B's 145-pounder is also ½ pound overweight. Both coaches agree that since both boys "balance out", why waste the time making weight and permit time to compete. May this be permitted? *Ruling:* No. In all dual meets, net weight shall be required. No overweight is permitted, nor should it be requested.

Situation: The coach, contestant, manager, or trainer leaves his restricted area and approaches the mat area for the purpose of coaching, directing, or encouraging his wrestler. Is this a violation? If so, what is the penalty? *Ruling:* Yes, the coach is expected to set an example of admirable conduct. The present wrestling guide provides that all personnel other than actual participating contestants be restricted to an area at least ten feet from the actual mat area during a match. Coaches are restricted to team benches except during time-outs or the end of the match. Officials are instructed to penalize promptly. First offense, deduct one team point; second offense, remove from premises.

Situation: A, who allegedly had injured his elbow during a practice session, reports to wrestle with a bulky, loose-fitting pad on his elbow. *Ruling:* If, in the referee's opinion, the wearing of such an item would prevent the opponent from applying normal holds, he will direct the wrestler to remove the pad before wrestling. If the wrestler is injured to the extent that he cannot continue without this equipment, the match shall be forfeited to his opponent.

Situation: A has B in a pinning hold and B's head supported by A's elbow extends outside the wrestling area. B's head does not come in contact with the line or the area outside the wrestling area. Can a fall be awarded? *Ruling:* As long as the shoulders of B are inside the wrestling area, A may be awarded a fall.

Situation: A has B in a pinning situation. B deliberately crawls or bridges off the mat. Can referee award A a near fall and a penalty point since B deliberately crawled off the mat? *Ruling:* No. If near fall points have been earned and are awarded, no penalty points can be given.

Situation: A is injured because of illegal action of B. B is penalized by the referee for the illegal hold. At the completion of the two-minute recovery time allowance, A is unable to continue. The referee awards the match to A. Is this correct? *Ruling:* Yes. Once the referee has penalized a contestant for an illegal hold and the opponent has been injured by that hold, the referee has no recourse except to award the match by default to the injured contestant. There is always the possibility that some coaches can and do take advantage of such a situation, and even though a referee may feel that the injured participant could continue, it is not his responsibility to make that decision.

Situation: A applies a Chicken Wing and Half Nelson on B and immediately places B into a pinning situation. The official stops the match and awards B a penalty point, claiming that the Chicken Wing was used as an illegal twisting hammerlock. The coach of B points out that the Chicken Wing is not listed as an illegal hold. *Ruling:* The ruling was correct. The Chicken Wing is legal as long as the pressure is applied perpendicular to the long axis of the body. When the pressure is parallel to the long axis of the body, it is illegal.

Situation: From a neutral position A, in attempting a takedown, lifts B from the mat, and: (a) brings him to the mat with force or: (b) brings him forcibly to the mat so the upper half of his body contacts the mat before any other part of the body. B does not appear to be shaken up in either case. *Ruling:* A slam in both (a) and (b). Whether B is injured is no criterion in determining the slam. The slam is defined as lifting and bringing the opponent to the mat with unnecessary force. It is entirely possible for a slam to occur without a wrestler being injured.

Situation: Contestants are in a neutral position. A applies a legal headlock on B and takes him to the mat. Both contestants are on their right sides approximately parallel with each other. B's right shoulder is touching the mat and his left shoulder is within two inches of the mat. A maintains this position for approximately ten seconds and the period ends. The referee awards no points. Is the referee correct? *Ruling:* Yes. Bringing a man to the mat with nothing more than a headlock cannot be considered a takedown and even though B's shoulders are in a near fall position, since no takedown is awarded, near fall points cannot be given.

It must be understood also that a simple headlock would not be considered a pinning combination, and although a "fall" could occur, near fall points should not be given in this or similar situations. A plain headlock affects only the near shoulder of the opponent and has little or no effect on the far shoulder. If and when contestant A adjusts his position and/or pressure within legal limits to the extent that B's far shoulder is endangered, then a takedown and/or near fall may be considered.

BIBLIOGRAPHY

1. Boring, Warren J. *Science and Skills of Wrestling*. St. Louis, Missouri: C. V. Mosby Company, 1975.
2. Gable, Dan and James Peterson. *Conditioning for Wrestling The Iowa Way*. Champaign, Illinois: Leisure Press, 1980.
3. Hopke, Stephen L. and Worden Kidder. *Elementary and Junior High School Wrestling*. Cranbury, New Jersey: A. S. Barnes, Inc., 1977.
4. Keen, Clifford P. and Charles M. Speidel and Raymond H. Swartz. *Championship Wrestling*. Menasha, Wisconsin: George Banta, Inc., 1976.
5. Keith, Art. *Complete Book of Wrestling Drills and Conditioning Techniques*. W. Nyack, New York: Parker Publishing Co., Inc., 1976.
6. Niebel, Benjamin W. and Douglas A. Niebel. *Modern Wrestling*. University Park, Pennsylvania: The Pennsylvania State University Press, 1982.
7. Perry, Rex and Arnold Umbach. *Wrestling*. New York City, New York: Sterling Publishing Co., 1976.
8. Umbach, Arnold W. and Warren R. Johnson. *Successful Wrestling*. Dubuque, Iowa: Wm. C. Brown Co. Publishers, 1972.
9. *Wrestling Rules*. Shawnee Mission, Kansas: National Collegiate Athletic Association, 1990.
10. *Wrestling Rules*. Kansas City, Missouri: National Federation of State High School Associations, 1990–91.
11. *Wrestling Rules Case-Book*. Los Angeles, California: Southern California Wrestling Officials Association, 1976.

Index